Education and Knowledge

Education and Knowledge:

The Structured Misrepresentation of Reality

Kevin Harris

University of New South Wales

Routledge & Kegan Paul
London, Boston and Henley

First published in 1979
by Routledge & Kegan Paul Ltd
39 Store Street,
London WC1E 7DD,
Broadway House,
Newtown Road,
Henley-on-Thames,
Oxon RG9 1EN and
9 Park Street,
Boston, Mass. 02108, USA
Set in IBM Press Roman
by Hope Services, Clifton Hampden
and printed in Great Britain by
Lowe & Brydone Ltd
Thetford, Norfolk

British Library Cataloguing in Publication Data

Harris, Kevin

Education and knowledge
1   Education – Philosophy
I   Title
370.1   LB17   78-41331

ISBN 0 7100 0137 1
ISBN 0 7100 0140 1 Pbk

Contents

Contents

Preface

If this work could carry a second sub-title, that sub-title would in all probability be: 'A New Introduction to Philosophy of Education'; for whereas this work is concerned mainly with its own thesis, the need to write it grew partly out of a general dissatisfaction with what philosophy of education has become, and with what philosophers have brought to the study of education over the past decade and a half. This secondary concern will account for what might otherwise appear as disproportionate attention given in the text both to philosophy of education, and to some of its exponents, especially R. S. Peters and P. H. Hirst.

The introductory nature of this work cannot be overemphasised, and towards that end I have attempted to reduce technicalities to a minimum while still giving a proper, and not oversimplified, account of particular philosophic positions. The balance, however, cannot always be held. This is a specialised work, and must employ some specialised terms: talk of 'epistemology', 'ontology', etc., cannot be done away with in this context. Also, certain aspects of particular theoretic stances have to be conceptualised and communicated with a high degree of precision; which accounts for the 'heaviness', and the resort to what might appear to be an unnecessary parade of jargon, in the second chapter: (for instance, to talk of 'labour' or 'theoretical products' rather than 'labour *power*' and '*determinate* theoretical products' would constitute a most serious misrepresentation of a particular theory). On the other hand, there has been some relaxation in the last four chapters: what has been presented there is a distillation, which should not be taken as a set of easily derived conclusions and prescriptions.

This work has emerged out of a particular social context, and it is 'mine' only in the sense that, along with having made some contribution to its substance, I have largely selected, put together and ordered what many people have contributed to a certain wider, ongoing discussion. Most significant among those people (as far as this book is concerned) are Alan Chalmers, Jean Curthoys and Wal Suchting (Department of General Philosophy, University of Sydney): Randall Albury (School of History and Philosophy of Science, University of New South Wales): Michael Matthews (Department of Education, University of New South Wales): and Jim Walker (School of Education, University of Sydney). More significant than any of these, however, is the person from whom I have learned most of what I profess to know, namely Peter Stevens - an exceptional philosopher and teacher whose talents, ironically, are not presently recognised by any university appointments board. If there is any credit to be gained from this book, Peter is deserving of most of it. (It should go without saying, of course, that the people mentioned above may not endorse what I have done with their material, nor might they support some of the conclusions I have drawn; and that I alone can be held responsible for the arguments that follow and the way in which they are phrased.)

Finally, I would like to thank Grenville Wall of Middlesex Polytechnic for his extremely helpful comments on an earlier draft of this work. Either now or after completing Chapter 5, the reader might care to give some further thought to the vast number of people, here unacknowledged, who also contributed significantly to the production of this book: for the appearance of my name alone on the cover and title page is the first single clear manifestation of the very misrepresentation of reality that this book is all about.

Kevin Harris

. . . like the irregular crab,
which, though't goes backward, thinks that it goes right . . .

John Webster *The Duchess of Malfi*

A general State education is a mere contrivance for
moulding people to be exactly like one another, and
as the mould in which it casts them is that which
pleases the predominant power in the government,
whether this be a monarch, a priesthood, an aristo-
cracy, or the majority of the existing generation;
in proportion as it is efficient and successful, it
establishes a despotism over the mind . . .

J. S. Mill *On Liberty*

the class which is the ruling *material* force
of a society, is at the same time its ruling
intellectual force. The class which has the means
of material production at its disposal, has control
at the same time over the means of mental production
. . . hence among other things [they] rule also as
thinkers, as producers of ideas, and regulate the
production and distribution of the ideas of their
age . . .

Karl Marx, and Friedrich Engels, *The German Ideology*

Introduction

Education is centrally and necessarily concerned with the transmission of knowledge. This is not to say, of course, that the transmission of knowledge is all that education is concerned with; nor is it to imply that knowledge is transmitted or gained only through education; but those matters are beyond the scope of this work, which will concentrate exclusively on the role that education plays in providing its charges with knowledge of the world.

'Education' has proved to be a slippery concept to handle, and so it is important that, right at the beginning, I make my particular use of it clear. By 'education' I shall be referring to a particular process, or group of processes, that are manifested in the deliberate provision, by socially approved institutions, of sets of learning experiences that are not narrowly confined either to restricted vocational ends or to the development of singular skills. Education, then, can be taken to include the provision of learning experiences or the transmission of knowledge as it occurs in places like schools, universities, liberal arts colleges, technical colleges, colleges of advanced education and the like; and to exclude the transmission (and gaining) of knowledge through travel, by incidental experience, at driving schools or ballet classes, or in institutions that do not have social approval for the purpose of providing learning experiences. The key features of education, then, are that it is formal and institutionalised, that it is provided by or sanctioned by the state, and that it is deliberately concerned to provide its charges with a broad understanding of the world. It should be noted, however, that the achievement of the last feature above need not be brought about solely through experiences with the overt set curricula of institutions; nor does the notion of breadth preclude the transmission and acquisition of highly specialised vocational, or even non-vocational, skills as well.

In being centrally concerned with the transmission of knowledge in a formalised way, education must aim to ensure that its charges, on leaving their particular institutions, know certain things that they did not know on arrival, and which they did not pick up elsewhere in the interim. It would thus appear that education, in helping people to gain knowledge of the world, embodies three particular functions. It selects, from the infinite body of knowledge, packages that are thought to be particularly worth knowing. It then provides the means and resources whereby those things can be approached and known. And finally, it applies pedagogical expertise in an attempt to ensure that these things are learnt and known.

Now one could hardly quarrel with any or all of these functions if it were the case that, in transmitting knowledge and methodologies for gaining knowledge, education introduced one to established truths and facts about the world, and did so in a neutral and objective way. The problem, however, is that neither knowledge nor education works in those particular ways. Knowing the world, or coming to know the world, is not a matter of learning or coming into possession of a set of facts or truths about the world, which are there in the world, and which the world yields up to those who are able to see them; it is rather, a matter of coming to perceive the world in particular ways, from particular perspectives, and from particular viewpoints, which are largely determined by and arise out of one's interactions in and with a particular historical and social context. Education, on the other hand, is a distinctly non-neutral political mechanism or institutionalised process that largely provides and legitimises the ways and perspectives by which and from which we shall come to know the world : it is also a process that, in certain political circumstances, transmits as knowledge structured distorted misrepresentations of the world. And to find those particular political circumstances one need not necessarily seek out totalitarianism or turn to horror regimes such as Nazism; one can look much closer to home – for in any capitalist liberal democracy education functions to transmit to each new generation a structured misrepresentation of reality.

Chapter 1

Knowing and interpreting the world

Introduction

This work is concerned with two central issues: how we can know, or ⓵ come to know the world; and the role that formal education plays in the ⓶ provision and structuring of our knowledge of the world. What follows, however, is not a philosophic enquiry specifically concerned with conditions of knowledge, nor is it a psychological treatise on how people learn; rather it is an examination of the factors that are involved in the act or process of knowing the world as it really is, or in making correct interpretations of what is really happening in the world. It is also an examination of the factors that impede us from knowing the world as it really is - but that consideration heads us far too quickly towards education, which is an area we would do better to arrive at after we have discussed certain basic problems that are more closely concerned with knowledge itself. Let us begin, then, with a detailed examination of what is involved in coming to know the world.

The individual and the world

It should go without saying that knowing the world, or coming to know the world, must involve both a subject, the knower or potential knower, and an object, the world to be known. The difficult question to resolve, of course, is the nature of the relationship between subject and object in the acquisition, generation or production of knowledge. This is not to deny that there have been some noteworthy, and less than noteworthy, attempts to 'remove' either the subject or the object from the process by collapsing or conflating one of them into the other. Classical idealists tend to play down the place of the real world in the process, or else see the world as something to be transcended; suggesting that real knowledge is to be acquired by contemplation, and that it is an 'object-less' production of the mind. This tradition can be found in varying forms as it proceeds (in Western thought) from Plato, down through such philosophers as Leibnitz and Kant, and receiving its most extreme expression in Berkeley. At the other end of the scale there have been those, like Bergson, and like some extreme materialists, who have taken knowledge to be a process or a product without a subject.

Neither of these positions is tenable. The denial of the world as a distinct object assumes an a-historical, a-social position which blatantly disregards the very arena in which people exist, act and acquire and produce knowledge. The denial of the person as subject similarly disregards the existence and actions of people who, through their actions, change and interpret the world to be known. Freire makes a telling comment on both extreme positions when he says:[1]

> To deny the importance of subjectivity in the process of trans-forming the world and history is naive and simplistic. It is to admit the impossible: a world without men. This objectivist position is as ingenuous as that of subjectivism, which postulates men without a world. World and men do not exist apart from each other, they exist in constant interaction.

As Freire indicates, people do not merely exist and they are not merely conscious; people exist in a real world, and they are conscious in and conscious of that real world. The world is the context for existing and for knowing – but that elementary recognition has been interpreted throughout history in a most misleading and dangerous fashion by what has become known as the empiricist tradition: a tradition that along with its effects, must now be met, challenged and exposed.

The empiricist–inductivist model

The notion of people interacting in and with a world has, not surprisingly, tended to result in a particular emphasis being placed on the nature of that interaction. People, as individuals, are finite, short-lived, limited and mortal. Mankind, as a species, might be longer-lived, but mankind too is mortal and limited. The world, however, is greater than man. It existed before man populated it, and it could conceivably exist after man has departed it; certainly it exists after individual people have departed it. Given this line of thinking, it is only a very small step from recognising the world as the context for human existence to interpreting the world as the *given* context for human existence; and from within that framework it would appear to follow neatly that tiny transient man gains knowledge and consciousness of the *given* world as he lives temporarily in it, and that increasing one's knowledge is a matter of coming to know more and more about an objective given existential world. This theme has permeated Western philosophy since the time of the ancient Greeks. And of all the philosophic legacies that the ancient Greeks left us, probably none has been as damaging as this particular one: this conception of gaining knowledge whereby the individual goes about the given world and comes to understand it, contemplatively in the Platonic tradition, more practically and empirically in the Aristotelian tradition. Modern and not so modern empiricists, and the rationalists, have shared the basis of these traditions, the former finding the foundation of true and sure knowledge in the senses, the latter in reason. Our purpose here is to concentrate essentially on the empiricists, and we shall proceed now to indicate the problems and faults inherent in an empiricist–inductivist approach and methodology for gaining knowledge of the world.

Gaining knowledge from an empiricist–inductivist framework has been described as 'the diligent gathering of facts and then the drawing out of generalities'. The empiricist observes, collects and infers. He goes out into the world and collects his data or facts diligently, he puts them together and analyses them, and then he draws out relations between them. For example, he decides to study the effect of heat on metal bars. He heats thousands of metal bars under a number of varying conditions, and in tabulating his data he finds that in all cases the metal bars expanded when heated. He then concludes that all metal bars (at least within the same net of circumstances from which he drew his observations) will expand when heated.

Now most of the problems with this approach come in the first step, concerned with data collection; but before examining those in detail let us quickly note a few well-known points with regard to the inductivists' logic, and the conclusions that are generated by it.

A central problem concerning inductively derived conclusions is that they are simply not logically valid, nor are they empirically binding. If ten million metal bars were found to expand when heated, *this* does not logically preclude there being a metal bar that will not expand when heated, and it offers no practical guarantee that the next metal bar will not expand when heated.

This, as indicated, is widely known; but inductivism has still found defenders in those who look at the whole issue in terms of probability. If something is found to occur a few times, it is argued, then we have little assurance that we have hit on a general rule or law. But if that thing is found to occur over and over again, then surely that is a different matter; and does not each additional confirmed instance at least increase the probability that a universal generalisation exists? The answer, unfortunately, is 'no'; for as Popper has clearly and consistently argued, when the population or set from which to draw findings is infinite, the probability concerning any finite set of findings is always zero.[2] But even that sort of argument will not satisfy some people, who see real significance in things continually being found to be the case by inductive methods; for surely, it is argued, we can infer something from a vast number of preceding, supporting instances. The problem there, however, is to determine precisely how many supporting instances shall count as sufficient; and that decision must always be arbitrary.

If the faith still remains, as it does in some, then yet a further challenge can be made against inductivism. Where could the faith in inductivism possibly come from, given the previous criticisms? Only, it would seem, from continued demonstrations that inductivism actually works regardless of the philosophic moves against its credibility. And it appears as though it does work. Metal bars always seem to expand when heated; repeated observations of ripe apples show that unless hindered, they consistently fall to the ground; daily observations in the eastern sky reveal a rising sun each morning, etc. Thus the faith in inductivism arises because it appears that every time we use inductivism it works. Or to put that slightly differently, it is a faith in inductivism that is arrived at inductively. And so what we find is that, regardless of any individual affirmations of faith that might find expression here, there is a basic logical point at issue: arguments from experience that attempt to justify the principle of induction must include the principle of induction among their premises, and are thus circular.

The apparent merit of inductivism is that it calls out generalisations from a number of particular instances (yet even here it can be faulty). The major problems with it, however, are that it neither *proves* those generalisations to be true nor establishes high probability levels of their being true. It thus not only poses great difficulties for us, even at the level of our simplest generalisations such as 'all metals expand when heated', 'the sun rises every day', 'frustration leads to aggression' and 'students who do well at high school will do well at university'; but it is also a most unlikely and unprofitable logic to apply in order to seek knowledge concerning things like the efficiency of school systems, the worth of economic policies, the function of free expression, the means of putting down student or worker unrest or the most desirable form of professional education for doctors.

Such are the problems with inductive logic. But as suggested earlier, even greater problems arise with the empiricist methodology of data collection.

There is a small number of basic core assumptions that are common to all variants of empiricism, but of these we shall be concerned with only one, namely the assumption that there are two types of knowledge, non-theoretical and theoretical. For the empiricist it is the non-theoretical knowledge that makes up the building blocks for his constructions, while the theoretical knowledge acts as both mortar and blueprint. This non-theoretical knowledge (the lengths of the unheated and heated metal bars in our previous example) is simply given; it is in the world and of the world, 'out there', waiting to be observed and known; and the empiricist merely reads this given knowledge as if the world lay before him like a book. The world, or parts of it, may at times be an extremely difficult book to read, but a book it is nevertheless.

Now clearly this basic assumption of empiricism suggests that there is a particular relationship between the individual and the world, and also that there is a particular valid way of gaining knowledge of the world. The relationship suggested is that, at one level, the individual and the world, or the individual's knowledge of the world, are not mediated by theory; and it is consequently suggested that at this level gaining knowledge of the world can be attained solely through sense impressions (perhaps assisted by sophisticated equipment). The non-theoretical knowledge, being 'there', does not have to be 'brought about' by people; it lies in waiting to be discovered (not created), and eventually to be understood by means of inductive generalisations. People, on the other hand, can only *discover* what is 'there in the world'; and they must gather what is given, and accept it as given, before they can theorise and make generalisations about the world.

This basic tenet of empiricism, despite its long history and its current widespread acceptance, is badly misconceived. There is no such thing as 'given non-theoretical knowledge'; and since theory always mediates between the individual and the world, knowledge is never merely a discovery of what is out there in the existential world (although some things we know might have correspondence with the existential world). These issues now require considerable elaboration; but first one procedural point. In contrast to the empiricist, I take it that there is a crucial difference between properties of the world, and knowledge statements about those properties: I shall therefore refer to the former as 'facts', and to the latter as facts (without quotes), while at a later stage some confusion will be eliminated by referring to the former as phenomena or instances.

Theory and concepts precede investigation

The theory and practice of empiricism-inductivism requires that an observer, investigator or researcher goes out into the world, there to observe, collect and record data or 'facts' objectively, that is, non-selectively, and with no *a priori* ideas about their relative importance to him.[3] He must then analyse what he has observed and recorded with no underlying hypotheses at all except those that relate to the logic of his thinking

7

processes. From this analysis he is then to draw out relationships and generalisations from among the 'facts' he has collected.

But this, for a large number of reasons, is neither feasible nor possible.

To begin with, one cannot investigate an object (record an instance or note a fact) without first having a concept of that object or a theory about what that object is; and further to this, the concept one has of the object will quite basically influence the methodology one employs in approaching and investigating the object. Let us consider an example.

Two people, A and B, whom we take to be in full possession of their faculties, are walking through a desert, and before them they see a small lake surrounded by sparse palm trees and a narrow grassy area. They decide to investigate this phenomenon. Now at this point they can conceptualise the object, or else, finding themselves unable to do so to their satisfaction, they can attempt to put themselves in a better position to conceptualise it – by walking closer to it, or viewing it through binoculars for example. But either way, the same thing is happening: conceptualisation precedes investigation. Let us now assume that person A conceptualises the object as an *oasis*. This sets up for him certain areas of investigation and certain appropriate methodologies. He knows he can use his sight to collect data; he can employ spatial relationships and consider measuring the depth and perimeter of the waterhole; he can use touch and taste to collect data, feeling the palm trees and drinking the water; and he can employ methods that assume that the phenomenon before him has a physical concrete existence, like climbing the palm trees in order to see what is hidden beneath their branches.

Let us now assume that person B considered the phenomenon and conceptualised it as a *mirage*. If this were so he would not expect the object to have physical concrete properties, and so he would not try to measure the waterhole, drink from it or climb the palm trees, for these are not appropriate methodologies for investigating the conceptualised object. Instead, given that he knows some rudimentary physics, he might plot the landscape, measure the temperature, and concern himself with looking for potential causes of light refraction.

It is important to note here that it is irrelevant to the issue at hand whether the object is an oasis or a mirage. A might approach it as an oasis, and set out to measure the perimeter of the waterhole, only to find it disappear before his eyes. B might, in carrying out measurements of the temperature, fall into the waterhole and get thoroughly wet. Presumably in these cases they would quickly reconceptualise the object they were studying. And it does not matter at what point the investigation is taken as starting from. A and B cannot say 'Let us investigate that object before we conceptualise it'. If they decide to walk closer to it they are already theorising (this, among other possibilities) that the object that looks like an oasis might not really be an oasis, and so they have already conceptualised it as a possible illusion–which conceptualisation is now determining their methodology of walking closer to it. If they decide to suspend judgment until they determine whether the water feels wet, again they have conceptualised a possible illusion which in turn suggests a methodology for investigation.

There is one further possibility that can be taken from this example. Assume that A and B have no experience of oases, mirages, palm trees or grass. They would then be in a position to regard their object in terms of: 'What is that unfamiliar thing?' But even this could not lead to a pre-conceptual or theory-free methodology of investigation. In agreeing to investigate the object A and B would still have to formulate some tentative hypotheses, such as that the object can be investigated; that it is a physical reality which can be seen, touched, smelt; that the perceived blue of the water, contrasted with the yellow of the sand, is a significant factor for attention; and so on. Some of these may be false hypotheses (especially if the object is a mirage), but the point would still hold. And the point comes not from a hypothetical reading of A's and B's minds, or an empirical punt that people formulate hypotheses and theories before investigating. The point simply is that this is inevitable.

We can thus conclude that when we attempt to investigate or operate upon some object we must inevitably have a concept of the object; a hypothesis, a theory, however tentative and preliminary, of the nature of the object; for it is only on this condition that one can devise methods of investigation and aims of operation. Each methodology of investigation is thus theory-laden; and this notion, of course, is quite in contrast to classical empiricist–inductivist theory.

It should be noted, however, that some modern inductivist accounts of scientific method and data collection attempt to accommodate this issue by distinguishing between the ways in which theories are formulated and the ways in which they are justified. They accept that theories may be formulated in many ways, and that the gathering of data is theory-dependent, not theory-free; but they still claim that observation and recording within such a context can provide support and justification for a theory. But the final appeal, in such cases, is usually made to probability–psychological experimentation employing levels of significance is a classic case–and the methodologies involved can usually be seen to contain some circularity and bias. This is not the place, however, to enter into the necessarily long and complex arguments required to counter these moves. Having merely noted them, we shall return to our own position, and move forward from what we take to be a completely unavoidable situation, namely that we can begin investigations only when we have some theory of the object under investigation.

Theory, concepts and methodology

At this point it is worth entering into a rather lengthy elaboration of the thesis presented in the previous section; first, in order to clinch it (for it is still not widely accepted); and second, to spell out in more detail how theory and methodology intertwine, and dominate even what appear to be paradigm *prima facie* cases of theory-free investigations.

Let us take as an example the task of counting the number of people on the university oval at a given particular time. Surely, it might be suggested here that nothing more is required than that an investigator simply goes down to the oval at a given particular time and counts. And surely if many investigators, given normal vision and the ability to count, were to undertake this task, then each of them (give or take a bit of human fallibility) would come back with the same total, which would in turn correspond to the number of people who were on the oval at the particular time of the test (i.e., to the 'given' data).

Actually, neither of these suggestions is correct. But this is not to imply that consensus could not be reached. Consensus could be reached in a number of ways. There could be a cancelling-out effect brought about by various inclusions and exclusions adopted by each investigator according to individual theoretic stances. And consensus could also arise if all the investigators agreed on the same theory, and employed the same methodology appropriate to the agreed-on theory.

Consensus is only marginally to the point here, however. What it is crucial to recognise is that the task at hand is not theory-free; and that different theories can account for different numbers of people being found on the same oval at the same time. There is an obvious explanation for that, and a less obvious one as well. The obvious explanation is that there are competing theories as to what counts as a 'person', and what counts as 'on the oval'; less obvious is the point that our answers to these questions will then determine what counts as appropriate methodology for collecting data.

Counting the number of people on the oval requires that we have concepts of the objects under consideration, and viable notions of what we shall include as instances. To begin with, we need a concept of what a 'person' is; and at first blush this might appear to be anything but a problem for us. By and large we know what people are, and in our everyday discourse we would rarely, if ever, find ourselves in discussion as to whether X was a person or not. We have a loose but adequate notion of a 'person', and a general theoretical framework determining what shall count as 'persons', and in most instances these work well enough for us. But they don't work well enough in all instances, or for all people.

There is a whole area of philosophy, an area that engages and continues to engage some of the sharpest minds of our species, that is centrally concerned with the very question our normal discourse takes as answered, namely – what is a 'person'? (and subsequently, how are persons differentiated from non-persons?). Common areas of debate centre round issues such as whether tiny babes and/or children count as persons – Mill excluded children from falling under the aegis of his principle of liberty, and virtually all societies deny children some rights and privileges which they afford to fully fledged persons–and whether human beings who do not, or who no longer, function as individual centres of consciousness (the severely mentally defective, or those reduced to a state of vegetation by a stroke, for example) still count as persons. Now this is hardly the limit of the debate: some argue that personhood is not achieved until something like Piaget's stage of formal operations is reached; others talk in terms of physical self-regulation or social self-regulation, and so on. And the arguments, and the issue, of course, have recently been vastly complicated by science fiction and science fact. The test-tube babies of Huxley's *Brave New World* can now be created in the laboratory as well as in the novelist's imagination: are they persons? Scientists are now able to produce computers far more 'intelligent' than man: if they are designed to look like people would they be persons? (Already we have had two ominous films, *2001* and *Westworld*, where super-computers take over, outsmart and destroy the persons who created them.) And nearer to home, science has learnt how to prevent conception, and how to abort prenatal development, which brings up the question 'Is the foetus a person?' This question underlies much of the current furore and debate over the matter of abortion; and if nothing else it should indicate that philosophic probing into the question of persons does not merely produce grist for academic mills in ivory towers. 'What is a person?' is an important question, with serious application to the real world. With all that said, let us now return to the university oval, and place some interesting people on it.

In the light of the above discussion let us start with a pregnant woman, a very obviously pregnant woman. Now remember that it has been suggested that our investigator has simply to go down to the oval and count the people on it; that is (presumably) to count the people he *sees*. Well, here he sees only one person, but he also sees enough to suspect that that person is carrying a foetus within her, and that the foetus is in a very well developed state. Now there is a theoretical and a practical issue involved here: let us begin by examining the theoretical one.

Is the foetus a person? Obviously the answer to that, whether it be 'yes', 'no', or ' "no" up to x months but "yes" after x months', will affect the person count. Let us now assume that our investigator marks only 'one' on his checklist, on the grounds that the foetus is not, or not yet, a person. Let us also assume that when we question that investigator on the matter of abortion he claims that abortion is wrong because killing the foetus is killing a person. Here we have a fascinating situation where the very concept or theory of what a person is changes for a particular individual according to contingent factors and purposes.[4] Clearly, then, there is even more involved in undertaking a task than just having a concept of the object, for that concept itself might be affected by the task at hand. Here the task is counting people; and the central theoretical issue can now be seen to be not just *what shall count as a person?* but *what shall count as a person with respect to a particular task or situation?* Our concepts and theories are rarely universals; it is more the case that they have sufficient flexibility in order to operate or be operated in task-specific ways rather than 'objectively' (which is by no means to suggest that people can wilfully use them any way they want to, or define things any way they wish). Consider, as a further example, the concept of 'woman'. At first glance it appears quite simple to determine what a woman is and which instances we shall count as 'women'. But if we were members of the International Olympic Federation, determining who shall be eligible to count as competitors in women's events at the Olympic Games, then for that particular situation we would employ criteria that would categorically exclude people who, for just about every other intent and purpose, would count as women.

Let us turn now to the practical issue on the oval. Assume that our investigator works on the theory that the foetus *is* a person. Clearly this theory alters or affects his methodology. He can no longer count the people he *sees*; to determine the number of people he must *ask* each and every woman whether she is pregnant or not (or more than *x* months pregnant). This methodology in turn presumes other theoretical standpoints; for instance, that the women will be honest, that they know and can know if they are pregnant, and that they know how many foetuses they are actually carrying. Now our researcher might not be happy about these three issues, and may conclude that, in order to get properly valid results, all women on the oval should be subjected to a different methodology, namely a full gynaecological examination. And thus we now begin to see the whole situation in a fuller light: undertaking a task, gathering data or collecting facts is dependent in the first place on concepts and/or theory, which may even be specific to the particular task, and which in turn affect the methodology employed in undertaking the task. Conversely, the facts or data that are gained *emerge* out of the particular investigation and all its facets rather than being merely given or 'there', they are theory-laden, situationally specific, and methodologically determined and influenced.

At this point let us return to the oval and place two more instances on it: one, a person fast asleep, and two, a 'person' who was not long ago fast asleep but who is now dead. From even a short distance away they appear very much the same. Again a theoretical and a practical issue arise. The theoretical question is whether the dead, or newly dead, count as persons; and here we can be fairly sure of large-scale agreement in the negative. But the assumption that the dead shall not count as persons, if we think on it, must seriously affect our practice and methodology. The idea of simply going down to the oval, having a look and counting would be inadequate; for we would surely have to determine which of our candidates were alive before we counted. This would preclude (unless everybody on the oval was in a constant state of motion) sitting in the grandstand and taking a global count, and it would certainly preclude the use of still photographs (which might have been employed as the only means of counting in certain particular situations, such as when vast numbers were constantly moving across the oval). Concern about the newly dead would require the observer to make careful observations of each case before including it or excluding it. And should he be unfortunate enough to run into a case that he thinks is dead he has great troubles indeed, because we are anything but certain ourselves as to just when a person is dead: this is an area of great controversy, wherein even the legal opinion on death and the medical opinion do not coincide exactly. Shall our investigator take a layman's decision, or call in a doctor, or a lawyer? The result could affect the person-count.

Our investigator could partly overcome the problems here by insisting that each instance demonstrate its mobility before it is counted (implicitly theorising that movement indicates life). This would, in all probability, be an odd way of going about counting the number of people on the university oval. And yet it is the standard way of counting the number of people on the parade ground of a corrective institution or detention area. In this case people are likely to want to escape, and perhaps to mask their disappearance by leaving behind a dummy figure, as one notable character did at Colditz. So those charged with the same task, counting heads, as it were, require the prisoner to move as he answers his name; this being a further example where specific contingencies and particular theories influence methodology; and a clear example of a point to be spelt out shortly – namely that motives also influence methodology.

We have by no means finished with the university oval as yet. Having decided on the person-status of dead people, we might be none too cheered to observe kindly nurses wheeling out vegetated stroke cases to 'enjoy' the fresh air and sunshine on the oval, including one who is being kept alive only by machinery. And it would be too cruel an act of fate to find a circus nearby, and the oval a relaxing ground for the two-headed lady, the half man – half fish and an assortment of Siamese twins. All we need now is a schizophrenic insisting to the investigator that he is *two* people, and we might expect the poor chap to give up in frustration.

13

We are, of course, beginning to overstep the limits of credibility; but well before this we have clearly exposed some of the hidden difficulties in 'simply' counting the people on the university oval. It is a task that is theory-laden, and the methodology used in carrying it out is theory-based; and in each aspect there are multiple dimensions of influence at work. If we ever did end up with a count of the number of people on the oval, thus completing the task of gathering data, it would be more correct to say that 'x people were found on the oval, through the application of theories $T_1 \ldots T_n$, and the use of methodologies appropriate to them'; than to say simply 'x people were on the oval'. We should note particularly here that the shorthand statement obscures certain factors that were essential in formulating the basic notion expressed by the statement. It thus disguises for us the reality of the situation it seeks to describe, for our knowledge of the number of people on the oval is determined by us through theory (and all that we have seen that goes with it), whereas the statement that gives utterance to that knowledge tends to suggest that we have merely read off the existential state of affairs down at the oval. In areas far more important than this one a great number of our statements work in much the same way, suggesting that things and states of affairs are merely given, and thus disguising how they have actually been brought about. This is one of the legacies of empiricism; and at times, as we shall see, it can be powerfully interest-serving, and not just harmless fashion.

It is important at this stage to elaborate on one of the dimensions that has been barely mentioned so far—this is the matter of motives influencing concepts and theory (and in turn influencing methodology). To do this we need not concern ourselves with the extreme situation where observers or experimenters 'rig' test situations to produce the results they want,[5] for we can simply consider more subtle instances where motives are allied with and woven into the purpose of the exercise. We have already seen instances approximating this sort of thing where observers or data-collectors apply *task-specific* concepts (as with 'women' and the Olympic Games): what I want to consider now is the application of *observer–motive-specific* concepts, theories and methodologies. Suppose, for example, that one of our investigators at the oval knows, or suspects (and we can't stop people suspecting) that he is undertaking the count in order to provide data for a *pro rata* grant based on the number of people using the oval. He could thus be easily motivated to come up with as high a total as possible; and he could easily achieve this without overstepping any acceptable bounds. All he has to do is interpret those fine distinctions that are open to debate in a way that serves his particular purpose. He could set his definitional parameters for 'people' and 'on the oval' as wide as is reasonable. He might simply allow for people sitting astride the oval fence to count as *on*, and for all instances distinguishable by sight from the grandstand as people to count as people. Thus he would not reject tiny children, nor would he examine his instances more closely, and in a different manner, to weed out any dead bodies from his count. On the other hand, should an investigator want as low a total as possible, he could narrow his parameters, and tighten up his methodology. For him, sitting astride the fence is *not* 'on the oval', 'people' would be more tightly defined, but still acceptably defined, and each instance originally included through a sight count might then be more closely investigated in the hope of weeding some out. More esoteric examples also come to mind. If the count is being made to assist in determining the number of showers to go into the new amenities block, our investigator might include those people straddling the fence who are obviously resting from some athletic activity, while excluding straddlers who are clearly spectators; if the count is a preliminary to providing seating around the oval, he might go the other way. Examples could be multiplied endlessly, but the point is surely clear. And it is very largely the same point that underlies the growing use of the 'blind' or 'double blind' in the more rigorous experiments in the behavioural sciences, the human sciences and medicine. In these instances the person doing the 'hack work' (giving tests, counting people, measuring responses, administering drugs, etc.) has his parameters strictly defined for him; he does not know the hypothesis under test and so does not know why he is doing what he is doing; he might not know who are subjects and who are controls, or which capsules are drugs and which are placebos. And in this way it is hoped (among other things) that greater rigour and objectivity will be achieved: which is only another way of admitting that conscious motives and purposes can, through influencing our concepts and theory, and with them our methodology, influence the results we obtain from an investigation of the world.

Two objections should now be countered before this section is brought to a close. The first relates to motives, for it might be claimed that if investigators have any motives other than the diligent collection of 'facts' and the pursuit of truth, then of course their findings will be biased. Thus to introduce investigators with other motives is to 'stack the deck' before the game is played. That may be so – but the real problem is to *eliminate* them. It is doubtful that such elimination is completely possible in a human context; and we have, as we shall see, an abundance of data from psychology that indicates how motives continually influence our judgment. Also, in most areas of investigation there is sufficient conceptual ambiguity (as with 'on the oval') to render different interpretations of single situations equally plausible. If these things are so, then there must be countless situations where, all other things being equal, and perhaps *because* all other things are equal, motives tip the scale one way or another. In investigating the world we might attempt to split off all our biases and specific personal motives; if we could the effort might be laudable, but this would neither remove the other problems, nor absolve us from at least being aware of the issue of motives, and how they can influence theory and methodology. As a final related point, the phenomenon of the 'Hawthorne effect' should not be lost sight of, either: that is, that the test situation, simply by being a test situation, can alter what is under study. In this case the finest motives of the most objective investigator might be ensured and controlled, say, by the 'double blind' or other means; yet the very test situation itself might yield to the investigator results that are affected by his investigation, rather than those that would have been 'given up' by the world independently of him and his investigation. As a fairly trivial example, some people might quit the university oval if they see or suspect someone counting heads there.

One final objection to consider is that the 'university oval' example was a bad or a loaded one, especially since it included definitional problems concerning 'people'. How about counting the number of cats on the oval? Or bottles? Well, a moment's reflection will indicate that these examples bring about substantive changes, but do not affect the principles involved. Cats get pregnant, but can't even tell us if they are or not. Cats can manoeuvre along the oval fence in ways people can't. Bottles still have to be distinguished from jars; and what shall we do about partial, or broken bottles? If we are to count only unbroken bottles, how carefully must we examine each instance? Obviously the problems were not introduced into our quest merely by basing an example on *people*; there could be *more* problems if the task concerned cats or bottles. But it could still be suggested that, even with cats or bottles, the task is still loaded. Do the same problems arise if we have to count the number of bottles on the table before us, or the number of red stripes in a given handkerchief?

The answer to that is 'yes'; but some qualifications need to be made. One can reduce the theoretical issues involved by progressively trivialising the task or enquiry at hand. But no matter how ingeniously we trivialise, we still cannot reach a theory-free task : all we really do is introduce lower level and/or less interesting theories. Counting the red stripes in a handkerchief involves certain problems; counting the red stripes *over one inch wide* eliminates some and brings in others, but still requires a concept of 'red', 'stripe', 'inch' and 'width'. We can never postulate a theory-free task or investigation, and rather than bend our wits towards trivialisation in the hope of approximating such a thing, we would do better to take warning that the investigations we carry on in the world are usually anything but trivial; they are also usually more complicated, conceptually, theoretically and methodologically, than counting people on an oval. And they are always theory-laden.

This recognition leads us towards a problem that is of the greatest importance in understanding the limitations and weaknesses of empiricist methodology in complex areas of research into social issues and social conditions. Strict empiricism must take the conditions it investigates as the end-point or result of some historical process or means of development. But social processes, issues and conditions are never just 'there'; their existence in the present is the result of at least two factors – the historical process that brought them about, *and the ongoing practical and theoretical conditions that maintain and reproduce them in the present.* Empiricism, by standing back and focusing on the conditions that 'exist', thus fails to account for, or even consider problematic, that social relations and conditions are also in a continual state of theoretic reproduction and reconstruction, and are never simply given empirically. Empiricist social research, then, is not a-theoretical; it is both theory-laden and mistaken in its theoretical stance; and the results it produces simply reinforce and legitimise its presuppositions, namely that certain social conditions and relations are given and natural, and that they can be seen properly in such a light. The shorthand language, identified earlier, in which the results are usually couched further reinforces this position. And we can now begin to see how empiricism can become a powerful interest-serving tool: by representing, or rather misrepresenting, certain aspects of the world as given, natural, and possibly immutable and unchangeable (a representation that is subtly bolstered in our ordinary language), it serves, in a positive manner, those people who have an objective interest in the maintenance of the *status quo*.

This particular matter takes us ahead too far and too quickly, and will be returned to when we focus more closely on 'ideology'. The particular aim of this section was merely to demonstrate that investigations, and methodologies for investigation, are necessarily theory-laden. Put crudely, theory determines what counts, and how to count it: there is no such thing as non-theoretical knowledge. In passing we have also (necessarily) shown that a fact – a knowledge statement (say, about the number of people on an oval) – is not a neutral description of what '*is*', but rather something that has been established as such by theory and methodology together, and which is also vulnerable to the effects of contingencies and motives. This essential theory-ladenness necessarily prevents empiricism from ever reaching the foundations of sure, objective knowledge, or from ever seeing the world unmediated as a prelude to revealing what it is really like.

There is still a great deal more, of course, that has to be said about the way we gain knowledge of the world; but in proceeding with this, while we shall continue to make further criticisms of empiricism, we shall also begin to lay some ground for answering a question that the previous discussion has left begging - namely, if all investigations are theory-laden, where does our theory come from?

Gaining data about the world

The claim we have made, that all methodology for investigation is theory-laden, and that data we finish up with are established by the theory or theories underlying our search, is not quite complete, for it does not as yet bite sufficiently against the basic empiricist epistemology which the inductivist account of gaining knowledge largely relies on. Empiricism, in brief, claims that we can gain true valid knowledge of the world through our senses; and the hard-core empiricist would claim that this is the only way that we can gain true, objective knowledge. Now our thesis, while placing theory between the endeavour to gain knowledge and the knowledge gained, has so far said nothing specific with regard to *sensory experience* which might suggest that there are faults in the empiricist account. The purpose of this section, therefore, is to focus on the place of sensory experience in gaining knowledge, and thus to show that the empiricist account of gaining knowledge, even in that respect, is a misleading one. We shall not, of course, deny that man gains sensory experience, or even that knowledge might (must?) begin with sensory experience; but we shall show that there are 'filtration mechanisms', some largely (but not completely) separated from theory, which operate in such a way that what is *sensed* and what is *known* could be two completely different things. In the discussion that follows 'sensation' is used to refer to activation of sense organs (sound waves striking the eardrum, retinal stimulation, etc.); while 'perception' refers to cerebral interpretation of sensations. The distinction will become clear as the discussion proceeds.

Let us begin at a very basic level. As we live in the world we do not sense things always as separate entities, nor do we sense things devoid of context. In all likelihood we sense an aggregation of an infinite number of things; and from these we select what we are after, and we order what we select, such that we experience a more or less coherent world. It is this phenomenon that led Kant, in his *Critique of Pure Reason*, to argue for the necessity of certain *a priori* concepts and categories acting as organisers of experience; and for modern-day Kantians like Piaget to theorise from a psychological viewpoint that the growing person learns to impose order on the booming buzzing confusion that he finds on his entry into the world. Certainly we do find order and coherence for ourselves, which allows us to live unbombarded and minimally confused, and we achieve this basic ability to undertake activities through selection of sensory inputs.

The notion of selection at this stage cuts two ways for our argument. In a strict empiricist-inductivist account of gaining knowledge, *a priori* selection is ruled out on methodological grounds, and in any situation the inductivist observer must note and record *everything* since, because he is ostensibly working in a theory-free way, all is equally relevant or irrelevant to him. Thus, in observing the moon's orbit, he not only has to record the length of his toenails, along with the phase of the moon, but he also has to get in the *whole* of the booming buzzing confusion; and this, if it is not impossible, would at least take all of eternity. This might leave us with little faith in inductivist attempts to ever come up with valid generalisations. And the second point about selection is that it appears to be a basic necessity for living and functioning in the world; so much so that it is tempting to postulate the operation of some natural psychological/physiological mechanism as a prerequisite for meaningful human existence. If this *were* so, then clearly perceiving (knowing) and sensing could be seen to be two different things, separated by a *natural* filtration mechanism.

We need not go to such lengths, or entertain naturalistic hypotheses, however, to illustrate the operation of selection and filtration; for selection, whether it be physiologically natural or not, is almost always a deliberate affair, and very often a sophisticated affair. When driving we do not read the billboards, which we can presumably see, and which our passengers do read, but we do read the road signs; and we watch out for potholes but not for interesting cloud formations. When searching a drawer for a missing piece of paper we hardly attend to the assorted odds and ends we dig out; we give more attention to bits of paper that look like the one we seek; and so on. The same applies when we are trying to find a comet in the skies, a particular property of a cell, or the causes of a significant shift in the political beliefs of a group. Put simply, we rule out or filter out what we take to be irrelevant, and we attend to what we believe to be relevant. Now there are obviously underlying bases for these things, such as efficiency and theory; for the nature of the selection process just described is anything but random. But what I want to argue now is that, while in all situations there may be a necessary element of filtration occurring, in deliberate goal-directed situations we necessarily find specific aspects or modes of filtration occurring between what we sense and what we perceive. The most common, and most important, of these are our existing knowledge, our preconceptions, our experience, forces like repression and other deluding mechanisms, and our linguistic categories; there are then slightly different, but still more significant, factors like prejudice, social pressure and mental sets. With some of these cases theory comes very much to the fore: but the point to be stressed is that, when theory enters here, it can do so in a different way from that discussed in the previous section – we shall find instances when theory, not merely concerned with conceptual issues, actually has us perceiving other than what we sense. Let us now turn to these 'filtration mechanisms', and begin with one that involves theory to a significant degree.

The issue of knowledge, preconceptions and experience can be illustrated by the well known 'anomalous playing-cards' experiment.[6] Subjects were shown normal playing-cards for very short periods of time, and were able to identify them quite well. But then anomalous cards were introduced, such as a red ace of spades and a black ace of diamonds. At first the subjects identified these as normal cards, perceiving the red ace of spades either as a proper 'black' ace of spades, or as a proper red ace of 'hearts'. Then one of two things began to happen: either the subjects came to realise that anomalous cards were present, or else they were told so by the experimenter. From this point on they correctly identified the anomalous cards. Now all that had changed was the subjects' knowledge, preconceptions and experience: what they saw, as a visual retinal image, remained the same; but the change in perception was quite marked.

Another example of this comes from the popular children's puzzle that involves finding a human face among the foliage in the drawing of a tree. What the subject sees at first is a tree. But once attention is drawn towards finding a face, and once the face has been detected, the whole thing is perceived differently. The same shapes that are visually seen are now perceived not as foliage but as features of a face. And once the face has been perceived, the same subject, at a later time, can very easily pick it out again: his knowledge and experience now allow him to perceive what others, without that knowledge and experience, are likely to have difficulty in perceiving, if they perceive it at all.

The influence of theory in these two cases is quite obvious. In the former case the subjects, having knowledge and theory of what playing cards look like, and no reason to expect anomalies, perceive anomalous cards (which they *saw* as anomalies) in terms of their theory of what normal cards should look like. In the latter example the perception of foliage arises in part from the theory that foliage is foliage. Only when the puzzle is put (barring pure accident) does the subject search for clues to fit another, and again less-expected, theory.

There are many other examples where knowledge and experience influence what one perceives, as distinct from what one senses, but where the issue of theory could hardly be taken to account significantly for the phenomenon. Sleeping mothers are known to be awakened by the cry of their babies while others in the same household, with presumably equal hearing faculties, do not hear and are not awakened by what must surely be striking their eardrums too. It is also well known that people long experienced at living near railway lines, or on farms, sleep through the roar of trains and the lowing of cattle, while their occasional guests have restless nights. Try sleeping in a house with a clock that loudly chimes each quarter-hour if you are not used to it.

We see from these examples that, right at the very basic level of what appears to be no more than sensory receptivity to stimuli, there is a gap between sensing and perceiving, between seeing and noticing. Thus Hansen claims that there is more to seeing than meets the eyeball;[7] and he could have added that there is more to hearing than meets the eardrum. These simple examples are sufficient to undermine any empiricist claim to sensorily derived objective knowledge; and they can be extended in two directions. At an even more basic level yet we could show how our senses can deceive us through simple illusions, thus feeding us information that is quite wrong; but let us take that as read and move instead into areas of increasing complexity.

Delusion also affects our perception, and as self-delusion it takes many forms. Shakespeare noted one form in Antonio, of whom Prospero says:[8]

> He thus being lorded,
> Not only with what my revenue yielded,
> But what my power might else exact, like one
> Who having unto truth, by telling of it,
> Made such a sinner of his memory,
> To credit his own lie, he did believe
> He was indeed the duke . . .

Freud notes several other forms, such as repression of things that are sensed but are too difficult for the conscious mind to accept; and reaction formation, where what is seen can call out responses to a totally inverted perception of the case; and regression, where things are perceived not as they 'are' but with a mind which has gone back in time and experience to perceive them in a more comfortable, acceptable way; and projection, where things are perceived in the wrong end of their context, such that what a man sees of himself he perceives in others; and rationalisation, where things which are deliberately fabricated are perceived as if they really relate to the situation at hand. In Freudian theory these are all defence mechanisms, and unless taken to extremes are regarded as *normal* parts of our *normal* everyday behaviour. The idea, over-simply, is that bits of life and bits of experience are usually, and more so in times of stress, too hot to handle. So each and every human being, in his own individual way, depending on his own individual experience, defends himself by making personal adaptations to the physical and interpersonal world he lives in and experiences largely through his senses.

21

We should note again that the above delusions, including Antonio's, are not abnormal ones, at least not until they are taken to such extremes that resultant behaviour pathology becomes clearly evident. A significant part of the legacy Freud left us is the disturbing notion that each person's world, or each person's perception of the world, can be regarded as a distortion, or a deluded picture, marked out by the necessary defences that each normal individual erects between himself and the world outside himself. This would further indicate that man, rather than simply reacting to an external given world, interacts with and in a world that he himself partly constructs, and constructs at times with little regard for the sensory experience (and rational knowledge) that he gains from the world.

There is, given the insight Freud has provided us with, something a little wrong in referring to the above phenomena as 'delusions'; but there are, of course, cases where the notion of 'delusion' is more appropriate. The paranoid might actually perceive guns in the hands of those he believes have come to kill him – guns that he could not possibly *see*, of course. The schizophrenic might perceive the same object or state of affairs differently while in two different states. The alcoholic might really perceive a world full of pink elephants, and this perception (or hallucination) could hardly arise from sensory experience. How are these phenomena to be explained? One thing is certain: they cannot be *explained away* as easily as they once might have been.

Let us consider hallucinations first. There is growing evidence that suggests that people under the influence of drugs, alcohol and even sensory-deprivation conditions do not simply see things that aren't there; it seems to be the case that, in such situations, certain neurological/physiological inhibiting mechanisms are rendered inoperative such that the people 'see things' that 'are there' but that are usually filtered out under normal conditions.[9] Such a thesis lends weight, of course, to the notion of 'ordering' the world through filtration of sensory inputs, but it also raises the question as to what are normal conditions. Here we might reconsider paranoia, schizophrenia and the notion of insanity in general; for again we are now not as certain as we once might have been with regard to when a perceiving mind can be judged to be insane or out of touch with reality. R. D. Laing's notion that certain forms of 'insanity' are really sane reactions to an insane world should, if nothing else, demand that we seriously reconsider the idea of human action as reaction to a perceived world.[10] The existential world can be neither sane nor insane, but the individual can perceive it as either, or as orderly or chaotic. Now insanity, virtually by definition, is reaction that does not follow the norm, even given that the norm might be widely defined; but once we take the emphasis off 'reaction' and place it on 'perception', i.e. that insanity is reaction to a *perception* of the world that does not follow the norm (as Laing seems to be suggesting), then we have an interesting problem, and with it full-scale difficulties, especially for an empiricist account of knowledge.

When, and on what grounds, can we say that an individual (or minority) perception or viewpoint is insane, as opposed to being just wrong? [11] Certainly the majority viewpoint need not necessarily be the correct one, and history has surely warned us many times of the folly of pitting consensus up against an unbalanced 'insane' individual. Galileo is probably the most famous example of a non-conformist who was branded insane in his time and yet was regarded as sane by later generations. But right throughout history a continual sequence of inquisitions, witch-hunts, Royal Academies and commissions has killed, discredited or ostracised people for preaching absurdities and heresies that were to become the orthodoxies of later times. One thing is sure: if it were not for 'crazy' people who perceived things differently from the majority, and who were willing to stand out against consensus and have their sanity brought into question, every area of human endeavour would be arrested at a long-distant point in the past.

None of this, of course, answers the question as to when and how we can say that one perception is right and another wrong, or that one is better than another. That shall be the subject for much of our future discussion: at this stage we shall simply note further features that mediate between sensation and perception.

The next aspect we shall consider that affects our perception is the linguistic categories or concepts we have, those things that allow us to say what we sense. It is claimed that certain North American Indians have only three number categories: one, two and many. (It hardly matters whether this is, or still is, the case, for the point will hold hypothetically.) A person with these linguistic categories would, when faced by five cows, say 'many'; and when faced by seven cows would also say 'many'. Now if visual acuity tests indicated that this person saw two different things, then we have a clear case where certain details of what is sensed are considered irrelevant or unimportant when a conceptualisation of what has been sensed is formulated. And given that we can only create discourse, and thus express knowledge statements around and with our conceptual schemes, it appears that our thought and knowledge of the world is formulated and bounded more by our perceptions/conceptualisations than by our sensory experiences. Man might sense many things, but he can only express what he perceives: and both the perception and the expression of it are together limited by the particular concepts (and symbolic systems) that are available in the situation, that is, in the particular socio-historical situation. If certain people had only one concept for those things that shine in the sky at night – 'heavenly bodies' – they would presumably *see* stars, planets, comets and the moon, yet perceive only 'heavenly bodies'. If at some time they came to recognise that some of these bodies shine of their own accord while others only reflect light, or if they had already noticed this but now decided that the difference was significant, the situation would have arisen in which they would be able to *perceive* stars and planets. It is in this way that knowledge can be seen to be the product of sensory experience filtered through conceptual schemes.[12] And concepts, and conceptual schemes, have more than just a strong historical-social character about them; the concepts that are available to people are actually determined by the socio-historical milieu in which those people live. This, however, in no way implies that conceptual schemes necessarily describe the world as it is; nor does it imply that conceptual schemes necessarily mirror or reveal our knowledge of the world.[13] But given, as we have repeatedly stressed, that concepts precede investigation, it certainly does imply that our investigations of the world are necessarily socio-historically determined. This is an issue of great importance to us, and will be returned to later; here let us now consider some further filtration factors, namely prejudice, social pressure, and mental sets.

Prejudice, in its non-pejorative sense, means pre-judging, and thus it can hardly be distinguished from knowledge, experience and preconceptions, all taken together. Thus it is a 'mechanism' wherein theory is operating to a large degree. I want to consider two aspects in the operation of prejudice; first, where prejudice operates more like a floodgate than a filter, bringing to our perception things not present at the sensory level, and thus allowing knowledge claims to be made on grossly insufficient sensory data; and second, where prejudice does act as a filter to bring about selective noticing from a multitude of sensations.

For the 'floodgate' phenomenon consider the experiment where subjects were shown photographs of men who fell roughly into two categories: clean-cut, handsome and smiling; and swarthy, cauliflower-eared and grim-faced: the subjects were then given a list of occupations ranging from doctor and lawyer down to criminal, and were asked to fit the occupation to the face. The results show a clear pattern and strong agreement. Now it would appear that all the subjects had to go on was a visual image of a face, but somehow that visual impression (sensation) 'told' the subjects a great deal more about the person they were looking at. The perceiving mind, it seems, does not simply accept the sensory message: 'black hair, brown eyes, broken nose, scar on left cheek, etc.'; rather, by means of prejudicial 'filling in' or the opening of floodgates, it perceives a lot more than the very scant data really offer.

In another experiment subjects listened to 'interviews' wherein, in one case, the interviewee gave answers to questions that generally fitted in with his job and life situation, while in the other case the interviewee gave answers that did not fit neatly (e.g. high salary, but disregard for luxury consumer items). The subjects then inferred considerably more about the latter's personality, presumably on the grounds that 'lack of fit' with one's life situation reveals certain fairly reliable criteria about a person.

An even more significant experiment is the one where two groups of subjects were given a check-list of personality traits and a photograph of a girl, the only difference being that one group was told that the photograph was of a *Jewish* girl. This group then found the expected stereotyped Jewish traits to an extent not found by the other group, yet both groups saw exactly the same thing. This sort of prejudicial response is, of course, quite familiar to all of us, and in everyday living we continually emit, and respond to, minimal data or sketches which we and others fill in with remarkably predictable consistency.[14]

Prejudice resulting in selective noticing is just as familiar to us. If our travel agent builds up Rome as the most exciting city of them all, we will probably find it that way. If we believe Negroes to be dirty we are likely to find dirt in their homes that we might not notice in a white home. If we believe a class to be dumb we will notice all the dumb things they do. And even worse things can follow from this; for such attitudes and prejudices can, as Rosenthal and Jacobson have shown,[15] set into motion self-fulfilling prophecies whereby subjects actually do come to act in accord with the prejudiced expectations of others.

In summary, two points can be taken from the notion of prejudice. On the one hand, prejudice enables us to perceive more than we see. On the other hand, it is instrumental in producing *selective noticing*: of all the stimuli that reach an observer some are especially singled out for attention. In both senses prejudice brings about perception of the world that is something other than a mere unmediated response to sensory experience of the world.

Social pressure is another factor that influences our knowledge of the world. It is a common phenomenon that certain people tend to go along with the majority, and to accept things that are generally agreed on, or that are supported by famous authorities or other types of power figures. This phenomenon is particularly relevant to education, which is usually characterised both by naive people getting their knowledge from authorities and by the attempt to bring about a form of large-scale consensus. But when we find that intelligent mature American college students can easily be brought to believe grossly erroneous claims of an emotionally neutral kind, such as that the average American family has five or six children, and that American males have a life expectancy of twenty-five years, simply by being 'worked on' by peer groups,[16] we should never dare to undervalue the power of group pressure to influence and determine an individual's knowledge.[17]

Social pressure also affects perception. A series of famous experiments by Asch, Deutsch, Krech and Crutchfield demonstrate this quite clearly.[18] Generally, although not all the experiments were the same, subjects were shown lines, and were asked to make judgments about their relative length. But they were also shown what they believed to be the choices that several of their peers had already made. When there was only a small difference between the lines the subjects tended to deny what they 'saw' and side with the majority. Now it is obvious that a third step has been introduced with this example. We have (1) what the subjects saw; (2) what they perceived; and (3) what they said they saw or perceived. But since it is impossible to know what someone perceives until he reports it, (3) may be taken as identical with (2), except where this is explicitly denied, in the form of 'I saw X, but I said I saw Y'. Some subjects in post-test interviewing admitted to this; yet we might assume that, in real-life situations, some of these subjects, having seen X to be the case, would still have acted as if Y were the case. But more interesting are those who continued to claim Y to be the case, denying their sensations[19] (and the worth of their own opinion) and accepting what the majority said. We see again a filtering mechanism operating between a person's sensation of the world and how he perceives the world: perception and knowledge again are influenced by mediating factors and are not merely a result of direct sensory response to a given external world. Incidentally, the problem of conformity to group opinion appears to have quite complex roots, for it has been shown that, in Western cultures, there is a strong relationship between emotional arousal and resistance to conformity.[20] This could imply that certain personality types are better fitted to resist conforming, which in turn could indicate that our perception and knowledge of the world are also filtered according to personality characteristics (and perhaps physiological factors as well).

The last 'filtration device' that I want to consider is that of mental set. Mental sets do not lend themselves easily to precise definition, but they have long been known to influence our perception. They can account for some illusions, like Ames's room or others involving size and perspective, where things seen or sensed as one size or shape are perceived otherwise because of the set that distant things appear smaller or things that are smaller must be more distant. They can account for the 'proofreading phenomenon' whereby a person reading a page for its sense may glide over spelling errors, while a proofreader may gain no sense from what he reads. And they can account for the fascinating things that happen when people are asked to read the following:

It is nothing short of amazing just how long it takes some people, even with directed prompts like 'point to each word', to realise that the figures do *not* say 'Home of the brave', 'Land of the free'. If we see the two 'the's' we do not perceive them; if we do not even see them then there are yet bigger problems for empiricist accounts. (Part of the 'set' effect is we never expect two consecutive 'the's' in a sentence; part arises from the phrases' familiarity; part from incomplete eyescanning.)

There is a great deal more that needs to be said about mental sets, but this shall be left aside for a moment. The purpose of this section has been to argue against a strict empiricist view of gaining knowledge of the world by indicating at least some of the filtration mechanisms that operate between our sensation of the world and our perception or knowledge of the world, such that what we 'see' and what we know (perceive) are two different things. We have pointed to basic selective mechanisms which let us get about our business with minimal hindrance. We have noted psychological delusions and defences which allow us, as individuals, to interpret and accommodate our sensations in our own particular way. We have noted factors like group pressures, where aspects not pertaining to the object under investigation also influence how we perceive it. We have seen that, through 'floodgate prejudice', certain forms of mental sets and the operation of prior knowledge and experience, we can and do actually perceive things that are not even there to sense. All of these mechanisms, and others like our conceptual schemes, in all probability interact in the most complex of ways; but we need only recognise here that they act as filters, mediating between the knower and what is to be known. Thus, not only are all our investigations necessarily theory-laden in terms of the concept of the object under investigation; but they might also be affected by the interplay of a number of other factors that come between us and the world, determining what we shall perceive and how we shall perceive it. With this notion established there is now more that needs to be said about mental sets.

Mental sets

Mental sets have a particular significance for us in a way that is not necessarily connected with sensory experience, but that is vitally connected with the way in which we gain knowledge of the world. In order to begin to understand this, consider the following elementary demonstration. Ask someone to answer the following three questions, being sure to deliver them quickly, as soon as the answer to each is given:

(1) What do we call a funny story that one person tells to another?
(2) What do we call the black substance given off from a fire?
(3) What do we call the white of an egg?

The chances are very good that the third answer given will be 'yolk', and that this answer will be given by a person who knows full well that the yolk is the yellow of the egg. The chances are also very good that you will be accused of *tricking* the person. And in a sense there has been some trick perpetrated, for the two previous answers (joke, smoke) have created and established categories of experience and response for answering the third question. The third question emerges *in a context*: it has implicitly been prefaced by an unuttered direction to think in a particular way before answering it. Consider now a far more significant example devised by A.S.Luchins.[21]

Luchins created a series of problems along the line of well-known children's mathematical puzzles dealing with obtaining required quantities of milk: e.g. if you only have a five gallon and a three gallon container how can you make up seven gallons in the simplest possible way? Luchins set a goal number and provided three numbers to manipulate. The problems read as follows:

a	b	c	goal
21	127	3	100
14	163	25	99
18	43	10	5
9	42	6	21
20	59	4	31
23	49	3	20
15	39	3	18
28	76	3	25

Each of the first five problems can be solved most easily by applying the formula $b-2c-a$. The next two can also be solved with this formula, but they can also be solved by *easier* formulae, $a-c$ and $a+c$ respectively. The last problem *cannot* be solved by $b-2c-a$ but can be solved by the simple formula $a-c$.

Luchins found that when people worked through from the beginning, 80 per cent of them used $b-2c-a$ for the sixth and seventh problems, and many were unable to solve the last one at all. People who began at the sixth problem, however, used $a-c$, then $a+c$, and had no trouble with the last one.

Luchins's experiment, of course, reinforces our earlier point against inductivism, for what was found to work seven times did not work in the eighth case. But more to the present point, we see that, when people acquire a set, or a way of thinking, or a theoretical framework, or a mode of operation, they tend to slot their experience, sensory or otherwise, into that set. Two crucial issues emerge from this. The first is that sets, as filtering mechanisms operating between the world and our knowledge of it, can be brought about in many ways. They can arise from common experience with the world – since two 'the's' never follow in a sentence one would not expect to find such an occurrence; since kangaroos commonly jump roads at dusk one ought to watch out for them then, etc. – but they can also be created for the individual, either overtly – 'always approach problems *this* way' – or covertly, as in Luchins's experiment. In this latter case we find that people can be given, or be subtly led, to give themselves categories, methods and sets with which to perceive and order the world; and that these categories for perceiving, experiencing and even thinking can simply be created or imposed by a form of manipulating one's experience with the world. Sets need not arise from direct interaction between an individual and the world; they can be imposed between an individual and the world to determine what he knows, what he does not know and what he cannot come to know. And their imposition can interfere with and distort, as well as assist or be neutral towards, the collection and ordering of data from sensory experience and/or rational cognitive processes. This leads directly to the second issue.

Sets do not necessarily offer solutions or unearth data and knowledge for us. They can impede such things just as well. In Luchins's experiment the set impeded some subjects from finding a simple solution when it was available; but worse, it impeded some from finding any solution when the set would not apply. Thus we see that sets can keep us working at certain methods while concealing other methods which would be more advantageous to us in gaining knowledge and solving problems. And sets can give rise to situations, as in Luchins's eighth problem, whereby if *the* method doesn't work it is taken that the problem can't be done. Sets (or theories) can exclude and deny us access to data; thus Feyerabend: 'there exist also facts which cannot be unearthed except with the help of alternatives to the theory to be tested, and which become unavailable as soon as such alternatives are excluded.'[22] Sets, or theories, are thus best seen both as revelations and as limitations: they both provide for, and deny, certain knowledge of the world. (Many people, for instance, are unable to determine the order in which the numbers 8, 5, 4, 9, 1, 7, 6, 3, 2 have been placed because of the operation of particular mental sets.)

Empiricism and the world

Our whole discussion so far has not had anything to say about the implications that empiricist theory and methodology have with regard to the other crucial factor involved in the issue of knowing, namely the object or the world. This can be attended to very quickly. Empiricism, like the mental sets we have been considering, also both provides for *and denies* certain knowledge of the world. What it provides for, and how adequately it provides, have already been hinted at; what it denies is far more important. Empiricism is a closed system, and as such it necessarily defines the real world according to its theoretical means, and confines the real world within the parameters in which its methodological tools can operate. And since the empiricists' basic tool is observation (or supposedly theory-free observation), empiricism simply cannot pick out that which is not observable, and the real world becomes reduced to that which is observable. What happens, then, to those things that are not observable?

Some non-observable things, like ethical principles, aesthetic judgments or theological premises, can hardly be said not to exist in the world; and these are simply dealt with by logical positivism (empiricism's philosophical backbone), which removes them from the realm of knowledge and places them in the categories of belief or opinion. They thus become parts of the world that we can have beliefs or opinions about, but they are not admitted into the real world that can be known.[23]

Other non-observable things, however, like Freud's notion of the 'unconscious', Marx's concept of 'class' or the nature of structures and the operation of forces in social relations, can be more easily dismissed, and are commonly dismissed by empiricists as either not existing in the world and/or as being not amenable to study (observation). Empiricist psychologists confine and define their study in terms of observable behaviour; empiricist sociologists concentrate on observable, measurable features of social relations and so on. Or at best, non-observables are restructured and reinterpreted in inappropriate and misleading ways. Thus R. L. Sears could make his famous claim that the great merit of social learning theory was that it made the insights of psychoanalytic theory amenable to the rigours of the experimental laboratory; whereas what really happened was that Freud's insights were reduced to 'drives' that could be measured on seven-point scales. Similarly, empiricist sociology took Marx's notion of 'class' and made it observable by defining classes in monetary terms rather than the relationist terms Marx employed. This 'redefinition', however, has neither accounted for nor done away with Freud's insights or Marx's concepts – which, like all those other unobservables, are hardly likely to go away just because a certain methodology cannot pick them out. There are more things, if not in heaven, then certainly on earth, than are dreamt of in empiricists' philosophy.

Having now noted the major weaknesses and limitations of empiricism,[24] the time has come for us to begin to draw together the positive points that have been won, and to set about the complicated task of building up a more satisfactory account of how we come to know the world.

Ordering data about the world

Given that we do not go about the world as random, all-collecting beings who read the world, gain knowledge as pure sensation, and store each and every bit of that knowledge somewhere in our cerebral mechanism, what really is involved in gaining and ordering knowledge? The answer we have been suggesting is that perception of any situation is characterised essentially by selective noticing or filtration, and that this process is determined in substantive fashion by our prior knowledge, our concepts, our preconceptions, our prejudices, our experience and our mental sets: it might even be influenced by our defence mechanisms, and by group pressures. These are the things that 'tell' us what to look for, what to notice, how to look, and how to categorise what we find. And it is these things, taken loosely together (for there could hardly be any strict ruling to determine their precise interaction), that make up an overall theoretical framework or matrix, containing areas of varying generality and specificity, in terms of which we select the data we shall notice, and into which we place that data for categorisation. This 'theoretic matrix' can be seen as a far more complex construction, which extends and continues the theory-methodology-contingency model established earlier.

To take a simplified illustration of its operation, consider three people on an archaeological site, one totally naive, the other two expert archaeologists. Place before them on the ground a small clay fragment. The naive person may not notice it, either because it does not capture his attention, or because so much is capturing his excited attention that he cannot isolate things in the booming confusion. The experts, however, because of their knowledge and experience, focus in on the fragment, and see it as a significant find. Knowledge and experience (and preconceptions perhaps) also make them perceive it as something specific. One expert, through specific knowledge and prejudice, perceives it as being part of the rim of a Mayan water carrier. The other expert, a member of a long-established respected school that denies the presence of the Maya in this area, perceives it as belonging to the stoneware of a different civilisation which never made contact with the Maya. For those three people then, at that point of time, the piece of clay is respectively a piece of clay, part of a Mayan jug, and proof that the Maya did not inhabit the area. It is to each person what that person takes it to be according to the particular criteria he has operating at the time for the purposes of

31

classifying and categorising it. (Perhaps there might be a fourth person present, for whom the fragment, for some strange reason, is a trumpet valve – but even this would not affect the present point.)

Given this notion, it again appears quite inappropriate to speak of a world of given 'facts', 'out there', waiting to be known by people. It seems more the case that we select particular 'facts' out of an infinite multitude, and order and categorise what we select in terms of all those things that pack into our particular theoretic matrix. Thus Gareth Stedman Jones, in speaking against the inductivist school of history, notes:[25]

> Those who tried to create theory out of facts, never understood that it was only theory that could constitute them as facts in the first place. Similarly those who focused history on the event, failed to realise that events are only meaningful in terms of a structure which will establish them as such.

And E.H. Carr has indicated that:[26]

> facts speak only when the historian calls on them: it is he who decides to which facts to give the floor, and in what order or context.

Carr also notes that:[27]

> the facts of history never come to us 'pure', since they do not and cannot exist in a pure form: they are always refracted through the mind of the recorder.

Theory, then, or the individual recorder or observer's theoretic matrix, constitutes 'facts' as facts, and establishes which events and occurrences shall be meaningful, and in what way. This recognition, however, raises two crucial problems which require some attention at this point.

In the first place, all the filtration mechanisms that we have identified are directly related, in substance, to historical and social circumstances, and at the same time to the individual's prior experience of and interaction with the world. This holds true even for Freudian defence mechanisms. Thus we can see on the one hand that gaining knowledge of the world is a process determined by the knowledge one has already gained of the world, and the adaptations one has made to the world; whereas on the other hand gaining knowledge of the world is determined, or at least limited, by what is 'available' in the world, that is to those things that the individual can gain access to as distinct from those things that are 'there'. (Neolithic man could not gain access to a round world even though the round world was there.) It appears, then, that an individual's theoretic matrix, or his way of coming to know the world, is a product of past and ongoing interaction with the world, but interaction within a very specific historical and social context. Now clearly much more needs to be said about the effect of historical-social factors in determining what we might know, but that shall have to be left to a more appropriate place. We turn here to consideration of our second problem.

It should be clear from our previous archaeological example that, while facts are constituted as such only by a theory that picks them out, it is anything but the case that a 'fact' can be picked out only by one single theory or theoretic matrix. 'Facts', events, instances and data can be selected for attention simultaneously from a great number of theories, and can be seen to be significant in terms of many theoretic frameworks, and as offering support for many theoretic stances – even conflicting ones (as with the two expert archaeologists above). Let us quickly illustrate this from three examples, and in doing so now put aside the sense of 'fact' that refers to the world rather than statements, and replace it, as indicated earlier, with 'phenomenon' or 'instance'.

The phenomenon known as the moon illusion, i.e. that the rising full moon appears to be larger than the full moon in the centre of the sky, can be picked out by the theory that humans are subject to optical illusions; by the theory that light close to large objects refracts; by the theory that the moon grows and shrinks as it orbits the earth; by the theory that the human nervous system, faced with a constant size retinal image from the moon, infers that the moon is further away at the horizon, and so relays a judgment of greater size; and so on. And the phenomenon itself need not merely be picked out by all those theories; it can also be taken as evidential support for any or all of them.[28]

Our second phenomenon is the appearance of a red-clad, bearded figure, in a sled driven by reindeer, on the roof of the home of Chicago's mayor, R. J. Daley, on Christmas eve, 1968. This instance occurred soon after the disturbing events of the Democratic Convention riots, at a time when authorities were especially on the lookout for subversive terrorists. And according to the 'report' in *Playboy* magazine they found a *prima facie* suspect. This S. Claus carried no papers, was attempting a forced entry into the house via the chimney, sported a beatnik Allen Ginsberg-type beard, wore black combat boots and *red* gear, and a hat of the type worn by terrorists in the French Revolution. He said he 'flew' to the rooftop, and was on a 'trip', these being dope-culture terms. He carried a hippie tote-bag full of riot weapons like baseball bats, and he continually chuckled 'Ho, Ho, Ho', reverently chanting the name of his 'leader', Ho Chi Minh. Now the annual appearance of Santa Claus might be fitted into a lot of theoretic frameworks, but hardly that of terrorist. And yet, as we see from this humorous example, if one begins with that theoretic framework, or merely wants to use that framework, then an inordinate number of details can be slotted in to make the interpretation seem quite plausible.

For our third example let us return to harsher reality, and consider the dismissal of a hundred or so workers from a car manufacturing plant, and the resultant walkout by the rest of the non-managerial staff. This can be seen as an attempt by the capitalist manufacturers to increase their profits by buying less labour power; as a good and necessary cutback in the face of economic crisis; as an indication that the government is not supporting the industry properly; as the result of a government squeeze so that it might nationalise the industry; as an example of fine solidarity among the workers; as irresponsible union action which can only further cripple the wounded industry; as the just results for workers who wanted too much, and finally cut their own throats; and so on. The phenomenon, the happenings, can be slotted virtually anywhere the observer wishes, depending upon his theoretic matrix or his way of perceiving things.

The second of the problems before us is now surely obvious. If instances or phenomena can be picked out by many theories (even competing and conflicting ones), and so be interpreted in many different ways, on what grounds can we judge any particular interpretation to be the best or the correct one? This is a problem that becomes far more complex, of course, when we go beyond identifying anomalous playing cards and accounting for the moon illusion, and move into the area of competing belief systems and interpretations of highly complex social relations.

A fairly glib answer to our question is that the best interpretation of any phenomenon is that which is given by the best available theory. We could, therefore, undertake a search for the criteria that make up a good theory, and then resolve to investigate the world using only the best theoretic matrices available.[29] However, we would also have to answer the question left begging some time ago – namely, where does theory come from? – for we would not only need to gain access to theories in order to investigate the world, but we would also require some understanding of the genesis of the theories we are employing. But if it is the case, as we have been suggesting, that theoretic matrices are determined by socio-historical factors, then this whole exercise could be regarded as rather futile; for if theories are merely products of socio-historical factors, then it could be claimed that no serious criteria for arbitrating between the worth of theories could possibly exist, and thus we are doomed either to relativism and/or anarchism.

The exercise, however, is not futile. The criteria of a good theory can be charted, the genesis of theories can be located, and relativism and anarchy can be avoided. These issues are the major concerns of our next chapter.[30]

Chapter 2

Theory and critical preference

Introduction

We have seen that facts are established as such only in terms of a theory that constitutes them as facts in the first place. It is obvious, then, that it would be a circular exercise to judge the worth of a particular theory only in terms of the number of phenomena it picks out and constitutes as facts. On the other hand, however, there would seem to be something odd about calling a theory a good theory if it picked out no phenomena at all in the world. The worth of a theory may be regarded as indeterminate if it has not been, or cannot as yet be tested; but otherwise some evidential support is clearly necessary if a theory is to be kept 'on the books' for continued, and possibly favourable, consideration. These simple realisations are enough to indicate that, while the matter of 'supportive evidence' is a necessary consideration in the issue of evaluation of theories, it cannot be a sufficient consideration. We shall now proceed to indicate other factors that are, or might be, relevant in evaluating theories; and in doing so we shall also lay the ground for taking a whole new perspective with regard to considering the place and role of theory in describing, explaining and accounting for the world.

One small methodological point should now be clarified. It will soon become obvious that I draw virtually all my substantive data from science, and virtually all my arguments from philosophy of science. This is not to suggest that I see theory in science, or scientific theory, as some kind of model or norm that theory in other areas ought to emulate or by which it can be measured. As it stands, I see no significant differences between the criteria necessary for evaluating scientific theories and those necessary for evaluating non-scientific theories; and in drawing from the literature of philosophy of science I am simply drawing from the most fertile and best articulated area available at the moment with regard to the issue of theory evaluation. This does, however, introduce a complication. The source material I am using speaks in terms of scientific theories, and at times of criteria that either distinguish the scientific from the non-scientific, or indicate the worth specifically of scientific theories. Now while many have argued that there really is no dichotomy between the scientific and the non-scientific,[1] I will at later stages in this work be making slight use of such a dichotomy. Thus, at this point I shall proceed by accepting the dichotomy between science and non-science, while claiming at the same time that there are no significant differences in the criteria for evaluating scientific and non-scientific theories. The main thing to note is that in what follows I will sometimes misrepresent my sources by talking about criteria for *good* theories, whereas they specifically meant good *scientific* theories. With that said, let us now begin again by examining a different approach to theory testing and theory evaluation, and see what light it sheds for us.

Falsificationism

Falsificationism (and here we shall deal with a simplified version of the general theory as articulated by Popper) recognises that neither the power of the intellect (rationalism) nor the evidence of the senses (empiricism) can provide us with proved knowledge, proved facts or proved theories. It thus 'retreats' to a sound logical basis, and begins from the point that, whereas no number of corroborating instances can prove a theory to be true or correct (as we saw in our discussion of inductivism), any single contrary instance can show a seeming universal generalisation to be false. The methodology of falsificationism thus operates in the following way: a theory, hypothesis or generalisation is conjectured or formulated in order to explain some phenomenon, and as long as it continues to be corroborated it is retained; but as soon as it is falsified it is rejected and replaced by a new theory, which in turn is tested until a falsifying instance occurs.

There are two basic principles inherent in a falsificationist approach. The first is that a good theory must, *in principle*, be falsifiable. The theory that there is a species on Mars that has the ability to vanish totally whenever earthlings try, in any way whatsoever, to observe them, is of course unfalsifiable, and thus would not enter into consideration as a good scientific theory. It is important to note, however, that the falsificationists' principle does not, as such, simply *make* this theory false – the species in question may actually exist. The second basic principle is that, the more falsifiable a theory is, through having either larger content or greater precision, the better a theory it is. Thus a theory (T_M) concerned with the acceleration rate at which all heavier-than-air objects fall to the ground near the earth's surface, would be better than a theory (T_L), which stated only that large stones dropped from tall buildings fall to the ground. This, however, does not simply give us licence to spin out weird theories with incredible content and claim they are good because of their high degree of falsifiability: the merit of T_M is that it accounts for all of what T_L accounts for and a great deal more, and accounts for it with greater precision. We see also from this example that if a theory (T_M) is falsified, retreat need be made only to those parts of T_L, or any intermediate theory, that may not have been falsified in the process. For instance, Galileo proposed a theory to explain the workings of a mercury barometer, namely that the vacuum at the top of the tube exerted a force on the mercury column, and from this hypothesis he was able to predict many other things. But the theory was easily falsified when the height of the mercury column was seen to vary at different altitudes. Galileo's theory was discarded, but not entirely. Only by sticking with the parts that were not falsified was Pascal able to produce the theory of atmospheric pressure; and when Pascal's theory was falsified, those parts that remained untouched were subsumed into the kinetic theory of gases. Falsificationism should thus be seen as allowing for steady progress through the ironing out of wrinkles, rather than insisting on the complete abandonment of a falsified theory.

The criteria of a good theory from a falsificationist account can be listed as follows.

(1) It should be able to explain all the acceptable observable phenomena that its predecessor could explain (i.e. it should have equal or larger content).

(2) It should be able to explain the observable phenomena or anomalies that refuted the old theory.

(3) It should be able to predict some new phenomena not previously known or not covered by the previous theory.[2]

(4) It should not be falsified by any accepted observable phenomena.

Now even though this may appear to be a significant advance on the inductivist–empiricist approach, there are however large problems inherent in such a falsificationist account.

To begin with, when a theory is put to the test there is more involved than just the theory. There are initial conditions, auxiliary hypotheses and the test conditions. Let us imagine that we are testing the theory that metals expand when heated. One of our initial conditions will be the pre-test size of our piece of metal; one of our auxiliary hypotheses will be that a bunsen burner will give out heat; another that our recording instrument will record expansion; and so on. Now we undertake the test, and our metal does not expand. Does this show the theory to be false? Not necessarily. There might have been a fault in the initial conditions, with some unknown factor preventing expansion from occurring. (The movement of Uranus appeared to falsify Newton's astronomical theory, yet was a result of an unknown initial condition, namely the planet Neptune.) Or there might have been a fault with the auxiliary hypotheses and/or the test conditions: our recording instruments might not, contrary to our auxiliary hypotheses, register expansion in the presence of the very heat required to produce expansion. (Flamstead's observations on the moon's orbit, rather than falsifying Newton's theory, resulted from a fault in Flamstead's auxiliary hypotheses, for he failed to account for refraction of light from the moon in the earth's atmosphere.) The point, then, is that every test situation is more or less complex, and it can never be determined unambiguously whether an instance of falsification can be attributed to a fault in the theory under test, the initial conditions, the auxiliary hypotheses or the test situation itself. Thus an instance of falsification is not sufficient for judging a theory to be falsified.

Let us quickly note an example here that has considerable relevance for our later discussion. The newspaper *Tribune* is printed and distributed weekly by the Communist Party of Australia, and communists are supposedly dedicated to 'the forcible overthrow of all existing social conditions'. Now the very existence of *Tribune* is taken by many as clear falsification of the theory that the media serves only the interests of the ruling class, of those seeking to stabilise existing social conditions. But it does not, of course, falsify the theory at all; the existence of *Tribune* is accommodated (at least) by the auxiliary hypotheses dealing with freedom of the press (and as we shall see, it will remain so accommodated while the threat it represents is considered insignificant).

A further large count against falsificationism becomes evident if we look at theories from a historical viewpoint. From such a perspective it becomes patently clear that virtually all theories that were, or still are, taken to be good theories were falsifiable, and falsified, just as soon as they were produced. The motion of Mercury was inconsistent with, and known to be inconsistent with, Newton's general theory of planetary motion. Reflection from plane mirrors is inconsistent with the particle theory of light. Examples could be listed from all fields of human endeavour; from which it could be seen that, if falsificationist criteria were rigorously applied, few if any theories would have ever got off the ground, and the development of knowledge would long ago have been arrested.

The most significant problem with falsificationism, however, is simply that it requires, as in point (4) above, that, should a theory clash with some observed phenomenon, then the theory must be rejected. However, as we have indicated earlier, what is observed about phenomena issues from us in knowledge statements, and these *statements* of observed phenomena are theory-dependent and fallible. The accepted observed phenomenon of the relationship between the sun and the earth in the medieval world would have resulted in statements like 'The sun moves across the sky'; and statements such as these were regarded by many as sufficient to refute and falsify the Copernican theory of astronomy. The statements we use to account for phenomena are theory-dependent, and further they are also likely to be false: thus the validity of the key criterion of falsificationism is ruled out - for in a proposed falsifying instance it may be the statement of the falsifying instance, not the theory under test, that is false. In the final analysis, falsificationism shares rather than avoids the problems of 'theory-ladenness' that bedevil empiricism.

The notion of theory-ladenness raises a further point which has particular relevance to the overall purposes of this work. We have noted earlier that our conceptual schemes influence our perception of the world, and that these conceptual schemes are theory-laden; but this implies neither that the theory underlying our conceptual schemes is correct or good theory, nor even that our statements reflect what we take to be the correct theoretical framework. Examples of the former point (from outside the realm of science) can be seen in statements like 'The nation has introduced new legislation to combat terrorism', or 'Criminals must pay their debt to society', where the concepts of 'nation' and 'society' are used in a way that suggests (or carries the implicit theory) that it is proper to speak of 'nations' and 'societies' in a reified manner. Such reification is very common in our ordinary language; so common that it is often very difficult to avoid embracing it even when one deliberately tries not to.[3] As for the latter point, again we need only consider our everyday discourse. Presumably most people who speak of the sun rising and setting, who talk of moonlight and how brightly the moon shines and who refer to green or white chalkboards in classrooms as 'blackboards' know full well that the sun neither rises nor sets, that the moon has no light of its own to shine with, and that the colour of the boards in front of them is not black. And for an example that spreads across both points, consider again our earlier problems with 'fact talk'. The concept of 'fact' has become so generalised that in ordinary language it fails to make, or make possible, an essential distinction between properties of the world and knowledge statements about those properties. In this way it bears poor or erroneous theory. But even those people who are aware of the distinction simply cannot make it conveniently with ordinary language: a special word such as 'phenomenon' has to be used for properties of the world, while the use of fact for knowledge statements still obscures the way those very statements are derived.

Ordinary language, then, can embody poor or erroneous theory; it can blur existing distinctions that the language-user might or might not be aware of, and that he might or might not be trying to employ; and it need not represent what we take to be the case anyway (as when we speak of 'moonlight'). It would surely follow, then, that examination or analysis of our conceptual scheme need not necessarily reveal to us the way things are; nor need it reveal what people think, believe or know to be the case, or even how they formulate their reactions to the world. The philosophic game of linguistic or conceptual analysis, an outgrowth of logical positivism, makes no bigger errors than presupposing that analysing language usage can be done in a detached theory-free manner, and that it can reveal and make clear the ways in which people order and structure the world. It is an exercise more likely to obscure and reinforce the 'treachery of language' than to throw light on the world, and its appropriateness to the study of education has been enormously misrepresented in the recent past.[4] That, however, must remain the subject of future discussion: at this point let us return to the more immediate issue of falsificationism.

It should be clear that falsificationism, as it has been presented here, is unable to indicate just when a theory ought to be rejected, and since it too shares theory-dependence problems it is also unable to place its knowledge claims on firm rock-bottom foundations. It thus might appear to be of no greater benefit to us than empiricism/inductivism; and yet there are some things that can be rescued from a falsificationist approach. Let us consider two points.

The first of these arises out of the falsificationist criteria that theories need be falsifiable only *in principle*, and that rejection (or partial rejection) occurs only *after* the falsifying event. Implicit in these criteria is the notion that rejection can and should take place only when the means are at hand to falsify a particular theory; and this notion clearly brings a historical factor into the consideration of theory evaluation. A theory may be judged highly in one historical setting (doing a far better job than any of its past or contemporary rivals), and yet be judged poorly in a later historical setting after new hardware and intellectual tools have become available for testing it.

Second, and of greater importance, it is clear from falsificationism (and clear to falsificationists) that theories are not to be judged solely by instances. As we have seen, a falsifying instance neither proves a theory to be false, nor alone requires the abandonment of a theory. Falsifying instances merely suggest that there is doubt around; but a theory is not seriously abandoned until, as in (1) and (2) above, another *theory* comes forward that can account for everything the previous theory accounted for, and the 'falsifying' instance as well. Thus inherent in a falsificationist account is that anomalous instances (ones that don't fit in with the going theory) are only warning signals; and that theories are really judged by other theories.

The appropriateness of placing 'history' and 'theory' over and above instances in theory evaluation can be demonstrated by a simple example. Consider the accepted theory in medieval times that the sun orbited a stationary earth, and our current theory that a rotating earth orbits the sun. Nothing relevant in the existential world seems to have changed since medieval times; and all the phenomena or instances that medieval man picked out as support for his theory (stones dropped from towers striking the ground immediately below, etc.) still surround us today exactly as they surrounded medieval man. The phenomena have not changed at all; but what we have in our historical setting is access to phenomena denied to medieval man, and a new theory, made up of new conceptualisations, that does the same job required of the 'stationary earth' theory, and seems to do it better.

Having indicated that historical considerations, and theories of 'larger content', are thus also relevant contenders in our quest for factors whereby theories can be evaluated, we shall now continue our exploration by considering a more sophisticated form of falsification.

Lakatos and methodological falsificationism

The most sophisticated notion of falsificationism we have available to us at the moment is that provided by Imre Lakatos.[5] Lakatos begins at the point where many modern philosophers of science begin; with the stark recognition that the notion of *proven* knowledge (i.e. that ideas and theories can be justified in the sense that they can be known to be true) has ultimately and finally collapsed. Two largely opposed reactions to this same recognition are found in the works of Kuhn and Popper. Popper, as we have seen, regards the quest for knowledge, or scientific progress, not as an attempt to prove, justify or verify theories, or even to probabilify them; but as an attempt to specify the conditions under which theories would have to be discarded. For Popper, nobody ever has the epistemological right to be absolutely committed to any theory.[6] Kuhn, on the other hand, rejects Popper's 'falsificationist' idea that science (and again, we apply this to all knowledge) either does or should proceed by attempted refutation of theories. For Kuhn, science consists in the elaboration of dominant theories or paradigms, and progresses by means of rare revolutions wherein existing paradigms are overthrown and new paradigms are instituted in a manner approximating gestalt shifts or switches.[7]

Lakatos stands closer to Popper than to Kuhn. He accepts Kuhn's criticisms of falsificationism, but claims that, whereas Kuhn can account for the growth of knowledge only in terms of changing consensus, and speaks only of a *psychology* of discovery, Popper's is the substantially correct position, providing, as it does, a *logic* of discovery. Lakatos thus sets about to extend Popper's notions, and to defend the principle of rationality and the canons of rational criticism against those (e.g. the sceptics, the anarchists, the relativists and the conventionalists) who saw all basis for rational criticism and critical choice necessarily disappearing down the waste chute along with proven, justified knowledge.

Lakatos argues that all theories are equally unprovable, equally improbable and equally undisprovable. He suggests, therefore, that talk of justification and proof in the area of theory must be dropped and be replaced instead with talk of 'criticism', 'evaluation', and 'critical preference'; and that a whole new tack must be taken; one that involves first and foremost not ontology, but methodology – a theory of criticism. (The methodology would, of course, have to make ontological assumptions; for example about the status of empirical evidence, and of theoretical propositions.)

The suggested theory is conventionalist in the sense that it is assumed, with Kant, that we cannot have knowledge of the world without interpreting it; that we perceive only through our conceptual frameworks; and that knowledge is therefore only such in the light of our expectations and theories. However, whereas Kant very largely saw these frameworks as prisons, and some of his followers drew the pessimistic conclusion that the real world is unknowable because of these prisons, Lakatos is more optimistic. Conceptual frameworks, he notes, 'can be developed and also replaced by new, *better* ones; it is *we* who create our "prisons" and we can also, critically, demolish them'.[8] But on what grounds are these frameworks (or theories) to be retained, or be replaced by better ones?

One possible answer is that, after a period of initial success in which a theory survives attempts at refutation, scientists may take a methodological decision not to allow the theory to be refuted. Having taken this decision, they may then accommodate apparent anomalies by auxiliary hypotheses, *ad hoc* hypotheses or other conventionalist stratagems. On this view, the older and more established a theory becomes, the less power does empirical evidence have with respect to it, and the less likely it becomes that empirical evidence will be brought to bear against it. This, of course, is very largely the way Kuhn sees science operating, with change constantly facing fashion, dogmatism and power.

A different answer to the question is given by Popper.[9] Instead of deciding to make unfalsifiable some universal theory or theories, the scientist decides to make unfalsifiable some singular statements with spatio-temporal reference, provided only that there is available some technique such that 'anyone who has learned it' is able by using it to decide that these statements are 'acceptable'. Statements of this sort may then be called 'observational' or 'basic', but only in an inverted commas sense. Now while the scientist treats some statements as if they are purely observational, he is fully aware that even in this decision-making technique there are implicit theories. He nevertheless applies the theory-laden techniques, *but not as theories*: they serve merely to secure background knowledge which is held to be unproblematical, in tentative fashion, while the theory in question is under test. He is, then, according the background knowledge tentative 'observational' status. This position, in which our most successful theories are used as extensions of our senses, largely overcomes most of the problems concerned with theory-ladenness; and it is the position that Lakatos adopts and labels 'methodological falsificationism'.[10]

The background knowledge or set of general hypotheses that is held to be unproblematical (e.g. Newton's basic laws, the psychoanalytic notion of the unconscious, etc.) is referred to by Lakatos as the *hard core*. This hard core guides research both positively and negatively, by stipulating which areas must not be challenged (the *negative heuristic*), and by suggesting guidelines for profitable development (the *positive heuristic*). Also, the hard core is 'surrounded' by a *protective belt*, and it is this that actually bears the brunt of testing, and that is continually modified or adjusted in order to protect the hard core. But the 'hard-core—protective-belt' complex does not, for Lakatos, represent a single theory, for he argues that to speak in terms of a single theory is to engage in a category error. What we really have before us at any time, Lakatos suggests, is no single theory, but rather a series of theories, or a *research programme*; and what we are actually involved in is not simply the evaluation of a theory but rather the critical appraisal of research programmes. And as far as the appraisal of research programmes goes, Lakatos sets out a rationale that, he claims, is applicable not just to science, but to all fields of intellectual and theoretical activity.

Lakatos's rationale includes a criterion for demarcating the 'scientific' from the 'non-scientific' and the 'pseudo-scientific'; and also rules for falsification. The acceptability criterion is that a theory is 'acceptable' or 'scientific' only if it has corroborated excess empirical content over its predecessor or rival; that is, only if it leads to the discovery of novel facts. As for the rules for falsification: we are to regard a scientific theory T as falsified:[11]

if and only if another theory T' has been proposed with the following characteristics:

(1) T' has excess empirical content over T: that is, it predicts *novel* facts, which are improbable in he light of, or even forbidden by T;

(2) T' explains the previous success of T, that is, all the unrefuted content of T is included . . . in the content of T'; and

(3) some of the excess content of T' is corroborated.

As indicated above, what is suggested here is that we have a series of theories, T_1, T_2, T_3 ... Tn. Each succeeding theory is a result of adjustments having been made to the protective belt, in the form of adding auxiliary statements or hypotheses or semantic reinterpretations, etc., to the previous theory to accommodate some anomaly. But what is of most importance in the whole scheme is whether the series or research programme is *progressive*, or able to achieve *progressive problemshifts*. Lakatos suggests that we call a series *theoretically progressive* if each new theory meets condition (1). Theories meeting this condition are said to constitute theoretically progressive problemshifts. In addition, a theoretically progressive series is empirically progressive, or evinces empirically progressive problemshifts, if it meets conditions (2) and (3) as well. A problemshift is progressive if it is both theoretically and empirically progressive, and 'degenerating' if it is not. Problemshifts are accepted as scientific if they are at least theoretically progressive.

We see, therefore, that in Lakatos's terms, a theory in a series is falsified only when a progressive problemshift is achieved, that is when it is superseded by *another theory* with higher corroborated content; and it is this very procedure that also provides the grounds for commenting critically on the whole research programme under consideration. In Lakatos's model, then, falsification not only takes on a historical character, but it also ceases to depend simply on the relationship between a theory and some supposed non-theoretical empirical basis. But of even greater significance, we see that falsification, and the achievement or non-achievement of problemshifts, is the basic indicator of the progressive or degenerative status of a research programme at a particular time. Programmes are never proved or disproved; and Lakatos clearly indicates not only the folly of ever totally discounting any programme, but also the extremely complex nature of bringing arguments to bear, either for or against the worth of any programme.

Let us now consider non-scientific theories. What makes them non-scientific, for Lakatos, is that, along with their lack of corroborated excess empirical content, they are not falsifiable. But this does not mean that they are worthless, or that they cannot be subjected to criticism. We cannot avoid non-scientific theories; and to suggest that we might and thus try to mount only strictly scientific theories of the nature of science is to make the kind of error made by the logical positivists with the verification principle. It is also to give to the scientific some kind of unjustified and unjustifiable status, and to create a hierarchy when all that exists are differences.

Nevertheless, we are still faced with the question as to how non-scientific theories might be criticised; and Lakatos leaves open for us an appealing solution. Criticising our total body of non-scientific theory, rendering such theory internally consistent and solving theoretical problems of a non-scientific sort is really a matter of applying the same general principles that underlie the specific process of scientific criticism in which falsification is possible. The difference between the two realms is seen to be marked out by the issue of *'empirical* content', which for Lakatos characterises the 'scientific'. What has to be recognised, however, is that empirical progress (the scientific) is not possible without theoretic progress, as we suggested in our previous chapter – but theoretical progress certainly is possible in the absence of empirical progress. Empirical progress and the achievement of falsification might always have the last say if we are intent on building scientific theories; but there is no practical or logical preclusion for operating with the Lakatos apparatus of research programmes, theory-series and problemshifts, outside of the realm of science. It is, as Lakatos himself claims, an apparatus that can serve us equally well in all realms of knowledge; so much so that, if we remain only with the rules for falsification, the notion of progressive series and the matter of theory evaluation in general, the distinction between scientific and other 'types' of knowledge and theory can be seen to be insignificant and irrelevant to the general application of the theory.

Some implications from Lakatos's thesis

Lakatos, as we have noted, overcomes some of the serious problems related to theory-ladenness; and he also breaks the awkward nexus once established between instances and theories, namely that theories are to be refuted if they clash with observed instances; or, more generally, that theories are always at the mercy of instances, and are to be judged in terms of the support (or lack of it) that they gain from observed instances. For Lakatos, a theory, a series of theories or a research programme deserves our favourable judgment, not because it stands up well to challenges, and not because it is regularly 'confirmed' and rarely falsified, but only if it meets the requirements of continuous growth. Theories are judged by the extent to which, and the rate at which, they are able to overcome difficulties thrown up by their predecessors, their competitors and even their own predictions; that is, by the extent to which they are progressive. There is a sting in the tail of this, however, for Lakatos's criteria (as he himself recognises) provide us with no means for deciding between the *absolute* merits of competing research programmes. There can be no rules for determining when a degenerating programme ought to give up trying to accommodate anomalies; and who can tell when the next ingenious adjustment to a protective belt will launch a programme into a new progressive phase? Thus while theories might be judged by the extent to which they are progressive, they can be so judged only in relation to their preceding and contemporary rivals. Two points follow from this. First, theories or research programmes are never static, and their content and auxiliary hypotheses can grow and develop, or decline, with the occurrence of intellectual shifts and conceptual modifications, and with the development of new hardware by which they might be tested. Thus it is clear that the merit of a theory, or the favour with which we judge it, must always be determined within a historical context; a context that includes contemporary rivals, intellectual climates and existing hardware. The second point is even more obvious: theories are judged by *other theories*. And these two points, taken together, indicate that there simply cannot be any a-temporal, a-social, a-historical, a-theoretical, 'objective' point from which we can make judgments or criticisms. When we judge a theory we do so from a social – historical – theoretical perspective; and we indicate its relative rather than its intrinsic worth. Thus Feyerabend again:[12]

> theories cannot be justified and their excellence cannot be shown without reference to other theories. We may explain the success of a theory by reference to a more comprehensive theory ... and we may explain our preference for it by comparing it with other theories. Such a comparison does not establish the intrinsic excellence of the theory we have chosen ... the theory we have chosen may be pretty lousy ... But it still may be better than any other theory that is available at the time. It may in fact be the best lousy theory there is.

It would appear, then, that Lakatos's thesis paradoxically turns against itself, in that, while identifying relevant criteria for making judgments of critical preference, those very criteria serve to make absolute judgments impossible. In practice we can judge whether research programmes are progressive at any point of time, and possibly which, of a number of competing contemporary programmes, is the most progressive,[13] but only with considerable hindsight can we judge whether one programme is really more progressive than another. It might be enough, however, simply to know that the programme with which we are working is progressive.

There are two further implications to consider. First, we should recognise that the logic of discovery that Lakatos has set out is an ideal, and an ideal in two ways. It is an ideal in the sense that it does not represent the only way in which we gain 'progressive problemshifts' or 'new, better' knowledge; and it is an ideal in that, for all its historical emphasis, it ignores (or idealises) the history of the discipline in which it attempts to chart the growth of knowledge. Lakatos, like Popper (and like Mannheim before them), seriously underrates the effects of politics, ideology and other non-scientific forces on the very activity of science itself, let alone its results.[14] But the particular point to extract from this is that, while Lakatos (like Popper) makes theory criticism 'subjectless' (*theories* judge theories), he does not make theory subjectless, nor does he adequately locate a 'subject'. He fails to account for where 'hard cores' come from, other than that they seem to be formula᾿ ᾿d or decided on by scientists purely scientifically, just as existentialists might have thought up existentialist philosophy purely philosophically. This is simply untenable.

Our final implication points to a further paradoxical turn, for as we shall shortly see it is actually Lakatos's thesis that can provide us with a context for considering a further approach to theory; one that can draw strength from the valuable insights Lakatos offers us, but which can also overcome the two major weaknesses in his theory. Before turning to examine that programme, however, it is necessary now, although perhaps not obviously so, that we consider the applicability of Lakatos's thesis in the realm of ideology.

Ideology and critical preference

Ideology is a subject that has a vast literature of its own, and it is hardly our purpose here to explore that literature meticulously. However, neither is it in our interest to give an oversimplified or misleading account of ideology, such as those embodied in notions like ideology being 'theory which continues to justify itself long after practice has shown it to be false'; or ideology being something that is mysteriously fabricated to provide a justification for the *status quo*. At this point, however, we shall make some simple, perhaps superficial, comments on ideology while at a more relevant later stage we shall fill in certain details.

Ideology can be loosely defined as a set of theoretic stances, involving attitudes, values and habitual responses (which are embodied in definite social practices), and which seeks to maintain the *status quo*, or to bring about a changed set of social relations and social formations.[15] In this way it is necessarily political. The point of ideology is the rationalisation of value and the legitimation of action, and in this way it can be taken as differing from science or scientific theories. The difference is further evident when we also realise that, in attempting to make coherence and sense of phenomena in the face of the necessity for ongoing social action, ideology has to make do with explanations and exhortations which may have little, if any, scientific or empirical support, and often little, if any, common sense support.

It should be noted that the distinction being drawn here between ideology and science is a practical one, and not a conceptual one. As both Kuhn and Popper have shown, scientific theories have social

47

contexts, and so can take on ideological status for particular 'schools'. Further, as Tranöy has indicated, scientists, philosophers and academics generally have their own professional ideologies;[16] and for Feyerabend, science 'is just one of the many ideologies that propel society and it should be treated as such'.[17] Science can, of course, become ideology; but our practical distinction can serve the purposes required of it without introducing complications.

If we consider an ideology (in the sense of a set of theoretic stances)[18] as a total belief system, it may be construed as loosely analogous to a Lakatosian research programme in several important ways. We could postulate, for any given ideology, its 'core', consisting of fundamental values and existential beliefs that would be relinquished only when it is judged that a rival ideology provides a more powerful and rational basis for action. For example, the rival might contain a more consistent and comprehensive set of value judgments, or a more elegant synthesis of existential and evaluative considerations, or both. Further, surrounding this ideological 'core' there will be a protective belt, in which minor accommodating adjustments are made in the light of fresh knowledge and changing social circumstances.

In addition to the analogies of core and belt, we may speak of positive aspects of the programme generated by an ideology in similar fashion to the research programme generated by a scientific theory. These positive aspects, ideally, are twofold. First, courses of action suggested by the ideology will continuously serve to modify, correct and refine it. Something analogous to falsification occurs in this interaction of theory and practice. Practical problemshifts, changes in the ideology designed to accommodate problems posed for the ideology by practice, are theoretically progressive if the revised ideology suggests and rationalises new courses of action, and are practically progressive when such action serves to enhance realisation of the values of the ideology. Second, rational holders of an ideology will attempt to accommodate the results of scientific and philosophical research pertinent to matters they deem important on ideological grounds. Such accommodation produces both theoretical and practical problemshifts. Feedback and challenges from these sources might be described as the intellectual and practical arena within which an ideology is developed, applied, criticised and modified. This interaction of ideological thought with practical action and attention to scientific research generates a continual series of problemshifts as new action-outcomes, awareness of changing social circumstances and cognisance of scientific developments are fed back into the ideological system, producing an ideology-series. And like a scientific theory-series, an ideology-series could be said to deserve our favourable judgment not because it may be able to stand up under crucial tests, but because it is able to meet the requirement of continuous growth within the context of social action, social change and scientific discovery.

We can thus see that what Lakatos says with regard to critical judgment and scientific theories can hold just as well for ideologies. We can conclude, therefore, by suggesting that (1) ideologies are not to be judged only with regard to their 'fit' with observed instances; (2) ideologies can be judged only in a historical context, with reference to their preceding and contemporary rivals; (3) ideologies can be judged only by, or in terms of, other theories (which might also be ideologies); and (4) ideologies deserve our favourable judgment to the extent that they are progressive. With regard to this last point, however, we must recognise that ideologies can present a distorted picture of the world yet actually function in an extremely effective and efficient way; and so clearly the favourable judgments we might make in Lakatosian terms must be made with regard to the ideology theory-series itself, and not in terms of how well the particular ideology functions in a particular society. When it comes to ideology, the best theory and the best functioning theory can be two different things. Lakatos's thesis tends to blur this distinction, whereas the theory we shall outline shortly overcomes this problem; but before turning to that theory some further things have to be said about anomalies.

The problem of anomalies

We have noted previously that instances gain status as facts only when they are called out by a theory. We have also shown that a single instance can be called out by many theories at the same time, even conflicting theories; and also that instances can fail to be noted when any one particular theory is in operation. What shall concern us at this point, however, is the noting of anomalous instances; those instances that appear, at first, as if they are unable to be accommodated by the prevailing theory or research programme.

There are three things that can be done with such anomalies. In the first place they can be neglected, rejected or discarded. The history of all branches of human endeavour bristles with examples of this tactic; and an interesting example is provided by the case of Mendel, who was greatly assisted on the road to fame by certain earlier researchers who gained data similar to his, but threw it out because it did not support their theories of genetic regression to the mean. Discarding instances, however, could hardly be regarded as a serious endeavour to gain knowledge of the world.[19]

The second thing that can be done with an anomaly is to attempt to accommodate it within the theory that picks it out. In this way it is

49

regarded as a *puzzle* to be solved *by* a theory or research programme. There are many ways that anomalies can be accommodated, from the invention of *ad hoc* hypotheses to modification of the theory itself. It is not to our purpose to rehearse these methods here, but we shall provide one simple example which will also have relevance for later discussion.

Let us take the theory that schools exist essentially to educate people, and that educated people can be defined by certain character-istics.[20] Let us now assume that a study of school graduates shows that the vast majority of them finish up with characteristics quite opposed to the expected and desired ones. Here we would have a large-scale anomaly. But it could easily be accommodated. For instance, it could be argued that increased class sizes brought about by a poorly planned building programme, or lack of good teachers owing to poor salaries, or lack of resources, or the impact of television, or whatever you like is making the job of the school that much harder at the moment. But, although the success rate isn't as good as it might be, schools do exist essentially to educate.

The third thing that can be done with an anomaly is to regard it as a counter-instance or falsifying instance for the theory or research programme.[21] Thus, in the above example the observed anomaly could be taken as evidence to suggest that schools do not exist essentially to educate. But we remember from earlier discussion that a falsifying instance does not necessarily show a theory to be false (although it can lend weight to such a suggestion, or initiate suspicion).

It should be obvious now that an extremely complex issue has been touched upon. Given that an anomaly has been found, it appears impossible to lay down any methodological rule for coming to terms with it (and even though Lakatos speaks out for 'continuous growth' through accommodating anomalies, his thesis itself is unable to tell us when we ought to give up attempts at accommodation, and either retreat to a simpler theory, which is not troubled by the anomaly, or else reject our theory and take another line). But if the detection of anomalies raises complex problems, both the *failure* to detect anomalies and the failure to detect them *as anomalies*, adds greatly to the complexity of the issue.

There are three ways that anomalies can escape detection. In the first place, the theory or research programme in operation may not be capable of picking out certain anomalous instances; just as the Ptolemic theory of the universe, and the hardware that accompanied it in its early days, simply could not detect the anomalies that would have discredited it.

Second, anomalies might go undetected because they are well disguised, and/or because there is no good reason for suspecting that they might be around. If a wolf came to us well dressed in sheep's clothing, we would see a sheep and never expect to find a wolf; just as, in the puzzle mentioned earlier, we see a tree and do not expect to find a face. In living in the world we take things to be as they appear until we have a particularly good reason for suspecting that they are not what they seem: if we questioned everything that came before us we would never get on with the business of living. And so only if our 'sheep' began to do certain unsheepish things, or if for some other reason we began to suspect its identity, would we call its status as a sheep into question (just as Uranus's status as a star, and then as a comet, was called into question when its behaviour was finally seen as befitting of neither of those categories). In these circumstances, detection of anomalies requires either a breakdown in disguise and/or strong suspicion (theory) on the part of investigators that something might be amiss – and so it is possible and likely that such anomalies exist in abundance, and could exist undetected for long periods of time.

This much, of course, overlaps with what we have said about 'mental sets' in our previous chapter. We showed there that particular instances could be accounted for by many theoretical standpoints; and that a mental set was a way of seeing things, a particular theoretic framework, which allowed for certain interpretations, and which at times excluded other interpretations. We showed that, if our mental set is directed towards hippie terrorists, we could conceivably take the red-clothed, bearded Santa Claus as one, and perceive his snow boots as combat boots. If we have the mental set that production troubles are caused by grasping workers incited by communist infiltrators, we could perceive factory strikes as attempts by the workers to cripple productivity. On the other hand, if we perceive the production situation as dominated by grasping capitalists out to exploit labour power to the maximum, we might perceive the same strike as a valiant attempt by the workers to defend certain basic human rights. If we are set in our belief that our education system is on the right track we might perceive its practical failures as resulting either from a lack of resources, or from the imperfect nature of the children it deals with: and thus not perceive those failures as indicative of any need to overhaul the system totally.

At this point, however, we must extend the notion of mental set slightly to indicate the third, and most important, way in which anomalies can escape detection. Again, let us recapitulate a little first.

In the oasis/mirage example, and other related examples discussed earlier, we saw many things influencing our theory and methodology: two of these were our concept of the object under investigation, and the theoretical framework or mental set within which we undertook the investigation. But in these instances, the object under investigation had little effect on the investigation itself. Having conceptualised the oasis/mirage as an oasis, theory and methodology were set into operation, but these would largely have been applicable to the investigation of any physical object. That the object was conceptualised as an oasis simply brought about specificity in investigation, such that the investigator did not dig for buried treasure or concern himself with the position of the moon at that time. Thus it would only be in a weak sense that the object of investigation influenced the perception of the investigator, and the investigation itself.

It is possible, however, to go to the other extreme, and find cases where the object under investigation very largely influences the investigator and creates the 'set' under which the investigation will be carried out. In these cases it is more than likely that anomalies will escape detection because of the way the object 'presents itself' for investigation, and actively interferes with the investigation. Let us approach this by means of an analogy. Imagine that doctors are testing two new drugs. The first is an anti-depressant, and the doctors are concerned to determine whether a person taking this drug feels less depressed than before. Now they can observe the subject to see if he exhibits non-depressive behaviour, measure certain bodily functions, and so on; but at some stage they would have to, or they should, ask the subject how he feels. Now, all other things being equal, the subject's report should be valid evidence regarding the efficacy of the drug, and the subject can validly report on the effect of the drug while he is under its influence.

The second drug is designed to alter perception. Here we have a clear case in which the subject, while under the influence of the drug, cannot make valid 'objective' statements about the effect of the drug. He might suspect that the drug is having an effect on his perceptions, but he cannot trust his perceptions to tell him whether the drug is having an effect, since it might be causing him to misperceive or even not perceive the effect it is or may be having. This gives rise to two particularly difficult problems. First, our subject is placed in this position the moment he *suspects* he has taken a perception-altering drug, regardless of whether he has taken one or not; second, the problem could be endless, for if he has taken, or if he suspects he has taken, such a drug it becomes impossible for the subject alone to tell when the effects of the drug have worn off. Now there is, of course, an obvious way around all these problems. All that is required is that a group of people, or even one person, not under the effect or the suspicion of the effect of the drug chart and indicate when the subject's stated perceptions cohere or don't cohere with the undrugged perception. But this, in turn, raises a further problem of considerable interest: what if everybody were under the influence of such a drug? Or, to complicate the issue further, what if everybody knew that there was such a drug around, but believed that it was a perception-improving drug, such that those who had taken it perceive better?

Leaving the complications aside for a moment, we have here a clear example in which the object affects and interferes with its investigation by continually acting back on its investigator. This would occur at a simple level when deep-water investigations were affected by the raptures brought on by being in the deep; but it is also a phenomenon that occurs to a highly significant degree in many of our most important investigations of the world.

Take, for instance, education. Investigations of education by educated people are influenced by the way education has taught those people to investigate: their set or approach to the object will be largely affected by the influence the object has had on them. And investigations by uneducated people would hardly be legitimated or taken seriously. Thus, if those undrugged perceivers saw things, including anomalies, that (because of the drug) escaped the notice of the drugged perceivers, their findings would not be likely to be attended to by the educated community – the community that believes education to be perception-improving, and so values educated opinions.[22]

Take, as another example, social relations. Investigations of social relations by people in societies are influenced by the social relations they live in: their set or approach to the object will be influenced largely by the way their experience of social relations has indicated to them what social relations are, and how they are to be characterised. They are quite likely even to employ in their investigations social relations that mirror their experience. Thus lived experience and investigation are interfering with each other: lived experience provides the context, theory and methodology – the set – for investigation of that lived experience. And again, as with education, investigations by undrugged perceivers (the uninitiated, the unqualified, etc.) are not likely to be legitimated or taken seriously. Thus we find areas wherein only the drugged perception of immersed investigators might be taken seriously and be considered valid. This would be likely to occur where all had taken the drug (and everyone has been educated, and lives in social relations), or where undrugged people see the drug as having improving effects, and so confer status on drugged people. We see that there could be fields of investigation where findings are legitimised only if produced by investigators who are so immersed in the field that their very immersion affects their investigation. In such cases, what an outsider might see as an anomaly could easily go undetected by the initiates, who, because of the effects of their initiation and their mental set, cannot perceive the anomaly.

Such cases go beyond what is involved in Kuhn's notion of investigations within a paradigm. The chemist in the days before Priestley and Lavoisier may have approached his objects with the mental set of phlogiston theory. But this set, paradigm or no-longer-questioned theory arose from the investigator's lived experience, *not* from the object under investigation, for there was nothing about the object itself that cried out: 'Think phlogiston!' In the cases we are considering the set arises from the object *and* the lived experience, for they are, in a large sense, one and the same thing: it is the *object* (and the action and effects of the object) – not only fashion, custom, or tradition – that largely determines the set, the basic assumptions, the no-longer-questioned theory by which it is to be investigated; and consequently what one will find when it is investigated.

In cases such as these we could say that investigators are working within a particular sort of mental set, one that is unlikely to be recognised by the investigator, and the operation of which he might rarely, if ever, be aware of. In this sense the 'drug' analogy works well, for the investigator 'bears within himself' a factor that determines how he shall approach and investigate certain objects, while at the same time leaving him unaware that his perceptions are necessarily drugged. And if there are many investigators who, through investigating the same object, all fall under the influence of the drug (as in investigating underwater phenomena while under the influence of 'raptures of the deep'), they would hardly be able to correct and adjust their perceptions, let alone recognise their perceptions as having been determined by a 'drug' operating on each and every one of them.

At this point we can compound the situation a little, and recall the matter of disguise mentioned earlier. Let us now imagine that the 'drug' and the disguise work together, so that it is not merely a matter of wolves being disguised in sheeps' clothing, but rather that the investigators are also drugged into believing that they (the wolves) are sheep, and are to be investigated as sheep. What arises from this?

First, as with all investigations, particular anomalies might not be noticed. And some others might not be noticed because of the general disguise that is operating. But in this particular situation the wolves in sheeps' clothing are even less likely to be noticed or arouse suspicion because any anomalous behaviour of theirs *will also be disguised*. If people were somehow convinced or drugged into believing that sheep can be investigated only by their clothing, and that howls were really bleats, etc., anomalous sheep could long go undetected. Similarly, if nations, rather than embarking on a programme of colonisation, gave massive foreign aid to underdeveloped countries with the avowed purpose of helping those countries to achieve prosperity and independence, and if people's consciousness was directed in these terms, and all the evidence (which counted as legitimate evidence) seemed to indicate that this was what was really happening, it would be extremely difficult to suspect and even begin to show that the process might be seen as one of crippling and enslaving. Again, while schools claim to educate, are thought of as educating, and actually do appear to educate, it is hardly likely that a person, especially an educated person, might ever suspect their role to be the production of a massive literate compliant alienated work force.

This whole general problem is the one that confronted Marx as he embarked on a critique of capitalism, for capitalism, he claimed, necessarily disguised itself, and presented itself as something that it was not.[23] It is also very much the problem that confronts us, or anybody, in attempting to investigate ideology; for ideology, arising as it does from lived experience, functions like a drug in that it alters or determines one's perception, so that when one comes to train one's perception on ideologies or ideological issues, one does so, usually unwittingly, in terms of an ideological set that has already been fixed. Further, ideology as rationalisation of value and legitimation of action tends towards disguise in that, like empiricism, it presents 'what *is* the case' as if it were naturally so, unquestionably given, and as the way things are supposed to be – instances are fitted to prevailing theory (which may require disguise), and are not displayed in a way whereby they might be seen as they really are.

If these things are so, then clearly it would be extremely difficult to criticise ideology, to find anomalies (and know what to do with them if one finds them), to recognise disguises when they are employed, and to expose what lies behind such disguise. And if certain ideologies distorted one's view of the world, and worked against one's best interests, yet indicated that they were not distorting, and were working *in* one's best interests, it would be very difficult indeed to expose their real function, and to present that *exposé* as compelling to others under the influence and effect of those ideologies.

At this point we have confronted a great number of problems, and have come up with all too few answers. However, the problems that have been encountered can, I believe, all be overcome by a single (if large) swoop; that is by reinterpreting the general problem of knowledge from a particular materialist framework (a framework that can be neatly defined and characterised as a Lakatosian 'research programme'). In the remainder of this chapter I shall outline what this materialist framework or research programme looks like, and I shall show how it both overcomes the problems we are left with while at the same time it embraces the points we have won. The materialist view should thus emerge as a *progressive* research programme or theory-series which is critically preferable to those contemporary rivals (concerned with knowing the world, and evaluating theories and theoretic frameworks) that we have already examined.

Knowledge as production

The 'knowledge as production' thesis has a very short history. Although it could be taken as a facet of the overall Marxian research programme of historical materialism, Marx himself devoted little more than a few paragraphs of his gigantic output to it; and the articulation of the theory comes to us mainly from the French philosophers Bachelard and Althusser. The thesis can best be approached by drawing an analogy with the Marxian notion of material production.

According to Marxian theory the production process can be described in terms of labour power transforming determinate raw materials by means of instruments of labour into a determinate product. The determinate raw materials and the instruments of labour together make up the 'means of production'; and it is the 'means of production' that are the determining factor in the productive process, since they both direct and limit how labour power can be employed, and they also make possible and determine what product can be produced. (Labourers working only with screwdrivers and tennis balls will never produce bread, regardless of their effort and ingenuity.) This is material practice or production; and in a well-known passage Althusser indicates how the application of the theory might be widened. Althusser says that '*practice* in general' can refer to 'any process of *transformation* of a determinate given raw material into a determinate *product*, a transformation effected by a determinate human labour, using determinate means (of "production")'.[24] From this basis then, *theoretical practice* can be construed as theoretical or mental labour power acting upon or transforming theoretical raw materials (concepts, previous knowledge, etc.) along with and by means of appropriate theoretical instruments of labour, to produce a determinate product, namely new theoretical knowledge.[25] And as with material production, it is the means of production (concepts, along with theories and theoretical tools) – now called the *problematic* – that is the determining factor in the production process. Let us here examine each aspect of the process more closely.

To begin with, the place of the knower or theoretical labourer, is greatly diminished, especially in comparison with empiricist theory, where a knowing subject comes to know a real object. In this theory, the theoretical labourer is always the agent of theoretical production who sets the production process to work; but rather than being the subject of knowledge, he is more like a bearer of relations of theoretical production, who has access to the world through theoretical practice. What more we can say about the labourer depends, however, on further understanding of the problematic.

The raw materials in theoretical practice must necessarily be theoretic ones. The individual labourer acts on the world through thought and observation, but he does not bring the real world (which has its own autonomous existence outside the head) into theoretical practice. Rather, the real object remains 'untouched', and it is 'observation transformed into concepts', or the *theoretic object*, that enters the process. Clearly, then, the theoretical raw materials are not bits of the real world or a-theoretic perceptions of real objects, nor are they experiences of the real world; they are the results of transformation, of previous theoretic production, already constituted as theoretical elements, and capable of being transformed further as they help set in motion further acts of theoretical production. We can note two things here. First, this theory postulates two objects of knowledge. There is the object of which knowledge is about (the real world), and there is the (theoretical) object from which knowledge is produced. The existence of the former is, of course, essential for theoretic production, but it is also totally independent of theoretic production. Second, recognition of these two objects overcomes the problem of theory-ladenness; for in recognising the *theoretic* object as being determinate in knowledge production, the notion that 'raw materials in the form of observational statements of knowledge are constituted by theory' is revealed as a lynch-pin of theoretical practice, rather than a problem that can be brought to bear against it.

The problematic (which includes the theoretical raw materials discussed above) is, in Althusser's words, that which 'defines the roles and functions of the "thought" of particular individuals, who can only "think" the "problems" already actually or potentially posed; hence it is also what *sets to work* their "thought power" . . . but according to its own peculiar mode'.[26] The problematic is the determining factor or means of theoretic production. As an underlying theoretic structure including concepts, techniques and methodologies, it transforms the theoretical raw materials into problems, and it then becomes the task of theoretic production to seek solutions to those problems. It is the problematic also (as with the screwdrivers and tennis balls above) that defines the parameters within which it is able to produce problems, and which excludes certain problems from its field of investigation. In this sense it is somewhat similar to Kuhn's notion of a paradigm, more similar yet to our notion of 'mental set', but closer still to Lakatos's 'hard core' (along with its positive and negative heuristics, and its protective belt).

We can now see more clearly the role of the theoretical labourer. It is not the theoretical labourer, but rather the problematic that poses problems and determines what the individual can do (just as in material production it is the means of production – e.g. screwdrivers, etc. – that determines what the labourer can do). Theoretic labour might be determinant in the process of transformation, but the theoretical labourer is determined by the very nature of the production process he participates in. The individual is a bearer of relations in the production process; but since the problematic necessarily structures what is essential or inessential for any act of production, and admits only those raw materials and means that are relevant, the labourer's activities within the process must be so structured, and can only be explained with reference to the process at hand. The individual is thus not seen as a subject of knowledge, but rather as an agent in the production of knowledge, which in turn is a process without a subject. And this, of course, is not only in direct contrast to empiricist notions; it is in contrast also to Lakatos's otherwise useful notion of a 'hard core', which, unlike the problematic, somehow results from scientists' decisions. It must be stressed however that, whereas the production of knowledge is seen as a process without a subject, the individual knower is simply not removed from or ignored by the process; rather, as labourer or bearer of theoretic labour power, he is seen as being crucial to the process, but in a different way from empiricist (and other) notions. All knowledge is recognised as having been produced by *people*; it is simply that their actions are structured and determined by the problematic.

Finally, we gain the theoretical product, the result of theoretical production, in the form of a new theory which provides an answer, or answers, to the problem posed by the problematic in relation to the theoretical raw materials. Gaining knowledge, then, is not a matter of reading pre-existing reality, nor is it a matter of sifting or engaging in successive approximations (falsificationism) to discover or reveal pre-existing reality: rather it is seen as a process of transformation activated by human labour power and utilising aspects of pre-existing reality variously as raw materials and as instruments of labour.

This, however, does not tell us the full story, for we have only considered a theory's relation with its *theoretical* object; and while this gives us an account of the origins or history or process of production of a theory, and at the same time an account of the production of its relation with its real object, it fails to tell us anything about the *nature* of the theory's relation to the real object; that is, it fails to explain why the production occurred, and why and how the theory functions (or fails to function) as knowledge. These things cannot be accounted for in an internal history of production (where the theoretical object is internal to the process of theoretical production); instead we must consider a separate and distinct question – how does a theory relate to its *real* object?

In order to answer this question we can continue our original analogy with material production. Like material production, theoretical production has both a social or external dimension and a theoretical or internal dimension. Theoretical practice does not occur in a vacuum.

Mental conceptions, as Marx indicated, are determined by social conditions (a thesis we shall return to); and in the words of Althusser, theoretical practice 'is founded on and articulated to the existing economic, political and ideological practices which directly or indirectly provide it with the essentials of its "raw materials" '.[27] The social dimension of theoretic practice, then, is comprised of those social conditions that make the process of theoretic production possible. These social conditions, determined by the specific form of a given society, affect the manner of theoretic production, but they also affect the functioning of the theoretic product, that is the nature of its relation with its real object. This leads us towards the central point in our overall thesis.

Clearly, theoretical practice can serve essentially towards the production of the real object, where the production of the real object takes precedence over social practices and social factors. On the other hand, theoretical practice can be dominated or distorted by social practice, such that what is produced is not the real object, but rather knowledge that serves certain social interests and practices. An important historical example of this is found in those Vatican astronomers who accepted and corroborated Galileo's theory of heliocentrism, but who refused to support him because of the social effects that the theory might have;[28] they thus supported a different theory on social criteria, and ignored the real object.

Now many Marxist and neo-Marxist epistemologists insist on an important distinction here. They take theoretic practice that has overcome (or might overcome) social practices, and that thus functions to produce the real object, as *science*, and theoretic practice that functions in the interests of social practices rather than in the interests of the theoretical product as *ideology*. On this point we part company with them, mainly on the grounds that it simply does not appear possible for theoretic practice, which is founded on social practices, to ever shake itself completely free of those social practices, at least while ever there is underlying conflict within those social practices.[29] But our refusal to accept the ideology – science distinction in no way harms our thesis; for if we simply keep our eye on the social or external dimension of knowledge production, two important things open up for us.

Firstly, we can see that if theoretical practice essentially serves social practices or interests rather than production of the real object then production of the real object (knowledge of the real world) must necessarily be subverted; and the theoretic products resulting from such practice must, barring coincidence, present distortions of the real world.[30]

Second, since the propensity for distortion and misrepresentation is seen to lie in the social dimension of theoretical practice (not in conniving individual's heads), it is both logically and practically possible to locate a particular distorted, misrepresentative picture of the world as arising from particular social relations and social conditions, and also to expect people living in those social relations and conditions to be bearers of that particular misrepresentative view. Further, it is also reasonable, having recognised that view as misrepresentative, to judge it adversely in terms of its relationship to the real world.

We can see, then, that we have almost automatically found ourselves in the realm of making judgments of critical preference. Once the social dimension of knowledge production is recognised and emphasised, the role and the extent of social practice and social interests in the very production of knowledge emerge clearly as central issues in evaluating the theoretic product (or knowledge). In evaluating theories, interpretations or knowledge, it becomes both relevant and necessary to consider which particular interests are being served in the production and promulgation of any particular theory, in what ways particular social interests are being served in any process of production, and how the various interests concerned are interrelated (and if necessary, disguised).[31] These considerations are not merely necessary for evaluating knowledge or theory; they are *crucial*: for, given the social dimension to the production of knowledge, the key question that we find embedded in and arising from the particular materialist framework under consideration is 'What functions do particular theoretic products serve in particular societies?' This question (and it does not preclude answers being given in terms of discovering or producing the real world) at once becomes both the focus of epistemological investigation, while also providing a means whereby we can make viable judgments of critical preference between competing interpretations, theories and research programmes.

Evaluation of the 'knowledge as production' thesis

The 'knowledge as production' thesis accounts adequately for both the subject and the object, and the relationship between them, in the production of knowledge. It makes no reliance on inductive logic or probability theory, and criticises rather than encompasses their faults. It is not troubled by any problems of theory-ladenness; it builds on rather than is troubled by the perception – sensation distinction; and it is not limited to the study of observables. Since the 'theoretical labourer – problematic – theoretical product' schema is independent from the real world, this system, unlike empiricism, is not closed. The flexibility and structure of the problematic accounts for our earlier identification of 'task-specific methodologies'; it explains 'mental sets' as a 'context of theory', and it explains also how anomalies can escape detection by not being presented as part of the problematic. The social dimension of the thesis accounts for the place of motives in the production of knowledge, for the operation of the Hawthorne effect, for the way objects of investigation can act back on investigators, and for the way lived experience interferes with investigation of the world: it further accounts for the historical factors in theory evaluation which are pointed to, but not properly accounted for, by falsificationism. It does not make the error of judging theories only by instances, and so it is not vulnerable to elementary falsifiability criteria. It makes far more of the falsificationist point that 'theories judge theories' by replacing 'third worlds' and similar idealist notions, where theories somehow grow from theories, with the notion of human (theoretical) labour employing determinate means of theoretic production; and it surpasses Lakatos's sophisticated falsificationism by developing the notion of 'hard core' into a more acceptable form and by adequately accounting for the social (non-theoretical) determinants of theoretical production. In short, it shows that theory 'comes from' the transformation, by human labour power, of aspects of pre-existing reality that are already constituted as theoretical elements, this transformation or process itself being determined by particular social conditions. Finally, the 'knowledge as production' thesis indicates a means for detecting and categorising ideology; and it explains how ideology can make phenomena appear as given, natural, eternal and unchangeable by human labour power by justifying those phenomena in accord with the interests that produce them.

Clearly, then, this thesis overcomes the difficulties inherent in the other positions we have examined, and thus can be considered as a progressive research programme; more progressive, it would appear (judged at this point of time), than those contemporary rivals that we have discussed. It is also a research programme that, unlike relativism, anarchism or scepticism, does not retreat from making judgments of critical preference; rather, it surpasses even Lakatos in that it provides workable tools and criteria for making such judgments.

Conclusion

We are now in a position to answer the question posed at the end of the first chapter; namely, if any instance can be picked out by a number of theories, how can we decide which is the best or correct interpretation of it? Or, put more generally, how can we arbitrate between different interpretations of the world? The answer comes in two steps.

First, we must recognise that in answering, or in attempting to answer, the question we must necessarily adopt a theoretic stance ourselves. And in terms of what Lakatos has shown us we would do best to adopt the most progressive research programme available to us. That particular programme, as we have suggested, could well be the materialist programme we have recently sketched. But there is more to it than simply taking a materialist stance. The second step in our answer comes from *within* the materialist programme itself, for that very programme (unlike its rivals) provides us with the substantive criteria for making the judgments we seek to make.

In the remainder of this work I shall continue to explore how we come to know and interpret the world; and I shall be mainly concerned to demonstrate that certain social relations and practices *necessarily* give rise to a particular distorted view of the world, wherein individuals are constituted as bearers of that view, such that they fail to recognise not only the distortions and illusions inherent in it, but also the way it actually functions against their best interests.[32]

This demonstration will rely largely on a consideration of the social dimension of knowledge production; and that declaration immediately suggests the theoretic stance that I shall be adopting. I can not, however, limit myself to the 'knowledge as production' thesis alone, for that thesis in itself is not completely adequate to enable one to carry out the whole of the task which has been set. The ensuing investigation, therefore, will be placed in the context of the larger research programme of which the 'knowledge as production' thesis is merely a part - namely historical materialism. Further aspects of this particular research programme will be outlined as they become necessary for the continuing discussion.

Chapter 3

Ideology

Introduction

The purpose of this chapter is to indicate in greater detail the way that ideology functions; and to outline certain conditions whereby ideology necessarily projects and presents distortions and misrepresentations, and disguises the real nature of the existing state of affairs. Our stepping-off point shall be Marx's classic statement from his Preface to *A Contribution to the Critique of Political Economy*:[1]

> the distinction should always be made between the material transformation of the economic conditions of production, which can be determined with the precision of natural science, and the legal, political, religious, aesthetic, or philosophic – in short, ideological – forms in which men become conscious of this conflict and fight it out. Just as our opinion of an individual is not based on what he thinks of himself, so can we not judge such a period of transformation by its own consciousness; on the contrary, this consciousness must rather be explained from the contradictions of material life, from the existing conflict between the social forces of production and the relations of production.

There are two important things to note in that passage. First, ideology is represented as the lived consciousness of the actual political/social events that are taking place (or are being aimed for). Ideology, then, is *perception* of the world, and as such it is governed and affected by those various aspects discussed in our opening chapter – it is a picture of the world seen from a particular standpoint, which is influenced by a multifarious collection of factors. The second point is that Marx builds in a pejorative sense to 'ideology' by contrasting it with science, such that ideological representations are necessarily distortions when compared with the precise determinations of science. For Marx (in this early passage at least) ideology is necessarily misrepresentative; and it follows that, if we could replace ideological representations of situations by scientific descriptions, then we would have automatically achieved a position of critical preference.

This reads all too simply, however, and as I have indicated earlier I fail to see either the logical or the practical possibility of replacing ideology by science in situations where theoretical products arise out of social practices that contain within themselves conflicting social interests (or even conflict between social and theoretical interests). But as it turns out, the distinction (and whether it can exist or not) is of little relevance to us, for all that I am concerned to show is that ideology is necessarily misrepresentative, and thus a target for judgments of critical preference, within a particular set of social relations – a set that is characterised by conflicting interests. In order to show this, however, further aspects of our research programme must now be filled in.

The world, from the perspective of historical materialism, is seen as dynamic; and throughout history, or at any time in history, it can be characterised in terms of the conflict of opposing forces which seek to attain predominance over each other. The interplay of these opposing or conflicting forces is both the stabilising factor at any particular time and the means by which development occurs; for when one gains ascendance a new interplay is set up, and the conflict continues but in a changed form. Now what holds at a macrocosmic level also holds at a microcosmic one as well, for the principle applies to *all* aspects of the world. Thus a *society* can be characterised in terms of the conflicting forces that both maintain its stability and impel its development. An example of such a force would be the interests[2] (and aspirations and desires) of individuals and groups within a society; and a society, or social system, can be meaningfully characterised in terms of the continual conflict between and among its interest groups. If the conflict is serious, which it would be if the interests really mattered, then 'struggle between conflicting interests and interest groups' becomes an apposite characterisation and description of the material state of affairs in any society, even though the extent and degree of struggle and conflict might vary from one society to another. Now struggle brings with it the notions, and use, of power and force. Thus what we would expect to find in any society (to varying degrees, of course) would be a situation where the conflicting interest groups held relative degrees of power and force, and where each interest group wanted the society to function in a way that, at least, served its own particular interests. In such a situation it is likely that all groups would want to disseminate their particular views, i.e. the views that serve at least their interests, and have those particular views accepted and respected by all; and it is also clear that the groups with most power, the ruling groups, would be better placed to succeed in this end. Thus the material state of affairs can be more simply characterised as a conflict between dominant or ruling interest groups and subordinate interest groups (there may also be 'self-contained' passive interest groups), where power becomes the key factor in determining which interests shall be served. And ideologies are spawned in the conflicts between interest groups, and become established as the rationalisations and legitimations of the ensuing actions and values, when the conflicts are, at least temporarily, resolved. Given this model then, it is clear that living in the world is not a matter of either living in ideology or not; it is a matter of living in one ideology or another. While there are conflicting social interests, and struggle, there is no escape from ideology; the best one can hope for is to live in the ideology that provides the best representation of the world.

As a partial illustration of this model, let us quickly take one simple example; the notion that there is, or could be, such a thing as the rightful ownership of private property. Now it is surely obvious that those people who did not possess, did not want to possess or did not believe in possessing private property would not have any interest in propagating views and instituting legislature to legitimate and protect private property. On the other hand, people with conflicting views and interests, who felt they had something to gain from the institution of private property, would try to make their views dominate, and to get 'everybody' to accept those views. If they were the ruling group they might disperse notions of the 'rightful' ownership of property when gained through inheritance or purchase; they might institute through the legislature bills concerned with trespassing and theft, and pronounce penalties for such crimes; the Church and the schools, if under their control, would pronounce theft to be bad, and teach respect for property; and philosophers might even seek justifications for the ownership of property from the unlikely fields of ethics and metaphysics. And if the ruling group won out, then an ideological belief would have developed into lived consciousness, whereby people would live in, and come to accept as given and right, a world that encourages, reinforces and protects a belief system, purely ideological, that was perpetrated by the ruling forces whose interests it actually serves.

There is, however, one very large problem with that example, even allowing for its oversimplicity. It could be argued that the institution of private property is in *everybody's* interests, that certain groups do not know what is good for them, and that it is the responsibility or duty or obligation of other groups to bring into operation those things that serve everybody best.

There are two ways to handle such an objection. The first embodies the classic philosophic concern of trying to determine what the good life is, and involves examining substantive issues to determine whether they are, or are not, in everybody's interests. This, however, is a tactic of limited worth, first because it must take each issue separately; and second because it is likely to become involved in a form of circularity, using what is 'given', whether it be methodology, substantive data or theoretical approaches, to examine the cases before it. Thus we are likely to find a general case similar to the one mentioned above where the object interferes with its own investigation and determines how it shall be investigated, and what shall be found; and we could find a replication of the instance of empiricist methodology that simply reinforces and legitimates its own presuppositions rather than provides insights into the world. Much of what passes as philosophy (and science) is really only ideological support.[3]

The second means requires not consideration of the substantive issues at hand (i.e. ethical, metaphysical or other debate about the legitimacy of *private property*) but rather an examination of the social dimensions of the production of the theory under consideration. A large part of that examination would have to concentrate on *interests* in order to determine whose interests, in any particular issue, are really being served; and if it is the case that *all* interests are being served, then to determine whether all interests are being served equally, or else whose interests are being served *most*.

The advantage of the latter approach is not only that it escapes from the ideological matrix in which the instances it wishes to examine lie (such that the object is less likely to affect its own investigation); but also that it enables us, through highlighting the social practices involved in the theoretic production, to reveal distortions, illusions and disguises for what they are. If it can be shown that any particular theory functions in order to favour one particular interest group (or favour them most), while at the same time it is displayed either as a 'truth' about the way the world is or as something that functions equally in the interests of all, then clearly consciousness that embraces what is promulgated rather than what is, whether that consciousness be in the ruled groups, the ruling groups or both, can be revealed as distorted consciousness growing out of disguises and illusions. And if it can be revealed as such, then clearly it becomes an object for judgments of critical preference.

We shall now indicate how, in certain social circumstances, lived consciousness or ideologies are brought into being such that they favour one particular interest group while working against the best interests of the majority; and yet, because of illusions, disguises and distortions, are not seen to work that way at all.

Conspiracy and self-delusion

When we consider again that ideologies are spawned in conflicts of interests, and that ruling groups, through the power that they have, try to disseminate and propagate their particular views in order to ensure that they are generally accepted, or at the very least imposed on everybody, this begins to sound like a combination of a huge conspiracy on the one hand and large-scale human stupidity or subservience on the other, working together to create a bizarre world of gigantic delusion. Well, the delusion might be there, but not necessarily the conspiracy or the stupidity. Nevertheless, we still have to account for the propagation and acceptance that commonly occur.

As far as propagation goes, one cannot simply look to cool, deliberate, calculated manipulation on the part of the ruling interests; at least not in any sophisticated form of society. On the one hand this idea is dreadfully oversimplistic, a-historical and humanly sterile. It conjures up images of dissociated people sitting around a table taking decisions out of a human context and somehow dropping them back in, in a fashion whereby they might take effect. This might work in *Brave New World* or *1984*, but these are caricatures with emphasised exaggerations, and it is the very detail that has been left out in order to create the caricatures that would militate against such an operation in the real world. On the other hand it is a naive view, for it sees the ruling interests merely spinning out ideas that they see as being *only* in their own interests: whereas in large measure the ideas are usually and commonly seen as being in everybody's interests, and as being anything but distortions and misrepresentations. Both groups, ruled and ruling, come to see the ideas as serving everyone's interests. For instance, capitalists do not tend to see themselves as exploiting workers, and certainly do not propagate any ideas along those lines. In all likelihood they see themselves as creating jobs, assisting the national economy and interests, and improving conditions in factories. The workers, on the other hand, tend not to see themselves as being exploited; rather they share the view that they are assisting the national economy; they are grateful for having jobs; and they appreciate the kindness of owners who offer bonus incentives and install hot showers in the factory and coffee machines in the office. Similarly, it can be assumed that politicians really believe in the 'democracy of the ballot box', and that voters, for good and tangible reasons, see their brief experiences in the polling booths as evidence of their equal participation in democratic procedures. And surely no teacher, while he might be doing little else than training his pupils to tolerate boredom, really sees himself as doing this, let alone doing this under the manipulation of capitalists who need workers who will tolerate boredom. Capitalists, teachers and children in all probability sincerely believe that schools are there to educate and disseminate knowledge and critical thought, and propagate *those* ideas. To suggest that the capitalist interests conspired to create schools to produce workers well attuned to boredom, and that they fooled teachers, parents and children into believing that schools do something else, is just totally naive.

A slightly more sophisticated form of the conspiracy theory, namely that ruling groups forged distortive ideologies so that ruled groups would accept the position of the ruling groups, was held well into the nineteenth century. The notion was embraced by both Feuerbach and Marx, who, while accepting the same general picture, gave different explanations of it in terms of alienation, whereby people make alienated or imaginary representations of their conditions because these conditions are themselves alienating. But that picture will not do either, as Marx himself came to realise in his later work. It is a picture, however, that can be refined considerably by adding some modern existentialist and Freudian ideas to explain further why people accept their position, or at least try to see their position in a favourable light, rather than expose and face the realities of it. It could be argued, from an existentialist point of view, that people project their own meanings on to material situations, and, feeling that they are totally bound to one such situation, project meaning that will maximally relieve their dissonance. Thus the family man – worker goes off to work, perhaps murmuring begrudgingly, because he feels he must feed his family, pay the mortgage, provide education for his children and give his family the 'benefits' 'everyone' else has, like a car and a colour TV. Never realising, or afraid to recognise, that he is totally free, he continues on as he is, thankful in retrospect for his good education, which has allowed him to acquire a job offering security and the opportunity to provide well for his dependants and himself. From a Freudian point of view, the acceptance of distortion can be related to any of the deluding defence mechanisms mentioned earlier, but most especially to rationalisation and sublimation. In terms of rationalisation people can be seen as accepting or creating theoretical frames of reference that will present their material conditions to them in the best possible light. Being consigned to earthly misery, they might create or accept an idea that there is another life where it all comes out idyllically; being consigned to poverty they might glorify poverty through cultural myths (the poor are happier) and warn against seeking riches. On the level of sublimation it is argued that people have sexual energy which, by and large, they fear, and seek to divert in other ways. Thus they readily accept socially sanctioned outlets for energy, and willingly serve the ruling interests, in work, in war and in their general life style.[4]

There is certainly more appeal when those notions are added; but what we have is still hardly sufficient to account for and explain the possibility that conscious people might come to accept and embrace a view of the world that is against their best interests. What is required now is a more feasible and convincing account of how such a thing can come about. We shall, therefore, attack the problem on many fronts in order, piece by piece, to build up a complete and satisfactory picture.

Ideology: a context of theory

Whether the new-born baby comes into the world in a Wordsworthian fashion, trailing clouds of glory, or arrives tainted with the horrors of original sin are difficult things to determine. But regardless of which (if either) is the case,[5] the child does arrive into a material world of already formed ideas, and means of human interaction; he arrives into a specific social and historical context within which he shall do his living and learning. Thus the child is not born with all his options open: his options are largely determined for him, and their parameters are set, by social and historical factors. The process of living and growing, then, is analogous not to development in an infinite number of possible dimensions, but rather to development within a wide, yet relatively fixed and stable, structure. As this discussion proceeds we shall say more about that structure, and we shall also indicate why people usually fail to escape, or even see the need to escape, from its constraints.

To begin with, the society[6] into which the child is born has, as does every society, an objective interest in the production of *certain kinds* of knowledge, and an interest also in the exclusion of other kinds. That knowledge that is encouraged and embraced by a society we shall call its *received view*, or prevailing paradigmatic way of seeing the world: it could also be taken as the current resolution of the competing, conflicting ideas of the time. Now there may be other factors that can be, and are, used to determine what a society is, like lines on a map, or natural geographic divisions – but these are not to our purpose. We are simply adopting the position that an essential characteristic of living in and participating in a particular society is being immersed in, and accepting (or just tolerating), a particular dominant view which generally characterises and strongly influences the actions, thought and human interaction in that particular society. Now given this, it is obvious that any individual lives in a great number of societies at one and the same time; but it also appears as if we are suggesting that societies, in their largest (national, legislative, or geographic) form, e.g. America, Britain, etc., are each monolithic, and that each espouse one individual precise received view. Let us consider these two issues in reverse order.

Our case would be easily clinched if we could simply lay out and quote the particular received views of particular societies. With smaller societies this can be done. The received views of the Boy Scouts, the Guild of International Oddfellows, the Ku Klux Klan and the Friends of the Earth are clearly and unambiguously spelt out for all to see; and anyone joining those societies (disregarding political infiltration) embraces the particular received views – perhaps tentatively, on a trial basis, but embraces them nevertheless. Anyone remaining in those societies continues the embrace; but resignation need not necessarily imply that the view has been discarded.

Complex societies, however, like nations and states, do not publish simple unambiguous statements of their received views; and the received view of a society seems to become more difficult to locate as the society increases in complexity. We often find slogans and platitudes, like 'the American way of life', 'a characteristically German outlook', and 'the unwritten principles of Catholicism', which suggest that there might be such prevailing distinctive views. More significant, and concrete, however, are things like the constitutions, manifestos and bills of rights, that are continually drafted, and published, as statements of what particular societies believe in. But to get right into the received view one has to dig deeper and further. Profitable areas to examine are the legal system, the education system, and the economic system, although these are not, of course, exhaustive. The legal system will indicate what is acceptable and unacceptable, both in behaviour and in punishment. The education system will give insight into what it is considered important for people to learn, and how they learn it. The economic system can reveal the development of social relations and the distribution of rewards with respect to the work people do, and their relationships to the mode of production. We could then look at whether people worship, and if so, how; how much time they have for leisure, and how they use it, and so on. Carry out that task carefully and we could gain a good idea of the values and the theoretic set of beliefs, the received view, that the society ostensibly operates under, and that characterises it as a distinctive society.[7] Of course it is quite likely that our investigations will reveal some contradictions and clashes within a society; we might even find gross pluralism in some or many areas; but these need not upset the thesis of an espoused monolithic received view as the current going resolution of the conflicting interests. Also, it is not contradictory for a monolithic view to embrace the principle of *pluralism*, a principle that all modern liberal democracies supposedly embrace.[8] However, should pluralism, or anything else, result in significant opposition arising to the received view, then social instability (and possibly civil war) could arise. It is thus in the interests of a society that its received view be held, accepted, propagated or just tolerated with a minimum of fuss; and to this end pluralism (or even directly opposing views), if they are encouraged or tolerated, are encouraged or tolerated within *limits*. There is always a point at which freedom of speech, or political expression, or the right to assemble, or the distribution of pornography, etc., is no longer acceptable, even in the most liberal of societies.[9] If there were not always an overriding factor, found at the core of the received view, then anarchy and the destruction of the society in its previously recognisable form would occur. When the received view no longer holds as such, either because of the development of incompatible pluralism, or because of its overthrow by another received view, then the society either collapses or changes fundamentally in nature.[10] A society wishing to preserve its interests would guard itself against such possibilities.

This leads us to our second issue, that people live in many societies simultaneously, each of which has its particular received view. These smaller societies exist, however, and publicly espouse their received views, only because they have been legitimated by the dominant society and its received view. The views, while perhaps pluralistic, are compatible. Thus an individual can function simultaneously as an American, a Jew, a Republican, a doctor, a country club member, a PTA member, a reserve officer of the National Guard and an anti-segregationist. But what of societies whose views conflict with the dominant society received view?

One possibility is to ignore them, which any society[11] does at its peril. A second possibility is assimilation. *If* Judaism conflicted with the 'American way of life', the view of the American way of life could be modified to encompass the principle of 'freedom of worship'. It is in roughly analogous ways that the Ku Klux Klan is allowed to exist in America and the Communist Party in Australia: their existence is assimilated under larger principles like 'freedom of speech'; and they continue to remain assimilated as long as they pose no significant threat to the dominant view.[12] A third possibility is repression; and a fourth is to ensure that societies with conflicting views never form in the first place. We shall return to these possibilities after we say more about the overall received view itself.

The received view, as we have noted, is a set of beliefs or theory, the prevailing way of seeing the world in a particular society. This is not to imply, however, that these beliefs are necessarily put into practice, or that they have to be put into practice. A society can cherish the view that all men are equal, and yet perpetrate the grossest of injustices, and oppress and subjugate the vast majority of its population. This sort of *volte face* can come about in two ways, which could at times be interrelated. On the one hand the situation might be accounted for in the received view itself. Part of the same received view that speaks of equality of all men might also speak of the principle of free enterprise. Thus while it is held that all men are equal or are created equal, it is also recognised that some will rise above the others for perfectly acceptable reasons, which are often related to equal opportunity. In much the same (but not exactly the same) way a society might espouse freedom of speech, but not until enemy infiltrators have been weeded out; or it might advocate principles of liberalism but forestall their implementation until the economy takes a strong upward turn. We should note here that, apart from being difficult things to pin down, received views are just as difficult to hold down, especially when, as in liberal democracies, they can easily embody contradictions.

The second way in which a received view can survive without being put into practice is if the illusion is created that it is being put into practice. If part of this view of a society is that all men are equal, and if people in that society believe they are being treated equally, that is all that really matters: whether they actually are being treated equally is largely immaterial. Thus, what is really important with regard to the perpetuation of a received view (and thus social stability) is not so much the material state of affairs that exists, but rather how people perceive that material state. It follows, then, that if a material state of affairs was to be perpetuated that was contrary to the prevailing belief system of a society, then members of that society would have to become convinced that the state of affairs was not contrary to their beliefs: they would have to take on, and become bearers of, a distorted, disguised or misrepresentative picture of the state of affairs. Similarly, people might go on living contentedly in a world that functions against their best interests, if they were convinced that the material state of affairs in which they lived was in their best interests.

But surely this begins to sound absurd. The received view is the view of a society: why would a society want to dupe itself?

A 'society', of course, would hardly want to dupe itself if this society existed in the form of a collection of largely homogeneous individuals who lived more or less together, and pursued common ends with no conflicting interests. Such societies do exist. But within a context where a society is characterised by conflicts of interests, differentials of power and a desire on the part of the ruling groups to have the ruled groups see the world in a particular way, the notions of deception and distortion do become a serious consideration: also, it becomes clear that, whereas the whole of such a society may be deceived, it is not the whole of that society that is deceiving itself.

From this point on we shall refer to societies that are characterised by conflicts of interests and differentials of power as *class societies*,[13] with ruling and ruled classes; and we shall now continue to indicate how, within class societies, normal rational intelligent people can come to accept and bear an illusory view of the world, and continue to live in social relations that appear to be, but are actually not, in their best interests. This requires, to begin with, further consideration of the formulation of received views within class societies.

In class societies it is hardly likely that the received view arises either out of a series of democratic decisions involving all people, or in a gradual fashion whereby folklore grows into value systems which everybody plays a formative part in establishing.[14] The case is rather that very few people have any influence in formulating the dominant beliefs in society, and those people who do have influence are the ones who have the power to be influential. They are, in short, the ruling class. Throughout the history of class societies, whatever form they have taken, it has been the ruling class that has been largely responsible for setting out the ideals, beliefs and values; the received views of those societies. And the potential to manipulate that such ruling classes have was well described by Robert Owen a century and a half ago:[15]

Any character, from the best to the worst, from the most ignorant to the most enlightened, may be given to any community, even to the world at large, by the application of proper means; which means are to a great extent at the command and under the control of those who have influence in the affairs of men.

Owen originally concluded: *'of those who possess the government of nations'.*[16] And Marx took this further:[17]

The ideas of the ruling class are in every epoch the ruling ideas; i.e. the class which is the ruling *material* force of a society, is at the same time its ruling *intellectual* force. The class which has the means of material production at its disposal, has control at the same time over the means of mental production . . . Insofar, therefore, as they rule as a class and determine the extent and compass of an epoch, it is self-evident that they do this in its whole range, hence among other things rule also as thinkers, as producers of ideas, and regulate the production and distribution of the ideas of their age; thus their ideas are the ruling ideas of the epoch.

It is important to note, at this stage, that Marx is referring to all knowledge, all ideas, not just to what we have called the received view. In this we concur with him, but wish to fragment his notion of ruling class just a little. When we look at specific areas of knowledge, and their propagation through education, we find the same thing that Marx identifies happening. A ruling group determines what subjects shall be taught. Within subjects, ruling groups, through their power on committees, their control over journals and publication in general and their 'positions', determine what shall pass as mathematics, history, geography, science, philosophy, etc., in any particular epoch. And this, as has been shown many times, is often determined on grounds quite remote from epistemological ones, or even a serious concern for 'the pursuit of truth wherever it may lead'.[18] Academic appointments are not made necessarily on qualifications and ability alone; books are not always published according to merit alone; authors rather than their articles are often included in or excluded from journals (witness the continued publication, and long-standing unquestioned acceptance, of the works of Sir Cyril Burt),[19] 'schools' of thinking (especially literary criticism) have their ascendancies and descendencies; the 'new' maths replaces the old maths on school curricula when power passes into other hands; and so on. Thus it can be said that what is learnt in schools and similar institutions, the subjects and their content, is determined by a number of ruling interests (who may be, as Marx suggests, coincidental with *the* ruling class - but this is not to our present point). Children do not simply learn maths, English, history and so on; they learn what certain ruling interests take as maths, English and history; and they accept as correct and worth knowing what those same interests count as correct and worth knowing.[20] It appears that all 'knowledge communities' have power structures and rule, and that ruling interests 'control' *all* forms of public knowledge.[21]

We have strayed a little from the notion of received views, and we must return to it now in order to complete this section. The one thing above all that has to be recognised about a received view in a class society is that it is a view serving the interests of a ruling class. If we ever pin down such a view in substantive form there can be much value in trying to ascertain who formulated it, how it came to be formulated (a crucial issue, for such views neither 'materialise' out of thin air, nor are necessarily formulated in committee rooms), and who it particularly serves and benefits. But what is more to our present point is to indicate how people whose interests are not served by the received view and its theoretic ideological content actually come to accept that it really does work in their best interests. Or to put that another way, how does the received view get to be received?

Repression

One seemingly sure way to create a situation where only one view (or one set of views) prevails or is tolerated is to use forces of repression to stamp out those people with contrary beliefs - by gaoling them, exiling them or killing them. There are, however, two very large problems with this approach. In the first place, it can really be successful only if the opposition to the received view is quite minor, or easy to break down by making examples of a few people. For instance, if in a capitalist society the small ruling class were to dispose of a gigantic labouring class which had somehow become aware of its exploited position, then obviously the ruling class would suffer badly for its own actions. In this instance only the 'reserve army' of labourers, or a number equivalent to them, could be safely disposed of. The technique of repression can be effective against individuals or minor revolt, but from there on it tends to become self-defeating.

The second problem with the overt repressive approach is that it may bring into practice things that are contrary to the espoused principles of the received view; and this would be a dangerous thing for any ruling class to indulge in, for it immediately exposes contradictions, not just between theory and practice, but *within* both theory and practice.[22] For instance, if a tenet of the received view was 'freedom of speech', it would be contradictory and odd to find repressive forces brought to bear against people freely speaking their minds. And this partly explains why there is always some form of public outcry (not necessarily a universal one) *within* society, and some change of consciousness or 'rethinking', when forces of repression move against political rallies, student meetings, demonstrations and marches in societies that espouse liberal democratic views including the right to assemble and freedom of speech. Such repressive action might be expected 'elsewhere', in other forms of societies, but seeing it occur at home can be sufficient to sow seeds of doubt and mistrust in people who otherwise believed that the espoused ruling principles really did guide the life and practice of their society. For instance, people in Canada and America were hardly stunned when Soviet tanks rolled into Czechoslovakia; yet only a short time later many of those same people were considerably disturbed when, in 1970, National Guardsmen opened fire on and fatally wounded students at Kent State University, and when, in the same year, tanks rolled into the streets of Quebec and 'secret' arrests were made following Trudeau's sudden midnight invocation of the War Measures Act. These actions, if nothing else, brought about a lot of rethinking, and a change of awareness, in many people who once believed they were living in a society where such things could not happen.

Repression is negative, untidy and dangerous not only to the repressed but to the repressors as well. It can actually promote the growth of the consciousness it wishes to repress. And, of course, consciousness, in the final analysis, cannot be repressed, at least not short of total brainwashing: machine-guns can stop people from acting in certain ways but not from thinking and believing in certain ways. But there is usually no need to resort to repression, at least in the first instance; consciousness and beliefs can be formulated and manipulated much more successfully through positive means.

The place of institutions

The received view of a society can be reinforced in a number of ways by institutions that serve to strengthen and stabilise the *status quo*; and thus it is in the interests of the ruling class to work through institutions, and to increase them in both size and number as a society becomes larger and more complex. Let us now indicate some of the ways in which institutions perform this reinforcing and stabilising task.

To begin with, institutions tend to depersonalise and disembody the ruling class as holders and formulators of the received view. For instance, to recall an earlier example, it appears as if it is 'the law', and 'the law' as represented by learned impartial judges, and as concretised through courts - not any particular individual ruling interests (who might have no obvious connection with the legal system) - that (somehow) decrees that there shall be private property, and that protects private property. Through such depersonalisation it becomes almost impossible to find the individuals who make up the ruling class, or any public exponents or formulators of the received view. Thus, while we all know the Rocke-fellers, a few bankers and some media magnates, it is difficult, in a sense, to associate them directly with the ruling class, or even to point out precisely who the members of the ruling class are. This point in itself is sufficient to convince many that there is no such thing as a ruling class, at least in a liberal democracy; and that Nelson Rockefeller, J.P. Morgan and John Fairfax are businessmen, bankers or newspaper owners, but hardly rulers (let alone people who largely influence our consciousness). In the one stroke both the ruling class and the formu-lators of the received view are rendered *unobservable*. Thus we see that institutions disguise and serve a mystifying function[23] along with their stabilising function: they give a false sense of the source of the received view, and so make that view, which is determined by social practice but also embodied in people, that much harder to locate, approach, and challenge. For example, if we wanted to find the received view on, say, education, or simply a definitive statement on what a society claims it is doing through education, in all likelihood we would go to an insti-tution - the Education Department - where our requests would be met (if they were met) not by the person in charge there, the Director-General, not by the elected parliamentary member, the Minister for Education, and certainly not by Mr Rockefeller, but by an 'official spokesman' for the Department of Education. And there are two things we can note about the received view as given by this 'official spokesman': first, it may not be his personal view; and second, in all likelihood he had little part in formulating the view he gives voice to. Institutions create the situation where a person, regardless of his own beliefs, can speak on behalf of the institution, the firm, the department or the ministry: and they also create the situation where, if we don't like what the spokesman says, we can hardly attack him personally, since he is only 'doing his job', mouthing a policy he may not believe in, and which he probably had no part in formulating. Institutions in this way separate policy as stated from policy as made, thus further masking the real policy-makers, and erecting in their places figure-heads who are merely doing their jobs. It has been said that many people would gladly attack 'the Establishment' if only they could find it. Institutions defuse such attacks, and confuse such attacks, and in this way protect the *status quo* and its engineers.[24]

Institutions further strengthen and stabilise the *status quo* through impinging more and more on the everyday existence of the members of a society. There was a time, not all that long ago, when a person could look after the education, health and employment of his children without passing through the hands of education departments, medical funds and employment offices. But not now; and not because it's illegal, but simply because that is not the way things work these days. This is not to say, of course, that everything about institutions is bad; what it is essential to note, however, is that institutions, having got the thin end of their wedge into society, have so insistently pushed their way in that the child born today enters a world where gigantic-scale institutional-isation and bureaucratisation is an existential 'fact', a *fait accompli*. Thus the only world we know and have experienced is a world largely operating through institutions that are overwhelming in their organis-ational size, their bureaucracy, and in their physical manifestation as concrete multi-storey skyscrapers. They give the impression of impreg-nability, both whenever one tries to do business with them – institutions muck people about, but people can't beat the system – and also when one merely looks at their massive permanent physical nature (how could you ever pull down and do away with a fifty-storey state office block which 'must' be necessary in its immensity since it was built to do jobs that 'have to be done'?) Both literally and metaphorically, institutions eclipse so much of the world that they make the possibility of a world without them unimaginable: they stand as given, necessary, and right. Thus by their bureaucracy, their physical presence and the constraints they exert on men's imagination, institutions, much in the fashion of a drug, create a static vision of society, and stunt the possibility of man thinking that things could ever be otherwise. In this way they effectively serve to prevent change; and by presenting themselves as a *fait accompli*, and as necessary for the smooth efficient running of a society, they become a serious radical constraint, a successful potent force sustaining the present social structure. Thus again they serve to legitimise the *status quo*; they restrict the possibility of alternatives, and so become a preventive force defusing and working against any form of cultural transformation or social revolution. Or in other words, they protect the vested interests of the ruling class, and bolster the received view of the society.

Institutions, of course, do not spring out of the ground like mushrooms; nor (except in circumstances of extreme repression) are people forced to accept them at gunpoint. Institutions are created; and they continue to exist because they are accepted. Institutions, in a class society, are instruments of the ruling classes that serve the particular interests of those ruling classes, and these interests are even better served if all alternatives are cut off such that conflicting views cannot even be formulated. For instance, towards such ends 'the state' could take over and institutionalise education, compel all children to go to school and close all non-state schools. Better still, it could keep up the facade of liberalism and freedom by *not* closing non-state schools but by exercising powerful non-direct control over them.

Recognising the place and function of institutions, however, takes us only part of the way, and what remains to be shown now is how the general disposition is brought about that will ensure the continued acceptance of the received view.

Supportive rhetoric

It has been said that if you keep people running all their lives they might become excellent runners, but they'll never learn to swim. This very largely is the principle that underlies the notion and use of 'supportive rhetoric'. Put oversimply at this stage, fields of discourse are mapped out and rules of discourse are established and legitimated (more correctly, they are determined by social practice), and then anyone who wants to can begin studying, talking and criticising for all he's worth. And this sort of thing is not merely made available and left at that: people are positively encouraged to engage in the discourse, and so build up the body of rhetoric, provided that they stay within the field, and play according to the rules. This again is largely analogous to what Kuhn describes as 'normal science'; in other areas it is often referred to as *mainstream* or *orthodox* philosophy, sociology, economics or whatever. It is, once more in Kuhnian terms, discourse within a paradigm. The scientist before Priestley bore and refined the rhetoric surrounding phlogiston theory; the nineteenth-century scholar of English literature worked in and built up a critical rhetoric devoid of reference to the metaphysical poets or their principles of poetry; the twentieth-century philosopher gave up being a Platonic spectator of all eternity and developed the rhetoric surrounding positivism and linguistic analysis. And on the negative side, all but a few of those radicals who have worked outside the prevailing fields of rhetoric have been packed away in history's silent dustbins: we know of Galileo, Darwin, Manet, Freud and Henry Moore; but they, and the others who have survived, were surely not alone in challenging particular orthodoxies.

An excellent example of defining orthodoxy and setting the parameters for acceptable discourse can be found in philosophy of education – the area in which this work is being written. The study of education, as a theoretic and practical discipline, had up until the 1960s sadly lacked the second-order philosophic probings that have been more common with, and so beneficial to, history and science. But then a school emerged that appeared likely to elevate educational discourse above the realms of platitudes and pious prescriptions. It was a school spawned by the Wittgensteinian 'revolution in philosophy', which applied the principles of linguistic analysis to education on the assumption that only after 'detached analysis' had clarified and given a clear sighting of the concepts concerned could other important philosophic issues be approached. (This is not the whole of the story, and disregards the attention also placed on ethics and epistemology, but it is enough for our present purposes). Early in the piece, R. S. Peters wrote in the Preface of *Ethics and Education*, one of the seminal works in the new study:[25]

> But this is one of the main reasons for publishing a book somewhat prematurely. The point is to provide a few signposts for others and to map the contours of *the field* for others to explore in a more leisurely and detailed manner. The important thing in the philosophy of education is that something should be there *to indicate what it is and to provide a determinate structure on which students can train their critical faculties*. The philosophy of education . . . will only develop as a rigorous field of study if a few philosophers are prepared to plough premature furrows *which run more or less in the right direction*.

One sentence later Peters states that advances in philosophy 'are made when two or three are gathered together *who speak more or less the same language* and can meet frequently. . .'[26] Then, in collaboration with one who speaks more or less the same language, P. H. Hirst, he writes: 'Philosophy, in brief, is concerned with questions about the analysis of concepts and with questions about the grounds of knowledge, belief, actions and activities'[27] and: 'conceptual analysis . . . is a necessary preliminary to answering some *other* philosophical questions'.[28]

Peters (and Hirst) had power and status. They were famous professors at the most respectable of universities. They controlled courses in philosophy of education. They controlled discourse, through supervision of higher degrees and through Peters's place in the Philosophy of Education Society of Great Britain. Peters controlled publications – through the Society's *Proceedings*; through his control with Routledge and Kegan Paul, the largest publisher in the area; as general editor of their 'International Library of the Philosophy of Education' (which contains the standard legitimised texts in the field); and through professorial power over staff appointments and the distribution of awards.

Given this, it is not surprising that philosophy of education from 1966 to the present – that is, what *really counted* as philosophy of education and made up the courses and reading in that subject – explored *Peters's* field, studied *Peters's* structure, and followed the direction of *Peters's* furrows. Philosophers speaking 'more or less the same language' turned out a plethora of books and papers analysing concepts as a necessary preliminary to answering philosophical questions about education. It became the height of orthodoxy to analyse the necessary and sufficient conditions of the concepts of 'teaching' and 'indoctrination' and to write counter-papers politely attacking other people's analyses, in the attempt to improve on them. The parameters were set; and within them people worked vigorously, at the same time both bound by and helping to develop the supportive rhetoric, and in all probability sincerely believing in the worth of what they were doing. And so a lot of people became excellent analysts, able to criticise the detail of other analytic works, but ill-equipped to criticise analysis itself; and unable to see, as they strived to detach themselves, that 'detached analysis' is a fiction. Further, this analytic philosophy, in true Wittgensteinian style, 'left everything as it is'; or rather, it spun misty cobwebs over educational discourse, but revealed little if anything about education (as defined for this work). Very early in the piece a student (thus not highly educated or initiated, or deeply committed to the analytic cause) said of his presence at a conference that he came from the trenches of teaching to the Pentagon, only to find the generals playing chess.[29] A decade later he is beginning to win applause.

In this specific example we see how the received view of the ruling class (Peters), fixed through institutions like societies, universities and publishing houses, came to prevail and be bolstered by a growing body of supportive rhetoric. Not only is it a classic case of what Kuhn calls 'normal science', in that it 'aims to refine, extend, and articulate a paradigm that is already in existence';[30] but it is also a representative and specific instance of what happens in all areas of study and investigation, and in society at large.

None of this is to suggest, however, that supportive rhetoric in wider fields is a transparently narrow thing, or that it cannot criticise aspects of the received view itself. Supportive rhetoric is usually as widely based as people can imagine (mainly because it encompasses all they have learnt to imagine, or all they have learnt to accept as orthodox critical methodology). And for this reason it is rarely seen for what it is, namely a *restriction* on criticism rather than a tool for criticism. It is criticism, certainly, but criticism in such a weak sense that what it really does is *refine* the received view. It gives the impression that criticism really is on, both in principle and practice; thus views are not seen as being imposed in a totalitarian fashion or as enforced by repression; and the small evolutionary steps that do occur bear constant witness to the serious way that criticism appears to be taken notice of and acted on. But the criticism that is encouraged by supportive rhetoric falls within the parameters of the received view, and as such can never be a serious threat to that view. Clearly, then, it is in the interests of the ruling class to ensure that such rhetoric prevails; for such rhetoric not only disguises the imposed nature of the received view; it also allows people, through critical discourse, to internalise that view as if it were their own, or at least to champion their own slight variations of it. Further, the rhetoric so occupies people's time and energy that they become incapacitated and unable to criticise from other perspectives: they either fail to recognise that there could be other perspectives, or they have no time to explore them. Formal education provides a neat example here, for it is a period characterised, from kindergarten to university graduation, by fixed 'time lots', in which the best a student can possibly hope for is to master the set pieces of work in the specific periods of time allowed for each. Education is a matter of learning the ropes, not of untying them or discovering who is holding them. But more of that later.

At this point, however, let us stay within the context of education, and illustrate by two extended examples how supportive rhetoric, while appearing to be critical, actually refines and reinforces the received view or extends and articulates the prevailing paradigm.

The matter of assessment in education has recently become the centre of considerable debate. The encouraged debates (i.e. those that get published, are joined in by respectable people in the field, are funded or are taken seriously where it counts) have been concerned largely with the mechanics of assessment: Should one-shot assessments be replaced by continuous assessment? Are exams, and essays, and reports, and attendance records valid and reliable forms of assessment? Should students participate in the assessment process? Should more complex grading be replaced by simple pass/fail assessments? Are particular assessment procedures compatible with the stated aims and ideals of courses? Do they have an adverse effect on the teaching/learning process? Do they actually assess what they set out to assess? Now there can be no doubt that all of these are important and highly complicated questions: and *each one* of them is capable of generating an enormous amount of discussion within a wide compass of relevance.

Take, for example, the matter of replacing single end-of-course exams by continuous assessment. Is the latter any more reliable and valid than the former? Would the problems of anxiety, illness and orientation for study be solved or magnified? Is the single exam to be replaced by a series of mini-exams? If not, what shall it be replaced by? Should attendance, class participation and even punctuality become assessment criteria? And if multiple assessment means are used how can marks given for exams, essays, reports, participation, etc., some awarded on ordinal scales and some on ratio scales, be meaningfully added and averaged? These are just some of the matters that would come up in any serious debate on the central issue; and overriding all of these matters, and others that might be raised, is the problem of evidence. What evidence is there to base conclusions on? And, since we are usually comparing the known with the hypothetical, what could possibly count as worthwhile evidence in such circumstances? Clearly, we have enough issues raised by now, all of them relevant and all of them important, to occupy the attention and effort of seriously concerned parties for a considerable period of time. And there are enough side-issues involved to catch the particular interests of individual protagonists; to bring the defenders and attackers of multiple-choice tests and normal distributions into the arena; to attract statisticians and educationalists and psychologists of all schools, along with all the others who might see a point involved that is worth their particular championing. And so a lot of people spend a lot of time and effort, with the hope that out of it all shall come a better means of assessment, whether it be continuous or of the one-shot type. And in all probability a better means of assessment will arise. Reform will have taken place.

Now given that sort of critical endeavour, and the changes that actually result from it, one could hardly say that the system was inflexible, that criticism wasn't encouraged, and that changes could not be wrought. But it is patently obvious from the example as I have outlined it that the entire criticism has been undertaken within the received view, or under the acceptance of the suppressed premise, that there *will be* assessment. This 'internal' type of criticism can hardly attack the received view, and so it is allowed to go on by the perpetrators of the received view. Usually it is positively encouraged. A commission set up by the Department of Education to investigate assessment in education satisfies most that something is being done, engages many experts and laymen in a form of occupational therapy, and helps ensure that assessment will remain by defusing attacks against assessment itself: many who would want to attack assessment are drawn into the internal debate, where they might win concessions that can be tolerated and assimilated easily.[31] The tactic of diversion should be generally recognisable.

So, too, should the general pattern. Virtually the entire corpus of

work that passes for educational discourse and debate is internal criticism of this type, whether it be localised debate like that which always
surrounds the publishing of a new report, or longstanding debate on
issues such as the merits of progressive versus traditional education.
Thus, wherever we find debate occurring on issues such as whether
secondary schools should be selective or comprehensive, whether they
should be coeducational or not, whether numerical marks should be
replaced by letter grades, whether junior maths should be taught by
coloured rods and so on, we find internal criticism that refines rather
than seriously criticises the received view. We find supportive rhetoric,
fostered by the dominant institution, which aids acceptance of the
general principles of the received view.

As our second example consider the following passage taken from
an article called 'The Educational Process From a Layman's Point of
View', an article that has pretences of being highly critical of certain
educational practices and theories. The author has already stated that:
'With relatively few exceptions, people are as lazy as they dare to be';
and that education should involve people 'in some substantial activities
from which they do not get instant enjoyment'. This sets the stage for
the following argument concerning extrinsic motivation, and compulsory constraints:[32]

> Almost everybody needs motivation from outside himself so that he
> can attain his maximum potential. This seems to be true even in the
> context of one's favourite activities. Even a champion athlete, a
> runner, needs the challenges of competition. Unless he is conscious
> of the inexorable testing he will have to face in a big race; unless
> he is aware of the relentlessness of the timing device against which
> he runs, he will never reach the performance peak which, otherwise,
> he could have attained. All business men would lapse into relative
> slothfulness but for the external pressures upon them – many of
> which they dislike. Challenges from competitors; drives for the
> personal satisfactions that are seen as corollaries to status and higher
> income; competition from others in search of the top job; pleasing
> the boss or the shareholders; the attitudes of the media; the market
> place; public opinion; consumer demand; parliamentary requirements
> and other factors force people into disciplined activities to which
> they probably would not have subjected themselves if left entirely
> to their own devices. Similarly the student, irrespective of age,
> cannot realistically expect to be free or to be freed from all the
> compulsions that society and experience suggest that he should
> face.

This 'argument' is based on two unsupported (and possibly unsup-
portable) generalisations – the notion of inherent laziness, and the

83

presumed necessity for external motivation in achieving maximal attainments - and the conclusion does not follow logically from what has preceded it. But these are not really to our point. More to the point is that there is no argument in the passage; instead it is a string of rhetoric supporting certain suppressed premises and a particular received view.

In the first half of the passage the author appears to be using runners and businessmen as illustrative instances of the general thesis that one needs competition and challenge to attain success and achieve maximum potential. What is really the case, however, is that the author has begun with a particular (suppressed) notion of success and the achievement of maximum potential that can be achieved only through chasing external rewards, and he has plugged in his examples accordingly. What is said of athletes and businessmen, even if it were true, would hardly apply to painters, potters, schoolteachers or anyone motivated by intrinsic reward; or who saw the achievement of maximum potential as, say, a Buddhist or a mystic might; or as Camus, Thoreau or the rural commune-dwellers of the world would see it. The particular notion of success with which this author begins is one of a relentless and endless pursuit of maximum potential which can be measured by material, extrinsic and extending criteria; the runner beats the clock and strives to beat it again and again, the executive goes from better job to better job to better job; and obviously this builds up and at the same time presupposes a context where 'competition', 'status', 'higher income', 'top job', 'shareholders', 'market place' and 'consumer demand' fit in so neatly. Clearly, the author has an 'unstated' view of what the desirable world would be like, and what would count as success and achievement in it. He does *not argue* for those things; but it is only in terms of *them*, not in terms of what he has actually 'argued', that his conclusions 'follow'. The need for self-discipline; distaste for slothfulness; the need to do things we dislike; glorification of competition; status gained through competition; pleasing bosses and shareholders; and recognition of the media, the market place and consumer demand as principal factors that force people into the activities they subject themselves to: all of these are *the terms of reference* for the argument, not things that follow from the examples. The author sees the world in a certain way, endorses what he sees, and claims that children ought to be educated to fit his world and to fit into it successfully.

But there is no argument (and where one is attempted it is fallacious). We appear to get the form of an argument, as part of a criticism of current educational practices, but what we really find is a piece of rhetoric shot through and through with suppressed premises and implied values and ideals, set neatly within a paradigm, and clearly more supportive of the prevailing assumptions underlying education than seriously critical of some aspects of its practice. Education, it is simply suggested, should be directed towards getting the student to buckle down and face the compulsions (*sic*) that society and experience suggest he should face.

As a final example of supportive rhetoric, consider the following statement by E.B. Castle:[33]

> On leaving school many of them will enter the world of the conveyor belt. In this world young persons are living two lives at the same time – a nut-tapping life and a dream life. The problem for teachers is : How shall we enrich the young worker's dream life? And the solution, which is thoroughly Greek, probably lies in rightly-educated emotions, so that while he is turning his screws and she is filling her cigarette packets, day dreams arise from a healthier subconscious.

This is hardly supportive rhetoric masquerading as criticism; it is unashamedly pure support for the *status quo*. Castle at least faces up to what few modern apologists for liberal education will face up to: namely that on leaving school many (most?) pupils will take on a life of dull, boring, dead-end work. But he does not challenge that or see *that* as *the* issue. He does not suggest that education might try to elevate all pupils beyond the life of the conveyor-belt, that education itself might call into question the conveyor-belt world, or that preparation for the conveyor-belt world is hardly *education* (in any liberal sense). Instead, Castle accepts the *status quo* and helps to legitimate it by defining *the* problem for teachers elsewhere; by suggesting what they might do to make a *necessary 'given' situation* a little more humane, and by indicating, through rather extreme rationalisation, the 'compatibility' between the principles of liberal education and the realities of the world of the conveyor-belt. This is in stark contrast to John Holt's recognition that: 'It is a waste of time and money, as well as a cruel deception, to talk about providing good education for children if the central experience of their adult lives is going to be pointless, stupid, stupefying work.'[34]

In concluding this section it should be noted that supportive rhetoric does not exist only in particular fields, subjects or academic areas, even though each will have its own version. Supportive rhetoric is also a totally pervasive thing legitimising the overall prevailing received view of a society. It is, in other words, ideology, a set of theoretic stances attempting to rationalise values and legitimate action. Such ideology in a class society, as we have argued, will attempt to rationalise and legitimate the *status quo* that serves the ruling interests in such a society (it might also attempt to bring about a new state of affairs that further serves those interests). In doing so it must also convince the ruled classes that the state of affairs is in their interests as well; and if the state of affairs is not in their interests (and it could hardly be in their best interests when it serves others better), then large-scale rationalisations and illusions have to be created and maintained to achieve this end.

Now it would be supremely naive to suggest that the picture we have drawn, concentrating on ideology as theory, could provide sufficient account for the majority of people embracing large-scale distorted and illusory views of the world. There are three large weaknesses in our thesis as it has been set out so far. First, even allowing for the language problems involved, what has been said still reads too much like a conspiracy. Second, our thesis underrates man's ability to judge the reality of his own lived experience in terms of its fit with the given theoretical rationalisations (or else it fails to account for how that lived experience reinforces the theoretical rationalisations). Finally, it fails to account for things like the received view coming into existence (for received views or prevailing ideologies, as we have noted, do not appear magically from the heavens); nor does it account adequately for the pervasive qualities that such things have. To overcome these weaknesses it is necessary to show how 'ideology-as-theory' is determined by, and rooted in, definitive life practices; and so we turn now to consider practical life-situations.

Ideology: a context of lived experience

We noted earlier that the child at birth arrives into a material world of already formed ideas and means of human interaction. The child is initially surrounded by a whole matrix of experiential ideologies, but only gradually does he come to live in, and participate in, them. These ideologies exist both in the form of various behaviours, habits and rituals, and in the form of images, concepts and ideas. Let us, at this stage, now concentrate on the first aspect.

To live as a human being is to engage in some particular sets of behaviour, to do specific things, to perform specific rituals and represent these to oneself in specific images, and to grasp and understand all of this through particular concepts and theories. Living really means living in a particular way, and the way that life is lived is not an accidental or chance matter: rather, it is an adaptation to a number of external conditions. The child, thus, is born into a set of lived relationships that are themselves determined by the particular conditions of existence. He witnesses them, comes to take part in them, and conceptualises them.

He learns, for instance, the marriage ideology;[35] and 'marital state' becomes a significant category for him. It becomes meaningful to trichotomise people into subdivisions of 'married', 'not yet married', and 'never been married'. He comes to regulate his own life in such a way that points to his getting married at some fairly specific time; he internalises the notions that married people are 'couples', that women change their names at marriage, that such couples are referred to as 'Mr and Mrs', with the male coming first. Through living in the ideology he begins to see the rituals, like family picnics, baked dinners on Sundays and others, evident in internal role expectations and relationships; and he begins to pick up a conceptual scheme that describes the situation, including such concepts as 'breadwinner', 'housewife', and 'little woman'. But the marriage ideology is only one of many that the child learns to live in. There is the church ideology (which lends support to the marriage ideology), the school ideology (which supports the work ideology), the work ideology (which supports the family ideology), and so on. Thus, for any individual the totality of the material form of his life, together with its related immediate conceptual representations, lies within the ideological matrix of that individual. And this matrix can be regarded as an ensemble of particular *lived* ideologies, each of which is a socially constructed set of practices, rituals and behaviours interrelated with one another and with certain concepts and images. A lived-ideology (e.g. religion, morality, schooling, family) is a coherent whole, and is distinguishable from other lived-ideologies, even though it may be linked to and influenced by them.

Now no individual carries out all aspects of all rituals of any particular ideology at any given time; and some individuals carry out few if any aspects of a particular ideology. For instance, a person may choose not to get married, not to have or live in a family, and to seek out only similar company. Another individual may remain atheistic and have nothing to do with the church. However, while they act as if the family or the church is the norm, e.g. by giving children presents at Christmas, they can still be regarded as living in the ideology. The line can be fine at times; but what we can say is that, when a certain range of a person's material acts and conceptual representations are governed by the organising principles of an ideology, the person can be taken as living in that ideology. And the group of ideologies within which an individual lives constitutes his ideological matrix. It is this ideological matrix that constitutes the individual as a social being, and which can be regarded as the determining force of his consciousness, in the sense that a person's awareness of himself, his attitudes and so on are the accompanying result of living in specific ideologies. This consciousness, of course, would also include what are generally referred to as unconscious or subconscious elements. Ideology, in this sense, more closely resembles Marx's use of it in later works, especially *Capital*, where the earlier pejorative sense is largely put aside, and ideology is seen not so much as a distortive (subjective, unscientific) picture formulated as the consciousness of an age, but rather as a matter of lived instances, related to modes of production, which *actually form individual consciousness, subjects, and 'personalities'.* Our discussion, from this point on, is embracing both senses of 'ideology', although the latter will be seen, eventually, to emerge as the more important.

We have been speaking of human existence and human experience all too glibly up to now, and at this stage it is necessary to make our discussion far more concrete. We can begin to do this when we add to our original research programme the recognition that there can be no human existence without production (except, perhaps, for very short periods in idyllic situations where food, clothing, shelter, etc., are readily and naturally available). Certainly there can be no long-term continued human existence without production. And continued production requires continual reproduction of the means of production (tools, machines, etc.), and continued reproduction of the producers. Now this latter does not simply require that children be born and grow up; it requires that children be born and grow up to think, believe and live in particular ways. This is occasioned because there is not simply one mode of production. There are many modes of production, but at any particular time and place there is one dominant mode of production; and *this*, we take it, basically affects how people live; it determines what sorts of work they shall do, how they will relate with other people, how they shall gain their means of subsistence, etc.; and how they shall conceptualise their lived experience, and thus develop consciousness. Herein lies the basis of Marx's claim that it is man's social existence that determines his consciousness (a claim that we are obviously assimilating within our research programme).

Now it is clear that, if the maintenance and reproduction of any existing mode of production is to occur in any society, then it is necessary that a particular consciousness be developed and maintained in that society. Thus the maintenance of people in a certain range of lived-ideological matrices becomes an important factor in stabilising and continuing a given mode of production. It may be very important, for this end, that certain lived-ideologies are supported (e.g. the family), or even institutionalised (marriage) or enforced (property laws). It is also important that each new generation be moulded, even forced (compulsory schooling), into pre-existing lived-ideologies which will be specific to the particular dominant mode of production in existence. In times of stability the prevailing lived-ideologies are usually sufficient to adapt people to their conditions of existence; but when necessary they can be backed up by political power or theoretical rationalisations. Also they have a great deal of self-perpetuating momentum of their own: the family tends to raise people who are best fitted for and desire family life; the necessity for school certificates to get better jobs supports the value of schools and the desirability of being schooled; etc. The individuals who are processed and produced by these social ideological

apparatuses and institutions:[36]

are formed with the habits, the attitudes and the conceptions which
are appropriate to the places in society that they have to occupy.
Moreover this 'processing' presents the existing system of social
relations as 'natural', as unquestionably 'given'. Thus the constant
reproduction of ideologies contributes to the reproduction of the
social formation as a whole by constantly forming individual subjects
who are suitable for insertion into the existing system of social
relations, while at the same time masking the reproductive aspects
of this process so that these relations seem natural and self-subsisting.

We now have a far better picture of the functioning of ideology; for
by attending to both the theoretical rhetoric and the lived experience
we can now understand the persuasive hold that ideology has on, and
the influence it has in, *determining* consciousness. With this understanding we can return once again to the question of when, and how, man
can accept consciousness that distorts his view of the world and works
against his own best interests.

Let us begin this time by focusing on the dominant mode of production in a society. If that dominant mode favoured all people equally,
there would be no need for any illusions to be 'created' in people's consciousness. But if that mode favoured one class particularly, it would be
in the interests of that class, necessarily the ruling class, to ensure the
continued reproduction of that mode, *and also* to 'bring about' a submissive consciousness in the dominated classes, so that the realities of
the situation were not obvious to them. We should note here, in passing,
that the capitalist mode of production is a paradigm case of a mode
that does not favour all classes equally. It is also illustrative of one of
the core factors of our research programme; namely that the world is
characterised by dynamic conflict and struggle. Under capitalism there
is continued struggle between the ruled and ruling classes (defined
according to their relationship to the means of production) wherein
the interests that are continually served most are those of the ruling
class, the owners of the means of production; and the interests that
are continually served least are those of the workers, who have nothing
but labour power to sell. Within such a mode, then, there would have
to be continued reproduction among the workers of a submissive consciousness which did not reveal the realities of the situation to them
(if that mode of production was to remain dominant, of course.) (We
see here that there is a double form of exploitation built in to the
social relations under capitalism; for both the labour power of the
working class and its consciousness are at one and the same time
exploited.)

The matter of 'producing' a submissive consciousness is relatively

easy. In class societies the ruling classes maintain institutions and in-formal lived-ideologies to produce the appropriate consciousness. They make use of their political power and control through state institutions, they provide economic support in some areas and withhold it in others, they use certain controls over the media, etc.; all to support certain institutions, and to develop and propagate theoretical views that endorse and justify the existing lived-ideologies. These theoretical views, which have built into them the class interest role and function, are the theor-etical ideologies or supportive rhetoric of our earlier section. The state's repressive instruments (the police, army, intelligence agencies, etc.) are also in reserve to deal forcibly with situations where lived-ideological-moulding fails with certain individuals who, (because they won't work, or go to school, or pay taxes, or be conscripted, or obey a law, etc.) threaten the existing mode of production.

This picture further serves to do away with the simplistic notion of ruling classes coolly plotting and calculating the domination of the masses. Rather, it sees the actions and ongoing existence of the ruling class as also deriving from their participation in, and acceptance of, lived ideologies. And these lived ideologies are very much the same lived ideologies in which the dominated class lives. This and related aspects lead us closer to our crucial question: if social existence determines consciousness, how can vast masses of people accept along with their consciousness states of existence that are not in their interests?

The answer is that, in class societies, one of three things happens: (1) there might be massive repression; (2) there might be an inbuilt ideological belief that a dominating/dominated set of class relations is the proper and correct way of organising society (such that the domi-nated accept their domination as part of the 'way things are', as with some caste systems); or (3) it might be that the real nature of social relations is *disguised*. In liberal democratic capitalist societies, where the capitalist mode of production, and beliefs and faith in liberalism and democracy must all be maintained, it is the third of these things that happens (although there are traces of the other two). From here on we shall now refer specifically to that type of class society (although parts of what is said might be applicable to other forms of class societies as well), and we shall proceed to illustrate certain further aspects of disguise that operate and occur in a capitalist liberal democracy.

First, if we consider the lived-ideologies in such a society, we find that they are largely the same across all classes (i.e. ruled and ruling). This in itself is sufficient to convince many that there is no such thing as ruling classes and ruled classes, or capitalists and proletariat. The disguise is also perpetrated by the theoretic production of a limp socio-logical theory of classes, defined in relation to clearly observable features like income, which speaks of upper, middle and lower classes and which,

along with all of 'orthodox' sociology, is unable to pick out capitalist and proletariat classes (members of both can belong to the 'middle' class). It is further unable to pick out that the (largely unobservable) dynamic nature of class struggle might be a powerful historical force, and so followers of such a theory tend not to see things in that way. As we showed in our first chapter, this theory, like all theories, selects certain instances in certain ways. It creates references and perspectives for knowing the world, but blocks off others; but we can now see that in doing this it is not merely (and objectively) describing the world; rather it is serving particular social interests within a particular set of social relations. Let us continue further with this example.

Rulers and ruled both live the family ideology, the marriage ideology, the religion ideology, the school ideology, the moral ideology, the legal ideology and so on. They might live them very closely indeed, attending the very same churches and the very same schools. And this coincidence of lived experience disguises the essential point that this lived experience is *class interest-serving*; for, it could be reasonably asked, if we all live the same sort of way, how could that possibly be in the interests of only a minority class? Very closely allied to this is the theoretical ideology that supports the lived-ideology. Schools, we are told, offer equal opportunity for all to advance and succeed; the law, it is insisted, applies equally to all people; and the very state itself, so the theory goes, is neutral as far as individual interests are concerned.

Now if these things were the case, then these lived ideologies would appear to be the very opposite of class interest-serving ideologies. And on the face of it they do seem to be the case. Also the supporting theoretical ideologies do appear, at many times, to be painting a picture of real relationships, which lived practice continually bears witness to.

There are countless instances where children of the labouring poor have risen, through schooling and education, to reach the ranks of the ruling class – so equality of opportunity really does appear to be on. There are again numerous instances where members of the ruling class have been brought down by the law, for murder, embezzlement or whatever – and so it really does appear that the law favours no particular class. And the state's repressive systems can hardly be seen to be working only in the interests of one class when they arrest murderers and rapists, prevent mugging, keep traffic flowing and protect the entire country from invasion. Departments of public construction, it appears, build roads and airports and bridges for all to use, not just for the benefit of the ruling class; and so on.

How are we to show, then, that education, the law, the 'state', the family, etc., do particularly favour one class in a capitalist liberal democracy rather than all classes equally? To show this would require, on the one hand, a great amount of evidence, evidence that would hardly be

picked out by any theory of 'impartial equality'. That evidence is available, although picking it out would be a mammoth (and possibly misleading) task; but the display of evidence is not to our immediate purpose (it will become relevant later). What we can simply recognise at this stage is that the class interest-serving nature of these institutions is necessarily picked out by our research programme, and the more important question to consider is why people living within the ambit of these 'institutions' or 'apparatuses' fail to recognise how class interests are being served.

To answer this question we can recall our earlier analogy of the perception-altering drug, and the way that objects of investigation can interfere with the way in which those objects are investigated. The issues in question make up the totality of lived experience, and also set the parameters within which they can be theorised about; thus a particular context for theoretical activity is established, which appears, for all intents and purposes, to fit well with the world as it is experienced, and 'thus' with the world as it 'is'. More technically, the individual, or theoretic labourer, although presuming himself to be the subject of knowledge and theorising, is really only a bearer of relations, and his theoretical activities are determined by the production process which includes the concepts and theoretic tools determinate to the process. The individual, 'drugged by immersion' in the social relations that he is living *and* that he is investigating theoretically, fails to see himself as *bearer* rather than subject of certain relations, and is thus unlikely to recognise the illusions and anomalies built into the theoretic and social relations that he himself is bearing. If class interest-serving aspects are built into, but disguised within, certain lived and theoretical ideologies, it is not surprising that the bearers of those ideologies, while acting as bearers (regardless of how they think they are acting), would fail to recognise the disguises, and also fail to recognise how those disguises are operating. And this even more so if the disguises are well perpetrated and have *prima facie* validity, as with the law or education, serving all people equally.

Once that is recognised we can finally dispense with any simplistic notions that people, offering great yawns of apathy and indulging in the blissfulness of ignorance, simply sit back and let themselves, and their consciousness, be manipulated by other scheming people out to pursue their particular interests.

Our account of ideology has, so far, done more than merely improve on a simplistic account of wicked manipulators and stupid manipulatees. It has shown how sets of beliefs grow out of perceived and lived relations. It has shown how perception of illusory relations is in part a product of the very illusion that the perceiver is subject rather than bearer of the relations he perceives. And it has shown how perception

of illusory relations can be facilitated by the way ideologies interweave real and illusory representations at much the same time, in much the same way. What is most important, however, is that our interpretation recognises and accounts for ideology as something that has a solid basis in lived experience. Ideology is not a set of illusions and dreams whose existence as theory is a total mystery; rather it can be seen as reflecting an illusory reality: and the illusion lies in the very way in which people live their relations to their conditions of existence, as manifested in the lived-ideologies of class societies.

Ideology, then, derives from the material way in which people live their relationships to their conditions of existence. Lived-ideology is a representation of a person's relation to his conditions of existence, a representation both material and conceptual. But in a class society, where a ruling class requires submissive consciousness in the dominated classes, 'mechanisms' can be put into operation whereby a disguise, an illusory representation, can be created, and instilled and perpetrated *in all classes*. In such a case we can concur with Althusser that:[37]

> What is represented in ideology is therefore not the system of the real relations which govern the existence of individuals, but the imaginary relation of those individuals to the real relations in which they live.

Given this, it is neither surprising nor startling that vast numbers of normal intelligent people come to have a view of the world that is not in their best interests, and that is a misrepresentation or distortion because it is both built on disguise, and itself disguises whose interests it serves, and how. And the ruling class, whose interests the view serves, is similarly unlikely to recognise the misrepresentation, distortion and disguise (although they might explain it a little differently), for they too are immersed in the lived relationships to the conditions of existence. So, again it is neither startling nor surprising that few people recognise this state of affairs, or that few are capable or motivated enough to do anything about it.

Chapter 4

Attacking ideology

Introduction

While the previous chapter provided little more than a sketch of the way ideology operates on and influences one's consciousness and the way one sees the world; there was enough in that sketch to suggest fairly strongly that, as individuals, we might never be able to escape the prevailing ideologies of our time and place. If this were so, then we could be regarded as victims of our social-historical circumstances, who in certain situations might have little alternative but to see the world in the disguised and distorted form in which it was misrepresented to us, or in which we misrepresent it to ourselves.

This, to a large extent, is so. We all live in historical-social settings, and we see the world as determined by those settings. However, this need not imply strict rigidity - that we always perceive things, and that we perceive all things, in much the same way: nor need it imply total uniformity and conformity - that everyone at a particular time and place perceives the same things the same way. There can, of course, be varying degrees of flexibility in frameworks, and some can be much larger and more accommodating than others. But the question that really faces us is whether we can ever escape our ideological immersion and put ourselves in a position to see the world in a different way. And a second question arises from that. Given, as I have claimed, that in general there is no escape from ideology (i.e. we either live in one ideology or another), is there any point in escaping or trying to escape from the prevailing ideology in which we live? The answer to this depends on the nature of that particular ideology. If it arises from, or is determined by, social relations and social conditions that work against our best interests, and that serve to distort and misrepresent the world to us, then clearly it is in our interests to break out and away from that particular ideological perspective. But not simply in a random fashion, of course, for we might land ourselves in an even worse position. It is in our interests only if we end up adopting a less distorted or undistorted perspective for coming to know the world, or, to put that in different terminology, if we forsake a particular ideological research programme in order to embrace a more progressive one.

We cannot, however, simply decide to go out and change our beliefs and perspectives, etc., for these things are determined by ongoing social practices, and short of changing social practices very little can be achieved. But what we can do, as a necessary prelude, is seek out the means and places whereby ideology can be attacked such that distortions, disguises, misrepresentations and particular class-serving interests can be revealed for what they are. If we can at least recognise the existence and operation of these things, then the possibility arises that we might begin the attempt to free ourselves from the ties they have on our consciousness.

Recognising the ideological

We can begin to attack ideology seriously or react against ideology only when we have recognised it for what it is. In some cases recognition is very simple; in other cases it is extremely difficult. Ideology, as the rationalisation of value and the legitimation of action, should be distinct from science; and ideology, in its interest-serving, distortive form, would be anything but descriptively neutral. Thus, it would appear that, in order to find ideology, or ideological statements, we should look for the non-scientific, and/or the serving of interests. Thus clear examples of ideological statements and standpoints are: 'Jews are an inferior race'; 'the white man was created especially to rule the earth'; 'communism is a pernicious evil'; and 'adult humans should live their lives within the confines and context of one monogamous sexual relationship'. Each of these standpoints could be supported by a series of arguments and further rationalisations, themselves ideological; but it is difficult to see how any of them could be clearly established as scientific and/or non-interest-serving, although if their ideological nature was to be disguised the attempt would certainly be made, and history has shown us that, for each of the statements, the attempt *has* been made. For instance, as support for the last statement it might be 'demonstrated' that monogamy was ordained by God, or that monogamous couples are happier, that children of monogamous couples have less neuroses and achieve well at school, and so on. On the other hand, it would not be mentioned that monogamy brings about a certain type of social stability and results in an unnecessary proliferation of consumer items (houses, television sets, washing machines, refrigerators etc.), both of which especially serve the interests of one group in society.

At the other end of the spectrum there are fairly clear non-ideological statements and viewpoints, in that they are either scientific and/or non-interest-serving. Statements of the type: 'all metals expand when heated' and 'Mercury is the nearest planet to the sun' are as close as we seem able to get to 'pure' scientific statements; and the viewpoint that 'noxious atmospheric pollution ought to be stopped' comes as close as we might expect to one that serves all interests, but no single interests in particular. This latter stands in complete contrast to R. S. Peters's reading of society:[1]

> Unless the wheels of industry keep turning the conditions will be absent which will allow any man to pursue a multitude of individual interests. And keeping the wheels of industry turning is a policy that favours no particular sectional interest.

Peters is simply wrong; but what he says can lead us into the crucial problem in this section: blatantly ideological statements are hard to find, non-ideological ones perhaps even harder,[2] which leaves a huge 'grey area' in between. And often (mostly?) in this grey area we find ideology dressed up as something else. Our purpose, then, in this section is to indicate how we might recognise ideology when it comes to us 'dressed up'. Let us approach this problem by means of a few examples.

On the occasion of the granting of independence to Papua New Guinea, HRH Prince Charles informed the population on nation-wide radio that: 'rulers are not feared by those who do good, but by those who do evil'.[3] Now this statement is probably empirically false; it is certainly empirically indeterminate, and could hardly attain scientific status, or be accepted as some sort of 'truth'. It seems more the case that rulers are not feared by those who do what the rulers want; and even this may not be so, for many people can obey and serve rulers and yet fear them at the same time. But what the Prince has done is build into his statement the notion that rulers, *qua* rulers, are necessarily good – a notion that any quick jaunt through history can call into question – and by strong implication in this context it emerges that those who fear rulers, i.e. are threatened by them, must be evil. The Prince's statement thus emerges as clearly ideological: it is designed to protect the interests of rulers, to ensure that rulers are supported and obeyed, and to brand as 'evil' any opposition to rulers. Thus a viewpoint is rationalised that blatantly serves the interests of one class (unless all rulers did rule in the interests of all people equally – which is not only denied by our research programme but which the very existence of Prince Charles and Windsor Castle close by the homeless people sleeping in the gutters at Charing Cross Station gives the immediate lie to).

A similar, now much-quoted, statement comes from Australia's

Prime Minister, Malcolm Fraser: 'Life isn't meant to be easy.' Mr Fraser has made a sudden jump from politics to metaphysics, but even if one looks favourably on metaphysical pronouncements there is still much to quarrel with here. The statement surely has no serious basis outside of a metaphysical context; but what are its political implications? Life, of course, often *isn't* easy; but that has nothing to do with the meaning of life. And life is not easy for a great range of people – the sick, the afflicted, the poor, the unsettled, those who have had to take a drop in their standard of living and so on. But one sure overarching factor in making life difficult (it may not be the only factor) is poverty; life is harder for the poor sick than the rich sick, as well as for just the poor as against the rich. But when we now note that Mr Fraser made his statement at the very time he was introducing stern economic measures, which were designed to make life harder for most Australians, especially the poorer ones (harder at least in the short run), then we can immediately recognise the 'rationalisation' and the 'interest-serving' aspects of his statement. If life isn't *meant* to be easy, as Mr Fraser has claimed, then there is little point in complaining about government policies or blaming the government when it turns out that life, for some, isn't easy. Further, if life isn't meant to be easy, how could one seriously, and morally, expect a government to try and make it that way? We see that Mr Fraser has simply rationalised and justified his policies by subsuming them into a declaration of the way things are or are meant to be, such that hardship and suffering might be more easily accepted, and not be seen to be a result of government (ruling-class) policy.

None of this is to suggest, of course, that the Prince and the Prime Minister were setting out deliberately to fool everybody. Given *their* lived ideologies, they probably believed what they said; even given that the educated white ruler–prince was addressing largely illiterate awe-inspired natives; and that the Prime Minister spoke in his millionaire's jacket on his country estate – both of which, he tends to indicate, were acquired the hard way.

Fraser's statement is anything but new, of course. It has its roots in countless notions that suggest that this world is a 'vale of tears', a hardship and a sorrow to be stoically endured for various reasons, the most common being a reward in the next world. Those notions too can be revealed as interest-serving ideologies when, on the basis of them, some people are kept in hardship, and at hardship, for the sake of a reward in another world, while those who keep them in hardship benefit from their labours, and so have ease, and get their reward in this world. Interestingly in this regard, Galileo's notion of heliocentrism was once considered to have ideological force, and it was originally rejected on ideological grounds. Although Galileo had some support from the Vatican astronomers, it was considered unwise to inform the peasants that the earth was not the centre of the universe, for it was believed that if they no longer thought that God had especially placed them at the centre of His universe, they would see no purpose in continuing at their arduous and poorly rewarded labours. But as we noted with ideology in general earlier, the class interest-serving nature of statements about a world of hardship and sorrow is partially disguised because it mingles illusion with what *is* the case – the rich or rulers also suffer from the same sorrows and hardships that the poor suffer from (sickness, accidents, family problems) although possibly not to the same extent; and everyone dies (and either comes out equal or gets his just reward) in the end.

At this point it would be relatively easy to draw out continual examples of interest-serving ideological statements and viewpoints that appear, at first glance, to have pretentions of the empirical, metaphysical or ontological about them, or else appear to serve all equally. Take, for instance, the rhetoric surrounding the notion that people can really fulfil themselves only when there is a strong but just authority structure in society. This is a most respected view, and has a strong philosophical tradition supporting it which goes back at least as far as Hobbes, in British circles alone. But interest-serving aspects are built right into it, for certain types of fulfilment are automatically excluded, and 'fulfilment' itself becomes defined in certain ways which are in line with the operation of a strong and just authority of a certain sort. The interests that are served best by this notion are those of a minority who stand to benefit most from such a social structure.[4]

Take also the body of rhetoric that begins with the notion of delayed gratification, emphasises the importance of education in the early part of one's life, talks about starting at the bottom and working one's way up in a career, and culminates with the prospect of retirement and enjoyment in the latter part of one's life. Built into this rhetoric, or running parallel with it, are practical aspects, like salary increases as years of service increase; superannuation, the benefits of which again increase with the years served, but which are largely forfeited if the job is given up; long-service leave; and retirement bonuses. This whole scheme, so the rhetoric has it, is in everybody's interests, especially in those of individual employees. And yet, if we look again at the scheme, we could say that it largely stultifies the individual. The 'best' years of life are to be given over to school, university and beginning a career; not to extensive travel, exploring other life styles and living more or less freely at a time when the mind is still flexible, and the individual is physically fit. And then the job or career takes a progressively greater hold over the individual. Given annual salary increments, promotion or the possibility of promotion *after* years of service, increasingly greater commitments to the superannuation fund, and the moment of long service leave getting ever nearer, it becomes harder and harder as the years progress for an individual, who is also not getting any younger, to make a break. Thus it could be said that people become locked into a lifestyle and a work situation that they might not like, that they might know to be against their interests, and that they hope will all be made worthwhile as they enjoy their well-earned retirement. And yet statistics show clearly that many never reach the age of retirement; of those that do few enjoy it for very long; and of those who achieve longevity most find the falling away of physical and mental capabilities an inadequate compensation for their extra years.

Clearly such a position is really in the interests of those who want stability and continuity among their employees. Otherwise, why not pay all teachers equally regardless of their years of service and position? For junior teachers tend to be worked hardest in a school, and while the principal might have 'responsibility', he does not have to prepare lessons at night. And why not make superannuation and long-service leave transferable, with different employers paying on a *pro rata* basis, if these things are *really* meant to benefit the employee, and be in his interests? Close examination of the whole situation would reveal whose interests were being served most, and how certain people come to accept benefits that, on the one level, really *are* tangible benefits for them (usually greater benefits than they, or their forefathers, have ever known); but are also benefits serving other interests to a far greater degree. And of course, that these things *are* tangible benefits makes it difficult for the receiver to recognise and realise that they may be keeping him away from other benefits or more fulfilling life-styles, and that the benefits *he* gets are really more beneficial to other interest groups.

Similar ideological positions, which appear to be metaphysically, ontologically or empirically supported, can be found in the rhetoric that surrounds things like the need for increasing consumption (to bolster the economy or the 'Nation'), notions of loyalty to employer, king or country, the wisdom of saving and protecting the future through life assurance, obeying the dictates of elected governments, living in nuclear families, the nobility and necessity of toil, the recognition of the state as a neutral body serving all people impartially, and the ascription of different status and worth to different peoples of the world – to name, of course, just a mere few.

Merely citing such examples, however, hardly justifies that there are interest-serving distortions operating within them; and even in my more extended examples I have not cemented the case that a strong authority structure is *not* equally in all people's interests, nor have I offered anything totally compelling to support my view regarding the career–retirement structure. I therefore wish to take two further instances and do two things with them: I shall attempt to give more support to my case; but mainly I shall indicate the difficulties that arise when one attempts to find the type of support I need. To make my job both easier and harder I shall consider two statements that appear to be strictly empirically descriptive claims, and that should therefore be testable as such: theoretically, ideology should not even enter the issue, either with regard to the statements or the testing of them.

The first statement I shall put in many forms:

(A)   More crimes (on a *pro rata* basis) are committed by people in the lower-income groups than are committed by people in the upper-income groups.

(B)   People in lower socio- economic groups tend more towards crime than people in higher socio- economic groups.

(C)   The poor are dishonest (as compared with the rich).

Now clearly, while the statements are related, they are not all of the same type, and they do not imply exactly the same thing. (A) is a statement that appears to be open to clear empirical testing, while (B) and especially (C) tend towards generalised value judgments. But it would appear that, if (A) *were* found to be the case, this would lend much support to (B), and some support to (C): whereas if (A) were found not to be the case, there would be no evidential justification for (B) or (C). Thus we could say that if (A) were not the case, (A), (B) and (C) would be statements that distorted the state of affairs. But what it is crucial to demonstrate now is that, if (A) *was* found to be the case, *this too* could be a distortive representation of the real relations between people and their conditions of existence, and thus an interest-serving ideological statement. Let us consider this further.

If we accept as a basic tenet of any civilised legal system that the law works impartially for all people and favours no group especially, then it is reasonable to expect that the law would not have to be brought to bear especially and significantly against any group that was not defined by specifically illegal characteristics. Commitment to destruction of public buildings is such a characteristic; poverty, or relative poverty, is not. Thus, if (A) were found to be the case, it might either be that:

(1)   the law does not work impartially; from which it follows that (A) has something of an interest-serving nature about it; or

(2)   there are characteristics about lower-income groups that make them more likely to break the law (or commit crimes).

We see, therefore, that evidential support for (A) is not sufficient to establish it as a neutral 'objective' description of the world; for if (1) is also the case, then (A) is revealed as an ideological statement dressed up in 'objective' descriptive robes. That, however, is only part of the problem; for how can (A) seriously be tested?

To begin with, we could look up court records, for, say, a period of fifty years. This would tell us how many people came into court, what crimes they were charged with, and how many were found guilty; it might also give us some indication of the socioeconomic status of those who passed through the courts. But this Herculean task would not tell us how many crimes were *committed*, for many of them either would have gone undetected, or else would have been settled out of court. So we might, if it were possible (but it almost certainly isn't) get into solicitors' records to track down some of the latter; and we might carefully analyse the distribution of the police force to gain some clues with regard to the areas where the possibility of detection is concentrated. (Perhaps we might find that higher-income groups settle out of court more frequently than lower-income groups, and/or that the police are concentrated largely in lower-income areas).

This would obviously be an enormous task, and one of great complexity in many dimensions; and it is unlikely that even a large research team, with more than ample funds and a great deal of time, would be able to gather enough data on which to base a solid conclusion. Actually, it is closer to impossible than unlikely, but let us pretend that they do gather the necessary data, and that the data support the hypothesis under test. Does this necessarily show that (A) is the case?

In one sense of course it does. But different sorts of things open up when we look behind this 'empirical truth' in order to analyse the nature of crimes and what they entail and in order to consider who commits crimes, and when. One crime that would have to catch our attention immediately is vagrancy, a crime that, by definition, could hardly be committed by high-income groups. Then there is the crime of driving a defective motor vehicle, which is more likely to be committed by those who cannot afford the necessary repairs than by those who can. Continued analysis would make it patently obvious that there are many crimes that are likely to be committed by people in poverty, but that would not, apart from exceptional cases, be committed by people in affluence (whereas the reverse is not the case). Theft is a case in point: by definition it is a crime, but at times (as in Dickensian England, or in some areas of America in the Great Depression) it is absolutely necessary for the very survival of some of the poor – which it could never be for the rich. Similarly there have been times and instances when the crime of prostitution has been the only viable alternative to hunger for many women, necessarily poor ones of course. There should be no need now to continue with these examples, for the point is surely clear that the very concept of 'crime' discriminates against lower-income groups (regardless of how impartially justice is meted out in courts) simply because lack of financial means places one in a position where, at times, certain crimes might have to be committed in order to gain the financial means for survival, or even in order to keep up with the social values, norms and ideals regarding consumption that are continually reinforced through all areas of society. Finally, lack of financial means itself is a crime, as with vagrancy, and can lead unwittingly to the committing of other crimes such as having no fixed place of abode.[5]

We can now summarise the points that have come out of this example. We began with a statement that appeared to be descriptive in a neutral sense and capable of being empirically tested. Testing it, however, turns out to be an enormous task, and almost certainly an inconclusive task. But even then, validating the statement in terms of showing that what it says is, *prima facie*, correct is not sufficient to indicate whether the statement is an accurate neutral 'objective' description of the state of affairs or a distortive and interest-serving ideological description; for the statement, as we have clearly suggested, may have disguised built-in factors that ensure its correctness, and that make its inevitable correctness interest-serving. If more crimes are committed by the lower-income group than by the higher-income group, this might have as much or more to do with what counts as a 'crime' and who makes the laws than it has to do with the respective morals and values of the rich and the poor. If crime is defined in the interests of the rich, and if the poor actually do commit more crimes, then we find here an excellent example of ideology in action; disguising interest-serving statements as neutral ones, and then mixing up together things that are the case (the number of crimes committed) with distortive interest-serving notions of what is the case (that crime is not defined in anyone's particular interests).

In examples such as this, the attempt to separate out and detect the ideological will rarely be an easy one, and it will require at least three things. First, there has to be suspicion that ideology is lurking within the descriptive, and a good methodological point in fighting ideology is to enter the ring with built-in suspicion of any empirically descriptive statement. (As with the children's puzzle mentioned earlier, the tree will appear as a tree, and the face will be found only if the puzzle is put.) Second, there must be evidence available that can indicate the ideological. And third, there must be methodology that can seek and gather this evidence, and that can expose the ideological nature of the original statement and its means of validation. This is the hardest aspect of all; for ideology, in accommodating anomalies, in building its interest-serving nature *into* its statements, and in building up an entire theoretical and practical matrix, will cover over the evidence required (as in disguising the notion that crime is defined in favour of the rich), and/or make it practically impossible to collect the evidence required (we simply cannot determine exactly who commits crimes, and the methodology of looking at court records favours the ideological position being promulgated). In the example at hand the methodology we employed was more concerned with the notion of crime and who defines it, i.e. with the social dimension of the theoretic product, than with the number of cases of crime that could be counted; and clearly it resulted in the production of a more comprehensive and accurate account of relations in the real world than would have been derived from a simple sociological-empiricist programme wherein counting what could be counted would almost certainly, and *inevitably*, have confirmed the empirical status, and thus the 'objective truth', of (A).

Our second statement for consideration is this:

(D) Economic inequality in society is rooted in genetically determined differences in intelligence.

Freely translated, it can also read as:

(E) The poor are poor because they are dumb; and

(F) Blacks are poor because they are dumb.

The sentiment expressed in (D) has had a great resurgence recently, spearheaded by the work of Arthur Jensen and Richard Herrnstein in America, and H. J. Eysenck in Britain,[6] mainly because of the mammoth failure of egalitarian education reforms such as Project Headstart in the 1960s and early 1970s. The basic idea of these reform projects was that everybody would be given the same educational opportunities, and that those who started in disadvantaged positions would be given compensatory programmes as well. The pious hope was that educational inequality and social inequality would thus disappear. They didn't. The poor, and the blacks, remained poor. And one seemingly good explanation for this was that intelligence, 'known' to be highly inheritable, was passed on within family and racial groups to such an extent that education simply cannot compensate for genetic difficiencies. Thus, it was concluded, education must (and ought) necessarily reward some more than others and lead to economic inequality, but the underlying basis of this is genetic differences. Before examining this issue, however, let us digress slightly to consider how intelligence came to be 'known' to be largely inherited.

A large part of the answer to that is that Sir Cyril Burt led us to believe this was the case; and because of his power and his reputation he achieved remarkable 'influence in the affairs of men', so much so that his work was not seriously challenged in his lifetime. But now a number of researchers have produced compelling evidence to indicate that Burt faked his research and findings in order to promote a personal and passionately held theory. Consider these extracts from a newpaper report of the affair; those I have chosen concentrate on the ramifications rather than the substantive details of the studies:[7]

> The strongly-based theories of inherited intelligence have been shaken by accusations that the works of Sir Cyril Burt, the eminent British educational psychologist, rested on false statistical evidence . . .

Sir Cyril Burt's work *profoundly affected the ideas and policies of Britain's secondary school system from the 1920s until the 1970s.* His papers gained acceptance in suggesting that intelligence was largely inherited.

His work also *has given credence to claims that race and intelligence levels are linked, with particular application to underprivileged black people.*

His works were not brought under scrutiny until after his death in 1971, largely *because he was held in such regard as to give his works virtually unquestioning acceptance* . . .

The conclusions have been that Burt did not make mistakes, because his brilliance would have prevented them, but rather *he dishonestly used data in supporting a theory which he passionately believed in.*

He was obsessed with the idea that heredity was the major factor in determining human intelligence variations, Dr Clarke and her husband suggested, as opposed to theories which support the influence of environment.

This obsession led him to mislead many researchers through his papers, they added.

Although a strong body of opinion still supports the concept of inherited intelligence, the so far undenied claim that Burt faked his findings has shattered much of the support on which this concept rested.

The Burt example provides us with a paradigm case of the propagation of knowledge, and ideological beliefs, by the ruling class, such that those beliefs become unquestionably the underpinnings of social practice (the school system) and social beliefs ('blacks are dumb').

Now Burt's evidence was most impressive (even though it might have been faked), and so too – to return to our example – is the evidence of Jensen and Herrnstein, which probably isn't faked (although Jensen's is suspect). But standing against their evidence is that of Bowles and Gintis, which shows that economic success tends to run in families almost independently of intelligence (as measured by IQ tests) – and this, of course, holds quite independently again with regard to the relative influences of genetics and environment on intelligence. Bowles and Gintis show that the rich stay rich and the poor stay poor virtually regardless of intelligence – the rich dumb child is likely to become rich, and the poor intelligent child is likely to remain poor.[8]

If Bowles and Gintis are right, then (D) can hardly be taken to be the case, and (E) and (F) are revealed as gross distortive ideological statements. But if Bowles and Gintis are also right in their *interpretation* of the instance described in (D), namely that economic inequality in society is rooted in the very structure of society itself, then (D) is not merely revealed as 'false'; it is also shown to be a statement that contains class-serving interests within it: it is thus both distortive and interest-serving - it is an ideological rather than an empirical statement. And of course Jensen's and Herrnstein's research and findings, and Eysenck's support of them, could be seen as providing supportive data and rhetoric for such an ideological stance, just as Burt's more dubious findings do.[9]

It is not to our point here to examine the protagonists' evidence, or even to arbitrate between their findings. We merely wish to indicate the obvious. Bowles and Gintis, by working through a different research programme, suspected that distortive ideology was lurking within an empirical description. They generated methodology to gather an enormous amount of evidence not gathered (or gatherable) by the opposing research programme, which tends to expose the ideological nature of the original theory. And what they proposed themselves, on the basis of their evidence, was compelling. Whether it is non-distortive, less distortive or more progressive is too complicated an issue to be taken up here. What we can note quickly, however, is that statements such as (D) locate faults, problems, deficiencies, etc., in *individuals* rather than in social relations. Their social function, then, could be seen as preserving the *status quo* by directing critical and remedial attention elsewhere. And in protecting social interests rather than 'producing the real world' they are again revealed as ideological.

One final point about recognising ideology that ought to be made is the less-than-obvious one that the technique that philosophers have recently brought to the study of education, namely conceptual analysis, as practised and inspired largely by Israel Scheffler and R.S. Peters, can be shown to be anything but the detached, neutral, second-order investigation it is set out to be. Much of the trouble with this approach, and part of the reason it lends itself so easily to internal debate or supportive rhetoric, is that too often the analysts have not recognised that, in answering questions about 'education', they have gone beyond purely 'linguistic' or 'conceptual' analysis into ideology without clearly realising it. Most of the supposedly linguistic or conceptual questions with which they concern themselves entail normative and ideological questions, such that supposedly 'neutral' philosophical analysis mostly masks educational theories. Both Scheffler and Peters, for instance, can be shown to hold educational theories that are implicit in, and that in subtle ways shape, their philosophical enquiries. This is, of course, again not the place to enter into the necessarily long and detailed investigation required to demonstrate this point convincingly, and we shall settle instead for one simple instance. Peters says:[10]

> There has been a lot of talk since the time of John Dewey about the school as a democratic institution, but one suspects that few schools deserve such a title in any full-blown sense. And why should

they? . . . There are some matters, e.g. the curriculum, the competence of his staff, about which it would be quite inappropriate for [the headmaster] to consult pupils, let alone give them any powers of decision. It is important, therefore, that any discussion of democracy within the school should be prefaced by a realistic appraisal of what the formal position of the headmaster is.

Clearly such a statement is shot through with values and theory, and entails a clear ideological stance. But the combination of the post-Wittgensteinian conceptual analysis tradition of English philosophy, and the theory that philosophers, *qua* philosophers, cannot pronounce on questions of value, has led philosophers such as Peters to hold a distorted view of their own educational philosophy which fails to appreciate its ideological significance. It is not the case that Peters, for one, denies holding a position in educational theory; he has set it down *quite* explicitly.[11] Rather, the point is that he oddly claims in various places that it is independent of anything properly called educational philosophy. Peters's view of the nature and functions of philosophy leaves him with an ideological blind-spot which can only lead to theoretical distortion, mislead educators and compromise the cause of the rational practical educational theory espoused by Peters and his colleagues. And more to our point, it leads to much 'neutral' analysis which is really the product of and justification for an ideological stance: while we continue to analyse the concepts underlying the *status quo*, we are hardly likely to produce the materials for changing the *status quo*.

We can conclude this section by restating that ideology, in whatever form it might take, can be recognised if we deliberately search statements and positions for implicit values, for distortions, and for the serving of particular interests; that is, if we examine also the social dimensions in their production, and the functions they serve in particular societies. We shall now turn to examine specific aspects of interest-serving, distorting ideology, and indicate how they might be recognised and grappled with.

Mystification

Mystification is an instrument of disguise; and as such it can take many forms, all of which serve very much the same end – to make things seem as they are not, to hide or divert attention away from central issues, and to cloak the real relations between people and people, and between people and the world. In earlier chapters we have already seen certain examples in operation. Castle, in suggesting that *the* problem for teachers is to enrich the process-worker's dream-life, diverts attention away from what the real problem for teachers is, or might be. The 'orthodox' sociological concept of 'class' picks out very little in itself, but diverts attention away from another notion of 'class', and thus disguises the possibility that societies can be meaningfully characterised in terms of particular class struggles, with 'classes' defined in ways other than by income. The philosophers who analyse educational concepts in a 'detached and neutral' way, and who in true Wittgensteinian fashion 'leave everything as it is', mystify the nature of philosophy; and, like the positivists before them who claimed that ethical discourse could and should proceed without ever considering one substantive ethical issue, they leave the important problems untouched, and possibly unrecognised as important. Similarly, people who argue endlessly within a restrictive paradigm, heaping complication upon complication rather than arriving at resolutions, could be seen as mystifying the situation; and Francis Bacon noted long ago, in *The Advancement of Learning* that: 'when a doubt is once received, men labour rather how to keep it a doubt still, than how to solve it, and accordingly bend their wits.'[12]

Mystification, of course, occurs in many practical ways as well. We find it when school principals list their university degrees on the nameplates on their doors; when authors (usually of school textbooks) also list their degrees; and when academics, lawyers, judges and the clergy (as distinct from the police and the army) wear their respective robes, wigs and other paraphernalia. In all of these cases an unnecessary and irrelevant aspect is introduced to influence the perceived nature of relationships. Degrees do not make a principal, but knowing that the principal has a degree can affect people's relationships to him: this is especially so with parents who, in discussing their children's schooling, tend to approach and interact with Mr R. M. Jones, B.A. Dip.Ed., M.Ed. differently from the way they might approach and interact with Bob Jones. That the author of a book has a degree (or a chair) is immaterial to the worth of the content of the book, but many people buy or prescribe the degree or chair, not so much the book, or at least are influenced by the degree or the professorial status of the author. And academics, lawyers, judges and the clergy can do their respective jobs just as well in ordinary clothes (as many are coming to learn), without the external trappings which give them an 'aura' and tend to place them in another category from ordinary people. When 'clothes', interpreted widely to include degrees, titles and so on, confer status on people, when they both make the man and hide the man, then mystification is at work, as relationships are set up on irrelevant or misleading criteria.[13]

Mystification can also be found in professional jargon, which seems to serve little purpose other than to exclude most people from ongoing discourse: lawyers and academics are experts in the use of such jargon, and create the image that their concerns are beyond the ken of the uninitiated. On the other hand, mystification can also be found in the appeal to common sense rather than expert knowledge. Before the 1975 Australian Federal Elections, Liberal Senator Margaret Guilfoyle laid the problem of growing inflation at the feet of the Labor Party's economic policy, and when asked to explain added: 'Women don't have to be confused by a whole lot of economic jargon, they know by their shopping basket week by week.'[14]

We have not properly accounted for mystification as yet, and this shall have to wait until aspects of the next section have been developed. But we can still note, if a little prematurely, that ideology can be recognised (and fought) by exposing mystifying features; by seeing them, and the relations they cloak, as they really are; by examining how and why they are produced; and by attempting to discover what lies beneath their disguise.

False consciousness

False consciousness is simply a matter of seeing oneself, the world, and one's relationship to the world in a distorted way. It is much like living under the influence of a perception-altering drug; or viewing the world from the perspective of a degenerate research programme (living in the twentieth century but still seeing the world in terms of Aristotelian cosmology); or being under the influence of distortive class interest-serving ideology. Now there would seem to be only two viable reasons for anyone wanting to promote false consciousness: first, the promoter might not believe his product to be false; and second, such promotion would be a good means of serving one's own interests by concealing or disguising from others what the real situation was. This latter reason indicates that promoting and establishing false consciousness could be a powerful ideological weapon; and therefore we would do well to consider the matter of false consciousness at some length. Let us begin by noting a few instances.

In the example we considered at the end of the last section, the senator could have been accused of promoting false consciousness in two ways: first by pointing to a very misleading and spurious index of inflation; and second by perpetuating the old myth that poor dumb shopping-basketed housewives would only be confused by economics. The same election that brought forth the senator's gem also brought forth one from the Anglican Dean of Sydney, the Very Rev. Lance Shilton, who in the midst of a very volatile political situation, by Australian standards, 'asked people to pray for the former and caretaker Prime Ministers, the Governor General, for rational debate, unbiased reporting by the media, and for an unselfish attitude by management and unions'.[15]

But for a more serious instance let us construct a hypothetical example.[16] Consider a person working as a tradesman in a light engineering factory. Suppose he takes some pride in his work, works steadily, perhaps even a little zealously, and cares enough for his family to go home to them promptly after work. His own relation to his work situation is expressed in numerous subtle ways. The boss encourages him, and hints at better prospects; he sees the privileges and lighter load of the supervisors who control him; other workers urge him to 'slow down', and otherwise shun him. This experiential situation probably results in his seeing himself as a good worker, deserving of his pay ('unlike some others'), and as one who 'keeps himself to himself'. He probably sees others as 'afraid of being shown up' and 'resenting his chances' of promotion or retaining *his* job should times get tough. He sees himself, therefore, as a deserving worker, isolated from the other workers.

Now this, for all intents and purposes, is a perfectly normal and justifiable way for the worker to see himself. The vision grows out of the lived situation, and everything in that situation serves to generate such an interpretation. Now *if* the worker was labouring under false consciousness, one important thing stands out most clearly, and that is that there need be *nothing pathological* in having false consciousness; nor is it necessarily a matter of displaying sheer stupidity in interpreting a particular situation. False consciousness, *if it does exist here*, grows out of, or is produced by, the very situation the worker lives, and by the way many factors interact to present the situation to him in a certain light.

And false consciousness *does* exist here. Rather than a deserving, isolated worker, keeping himself to himself, what we really find is an exploited worker engaged in a highly specialised labour process involving extensive co-operation with other exploited workers.

But now one crucial question is immediately thrown up: who is to arbitrate on the truth or falsity of consciousness, and how? Perhaps the Dean of Sydney is right, in that what he sought *really can* be won by prayer: perhaps our worker is right, and it is my consciousness of the situation that is false, and my perception that is drugged.

The question has been partly answered twice before. Our discussion of ideology has indicated how, in a class society, people can come to accept, and bear, illusory notions of the real relations in which they live; and our worker would simply bear these illusory notions or have false consciousness. Also, when we noted that any instance can be picked out by a number of theories, we also argued that choices of critical preference can be made between theories within a research programme, or between research programmes (given hindsight); it can be taken as following from this that if our consciousness results from a theory or research programme that can be *shown* to be more progressive than another theory or research programme, then consciousness that is generated from the latter can be said to be 'false'. For example, anyone looking at the universe in terms of the Ptolemic research programme would have false consciousness, since we now have more progressive research programmes in both Newton's and Einstein's theories. Similarly, anyone approaching or explaining human illness in terms of Hippocrates' humours, or accounting for thunder and lightning in terms of warring and angry gods, would have false consciousness.

In these examples, however, it is relatively easy to make choices of critical preference, and to decide which of the contending theories or research programmes is more progressive. But when we come to ideological issues the matter becomes far more complicated for many reasons, most of which have been indicated earlier;[17] and so it might be worthwhile to illustrate the issue of critical preference in some detail. In order to do this let us take a single instance, more serious than Santa Claus this time, and see how three theories handle it. The instance is that *in capitalist societies there are rich people and poor people.* The three theories we shall consider (and they are not the only ones that could account for our instance) are:

(A) God willed that this be so; just as He willed and ordered everything.

(B) People sort themselves out on a natural hierarchy through ability and effort, and their wealth largely reflects their ability, effort and talent.

(C) Such relationships are necessarily built into the capitalist mode of production.[18]

Let us consider each of these individually.

The allocation of riches and poverty by God is a very widespread belief, although it is possibly less accepted now than it was up to a century ago. In *Fiddler On The Roof* Tevye begins his song 'If I Were a Rich Man' with a plea to God: 'Lord you made so many poor people . . .'. But you don't have to be Jewish. The third verse of one of the most popular, most sung, Christian hymns, 'All Things Bright and Beautiful', reads:

> The rich man in his castle,
> The poor man at his gate,
> God made them, high or lowly,
> And ordered their estate.

And one only has to skim quickly through popular literature, parliamentary speeches, magazines and quarterlies; and through statements from the clergy, social philosophers and men of letters, especially of the nineteenth century, to find the view continually expounded and reinforced. It is, of course, still with us today: and if we take the viewpoint just a little wider we can easily find examples of the claim that God has ordered things that men are not to tamper with or rise up against. In that same memorable speech on the declaration of Papua New Guinea's independence, Prince Charles told the nation what Paul told the Romans: 'Everyone must obey the State authorities: For no authority exists without God's permission, and the existing authorities have been put there by God. Whoever opposes the existing authority opposes what God has ordered . . .'[19]

And the Fraser ministry, not to be outdone, expressed through Senator Cotton the similar sentiment that what God ordains man can not be responsible for (or undo): 'No Prime Minister or Treasurer, past, present or future, can be held responsible for acts of God.'[20] Presumably, then, if poverty (or inflation) is an act of God, one can't blame the prime minister or treasurer for it, or expect them to be able to do much about it. Similarly, insurance companies still build the notion of 'acts of God' into their policies, disclaiming responsibility in instances where God is apparently the casually predominant factor.[21]

What worth does this theory have as theory? The initial temptation is to say that it has little, if any, worth at all. On the one hand it is not falsifiable. Then, as far as supportive and falsifying instances are concerned, none could be brought to bear for or against it. With regard to Lakatos's criteria, the first two of his rules, and probably the third,[22] could hardly be applied because no new theory could possibly have excess empirical content over the one under consideration; nor could any new theory explain the success of this theory *if* it were correct. Thus, in terms of Lakatos's model, the theory is static, non-progressive, and non-degenerative; it can neither fit into nor generate a series. It might contain the ultimate truth or the ultimate nonsense, but its worth as a theory simply cannot be determined. Thus in one sense we cannot judge the worth of the findings or conclusions that it generates, yet in another sense we can. We cannot judge what is generated in terms of how well it explains and accounts for the real world; but if we switch to the social dimension of theory production and consider how the theory functions in society we can see immediately that the theory, and what it generates, has been used continually throughout history to serve the interests of particular ruling classes: it has been a major weapon of the ruling classes in keeping the ruled classes in 'their places' by convincing them that their position has been divinely ordained (not humanly contrived), and as such is not to be opposed. Thus we can at least judge the theory to have vast class interest-serving potential, yet potential possibly in that area alone.

Our second theory, the 'natural selection' thesis, has also had a long and influential run throughout history, and is still widely accepted today. Countless examples of statements to the effect that some people are better endowed than others to do the more responsible tasks, and the higher-status tasks, could be brought forward to illustrate this. Plato's Republic was based on this notion, as was the social Darwinism preached by Spencer and Sumner last century; and Jensen's current genetic theory has similar roots. And the notion that one gets what one deserves, which relates efforts to reward virtually to the extent of intimating a causal relationship, is surely a familiar enough part of modern liberal rhetoric not to require detailing here. Actually it is a cornerstone of liberal rhetoric. As two notions began to slide into some disrepute, namely that God had ordained each man's place in the world; and that inheritance, birth, or breeding solely determined, or should determine, each person's place in society; a rhetoric developed, largely in the nineteenth century, which emphasised the notion of the individual as the architect of his own social destiny. The State, it was suggested, ought minimally and impartially to interfere in the lives of individuals who, through their ability and application of effort, are to find and secure their proper place in society.

Such a rhetoric could hardly be taken seriously, of course, if people were born unequal, and if they were never given the opportunity to develop and show their worth. One solution to this problem was seen to lie in compulsory universal education, which, not coincidentally, emerged as the rhetoric gained force. No longer, it was claimed, would heredity be the major social sifting device, whereby children of poor illiterate labourers would necessarily become poor illiterate labourers and raise a progeny of poor illiterate labourers. The school would now become the sifting device, offering equal opportunity to all; rewarding those with ability and those who would work hard at their tasks, while dumping those who had been given every chance but who were found to be dumb and/or lazy. The successes, regardless of their background, would rise in the world, take positions of responsibility or requiring great skill and become rich; while the failures, through their lack of ability and effort, would be consigned to lowly positions and remain poor. The rhetoric is, of course, still with us, and even today we hear that any person can become president of the United States, managing director of BHP or a millionaire if he has the ability and application.

How shall we judge the worth of this theory? To begin with, it stands up very badly in the face of evidence. Supporters of it are always quick to come forward with confirming instances, but these are always isolated, atypical cases of log-cabin dwellers becoming presidents of the United States or children rising from poverty to top positions in society, politics and industry.[23] These atypical instances, however, are swamped by counter-examples, and they have been put into proper perspective by recent findings where, time and time again, it has been and is being shown that wealth does not correlate highly with ability and effort, and that, despite compulsory universal schooling, children of poor dumb labourers become poor dumb labourers and produce poor dumb labourers. It has been shown (as we would expect) that those at school longest get the best-paying jobs; but staying at school longest and thus getting entry certificates for well-paid jobs has now been shown to correlate strongly with personality, sex, race and *especially* social background (wealth), and only minimally, if at all, with ability as measured by IQ.[24] Thus it would seem that, regardless of ability and effort at school (and disregarding a few atypical cases), the rich get rich and the poor stay poor. It would also appear that, regardless of finely expressed sentiments, schools do not offer equal opportunity at all.

Of effort very little will be said. On the one hand it is a vague aspect to pin down in these circumstances, while on the other hand it might appear that the quantity of effort is not as important as where the effort is put in: expend tremendous effort at the coal face and riches are not likely to follow; expend a little at the stock market and anything could happen. Finally, there is little effort involved in inheriting fortunes, which is the way most of today's rich became rich.

Up to this point we have considered only empirical evidence, and it will be remembered from earlier discussion that the production of evidence, in the form of either confirming or falsifying instances, is not in itself sufficient to judge a theory (although it may lend weight towards making a judgment). We shall, therefore, now attack on another flank. Note this statement from an apologist for the liberal tradition and the ability/effort thesis:[25]

Nevertheless societies cannot be perpetuated unless many menial and instrumental tasks are also performed and *vast numbers* of people are also trained in them. The Athenian way of life was made possible, to a large extent, by the slaves and metics who performed such functions. In modern industrial society all such tasks have to be undertaken by citizens; for many of them training is essential. The school, therefore, has also an instrumental function in training and selecting people for such tasks.

Note also this one made by D.H. Lawrence, forty years earlier:[26]

90 per cent of these board-school scholars are deliberately taught at school, to be malcontents, taught to despise themselves for not having 'got on', for not having 'got out of the pit', for sticking down all their lives doing 'dirty work' and being 'common colliers'. Naturally every collier, doomed himself, wants to get his boys out of the pit, to be gentlemen. And since this again is *impossible* in 90 per cent of the cases, *the number of 'gentlemen', or clerks and school-teachers, being strictly proportionate to the number of colliers,* there comes again the sour disillusion. So that by the third generation you have exactly what you've got today [1929], the

113

young malcontent collier. *He has been deliberately produced by modern education* coupled with modern conditions, and is logically, inevitably and naturally what he is: a malcontent collier. According to all the accepted teaching, he ought to have risen and bettered himself: equal opportunity, you know. And he hasn't risen and bettered himself. *Therefore he is more or less a failure in his own eyes even.*

Lawrence points to what many modern critics of schooling (Illich, Reimer, Holt) point to, and what Peters points to but appears to be un-ruffled by: the number of gentlemen is proportionate to the number of colliers; or there must be, in a capitalist society, more workers than bosses, just as there must be few executives and professionals and 'vast numbers' of factory workers and menial labourers. The point to recog-nise, then, is that the ability/effort thesis is not on *in theory*. Regardless of ability and effort, only a few can succeed, not only because there is no room at the top, but also because the base at the bottom must be secured if a particular form of society is to be perpetuated. As more people apply more ability[27] and more effort more people can't rise and don't rise: what happens is that the 'standards' are pushed up. Today one needs qualifications to teach which were not required a generation ago, and the joke that soon one will need a PhD to become a garbage man in New York is ceasing to be funny. All that can happen if every-body raises his ability and effort is that most will end up in jobs that will require far less of them than they are capable of, and consequently many will suffer dislocation and discontentment with their place in life as measured largely in relation to the work situation.[28] As it turns out, schools must produce a broad base of 'failures', and most children do leave school as 'failures'; but they are 'failures' largely because of the way school functions in a capitalist society, and largely because capi-talist societies require these 'failures' to do the necessary menial jobs with a minimum of discontent: it really has little to do with the ability and effort the children put in. *Now* if we plug in the evidence that success correlates with wealth rather than with ability, we have a telling criticism of the theory under discussion. It is internally contradictory because, if all applied ability and effort, all could not rise or settle at appropriate levels; and there is also massive counter-evidence to suggest that it is not necessarily ability and effort that are rewarded either in school or society. But once more, if we examine the social dimension of the production of the theory, and how the theory functions in society, the serving of particular class interests is clearly revealed within what is put forward as an 'objective truth' or an empirical description of the state of affairs. The theory, even as put forward by Plato, but especially in the forms that Sumner, Spencer, Jensen and modern liberal apologists put it, rationalises the inevitable success of one class by giving a distorted account of the means whereby that success is achieved.

Our third theory is a relative baby, which was fully articulated just a century ago by Marx. There are tremendous dangers in reducing the three volumes of *Capital* to a mere handful of lines; and it is with those dangers in mind that I now spell out Marx's thesis. Marx sees a social formation as a totality of people in certain relations to one another, and to nature. These relations are mediated by material objects of certain sorts. Now the causally predominant factor in determining the character and structure of a social formation, and the change it undergoes, is for Marx the productive network, or the mode of production. Capitalism is a mode of production wherein there is a class of capitalists who own the means of production, and a class of workers who produce, selling their labour power to the capitalist. The capitalist is 'driven' by a profit motive, and derives his profit by extracting surplus value from production, i.e. by paying the workers less than the monetary value of their labour to him, which is a form of direct exploitation. Now the workers must consume to live and reproduce: thus they continually use up their wages, and must continue to sell more labour power. And since the products they consume come to them at a price that includes some surplus value, they simply cannot get far ahead financially while all they have to sell is labour power. The capitalist, on the other hand, if he is to remain a capitalist, must continue to draw profit, and if he is successful he continues to draw further and further profit – this is something like the principle that 'money makes money', but not quite. Given this process, especially its latter aspect and the *continued* extraction of surplus value, it is likely that some capitalists will fail, and that eventually capital will become concentrated in fewer and fewer hands. And so, while capitalism is the dominant mode of production in a social formation, there will be a small number of rich people and a large (growing?) number of poor people – this is inherent in the operation of the system.

How much worth does this theory have? A proper answer to that would require a thesis on Marxism itself; and we must surely settle for much less here. It could, I believe, be shown that this theory alone of the three under consideration can meet the requirements of continuous growth within the context of social action, social change and scientific discovery; but I shall settle for smaller points. To begin with, it does not build in any metaphysical assumptions about the nature of man, as (B) does. It is falsifiable in a way that (A) is not, and there is nothing like the 'falsifying evidence' against it that has been marshalled against (B). Given other parts of the materialist research programme, which we have examined earlier, it can explain the successful functioning and acceptance of (A) and (B) in terms of their class interest-serving nature and potential; and while there is no evidence that could refute (A) (other than God himself coming to earth and making a public denial)

(C) can account for the evidence that refutes (B) (as has been partially shown in the discussion of (B) above), while retaining all the unrefuted content of (B). On the other hand, (B) cannot explain the success of (C) without falling into contradictions, nor can (B) retain the unrefuted content of (C) and at the same time account for any content that refutes (C).

Some slight expansion of the latter points might be in order here. (C), if fully articulated, could show that (A) and (B) were class interest-serving; i.e. that they were rationalisations that favoured the ruling interests in society. (A) is a 'religious' view, espoused by the Church institution, whose views and existence have been generally supported and encouraged over the last 400 years by the ruling interests in capitalist societies.[29] The ruling interests, 'decreeing' that the miners and the mine-owners sing 'All Things Bright and Beautiful', thus reinforce the theoretic ideology that God made rich and poor people, and the poor labour on in poverty, and against their own interests, because 'this is God's way'. Such a belief favours only the ruling interests. (B) works in a similar, if more complicated, fashion. The practical and theoretical ideology of schooling produces the illusion of equality, but really favours the ruling interests who set up schools and employ the graduates, with the highest graduates generally coming from the ruling class (now 'qualified' to do the work of the ruling class), and with the lowest 'graduates' generally coming from the working class (now 'properly' consigned to the working class). Those being schooled, however, come to believe that schools act equally in the interests of all, whereas it can be shown that they do not. But can (B) judge (C)?

It might be argued, from the point of view of (B), that (C) is a rationalisation formulated by malcontents who had the chance, but either didn't see the opportunities or weren't smart enough to grab them when they appeared. They could have bought mills and factories and mines, but, through either stupidity or lethargy, or otherwise, they did not; and now they simply provide a rationalisation to excuse their resultant poverty. A second argument talks about the risks an owner takes in starting a business, the investments he has to make, the decisions forced on him and the impending ulcers and heart attacks. The owner puts up a fortune, probably borrowed at interest, to start a factory, and it is on his decisions that it stands or falls. If it falls he loses everything. The worker, on the other hand, risks nothing and decides nothing, and if the factory falls he simply moves into a similar job next door. Now surely the owner deserves a greater share of the lolly if the factory stands and expands! He deserves to get rich, if he is successful, but the worker can really expect little more than basic comfort.

The problem with this line, for all its seeming plausibility, is that it brands (C) as a class interest-serving rationalisation (yet not serving of the ruling class). It therefore accepts the *principle* of 'class interest-serving ideology' (although it would not use those terms), yet proponents of (B) see their view as 'natural' or 'neutral', as the view of the way things really are, and not as class interest-serving. But to recognise the principle of class interest-serving ideology, and to find it in (C) yet deny it in (B), is to be aware of a research programme or theoretic framework, but also to fail to see its implications for the position being held; it is also to ignore the myriad of historical and theoretical contradictions and instances that that very programme highlights in (B) – for instance, it never was the case that *anyone* could grab an opportunity, or become president of the United States; it never was the case that schools offered equal opportunity, and so on. But even if proponents of (B) accepted the class interest-serving nature of *both* (B) and (C), they would surely have to back down from their position of 'naturalism' (i.e. the belief in natural abilities, etc.). Also, they would have to account for the widespread successful social functioning of their theory in class interest terms, and thus would have to accept one of the basic tenets of (C): ('ruling ideas being the ideas of the ruling class'). Although there is hardly space to argue this fully, it should be clear that any attempt to justify (B)'s relative superiority over (C) (as distinct from arguing only for the worth of (B)) must end up in contradictions or else suffer from gross myopia.

One final point. As for content that refutes (C), there appears to be precious little around; and if proponents of (B) call on those things mentioned above, e.g. the capitalist's risks, investments and seizure of the initiative, they are drawing out content that actually bolsters (C)'s auxiliary hypotheses, and thus serves to *confirm* rather than refute (C). If they retreat to 'natural qualities' they are not only being naive; they are denying the content that supports (C).

Although the previous discussion has been necessarily short and slight, hopefully enough has emerged from it to show that judgments of critical preference can be made among theoretical interpretations of instances, and that in the examples we considered (C) could be shown to be the most preferable account of the coexistence of poverty and wealth under capitalism. Unlike (A) and (B), (C) functions in terms of the theoretic product and real object (i.e. it accounts for the phenomenon) rather than in the interests of social practice; and it is thus not a rationalisation that serves the interests of the ruling class (nor does it promulgate the misrepresentation among the ruled class that it serves their interests equally as well). Also, unlike (A) and (B), (C) is not distortive in that it does not depend on or promulgate illusory notions about the real relations between people and the world. Thus, in the terms being used in this section, we can say that people holding (A) or (B) have false consciousness.

One caveat should now be put, and it is that recognising and rejecting false consciousness might not always be a blessing. Theories, including ideologies, we remember, must be judged in a historical context and so there will always be a historical factor involved in labelling anything as 'false consciousness'. Yesterday's consciousness (e.g. a belief that the earth is flat) may be shown tomorrow to be false; and unlikely though it might seem now, who can know when God might come to earth and admit that he created rich and poor.[30] Perhaps it will be shown in the future that the positions of the planets determines people's wealth; but anyone holding that theory *now* would have false consciousness. But the fact that we are necessarily bound by our present knowledge and understanding, and are thus fallible, should hardly daunt or deter us from making judgments of critical preference: we need not automatically refrain from declaring that certain ways of seeing the world are, given the historical intellectual circumstances of the world at the present time, examples of false consciousness. Rather than abdicate from decision-making we should attempt to ensure that our tools for decision-making are as suitable and adequate as they can possibly be.

In concluding this section we can now recall the notion of mystification. Mystification is hardly as we represented it previously, namely as a series of isolated aspects. Mystification and false consciousness go together, the former providing part of the substantive data for the latter. Together they disguise reality, mystification usually working on the substance while false consciousness builds up a theoretical framework of explanation; and clearly a crucial aspect in identifying and overcoming distortive ideology is to recognise mystification and false consciousness when and where they arise.

We shall now turn to examine some further methods and techniques for exposing and criticising ideology.

Internal contradictions

The most effective immediate critique of any thesis, stance, theory, body of thought, ideology and so on is what we shall call an immanent critique. This is a critique that attempts to show that what is being criticised cannot or does not attain the end that it proposes for itself, and/or a critique that points out anomalies and contradictions that are otherwise comfortably contained and accommodated in the theory under scrutiny. Such a critique differs markedly from the internal criticism that goes on in supportive rhetoric; and, while it also differs from making judgments of critical preference between theories, it can be a valuable aid in marshalling the ammunition necessary to make those judgments. At this point let us give a few simple examples of the operation of such a critique: in doing so we shall stay within the field of education.

In New South Wales the Department of Education lays down strict guidelines for prospective secondary teachers regarding the courses they, as scholarship-holders, must undertake during their undergraduate years, where such undergraduate study precedes any formal and specific teacher education course. Briefly, and roughly, the students must study, as the major part of their course, the actual subjects they propose to teach; and while there is some possibility of getting round this at the training level, having undertaken the required studies later becomes a prerequisite for promotion within the teaching service. And by and large, the department polices this policy carefully; scholarships can be, and are, terminated if the undergraduate follows an 'inappropriate' course, and promotions are often denied on the basis of incorrect or unsuitable undergraduate studies.

Now the rationale for this appears, on the face of it, to be quite sound: if someone is going to teach subject X at secondary school level he should first have studied X at a far higher level himself. But at least three things can be said against this. First, it is not necessarily correct. There is no compelling evidence available to show that one's mastery of X at a high level makes one a better teacher of it at a lower level – university teachers on campuses across the world demonstrate this continually – and it is well known that much effective learning goes on when one who has just mastered something passes it on to someone else, as in the interactive learning process among peers. Second, the rationale assumes a certain teaching/learning structure and process, and perpetuates it without question. But third, and this is where the internal contradiction comes in, when the department places its graduates in schools they do not necessarily end up teaching the subjects they studied. Perhaps the department tries to place students who studied A and B in positions where they will teach A and B – this does occur in most instances. But there are thousands of cases where people studied A and B, were trained to teach A and B, but are actually teaching X and Y, and teaching them well.

In the face of that contradiction (and perhaps in the face of a possible contradiction in the first point) we are now in a position to ask why the system of prerequisite studies is really employed. Is it because the degree the scholarship-holders get, loaded as it is, is good for nothing but teaching, and so the graduates are trapped in teaching? Or is it because the loading of teaching subjects forces other subjects out, so that teachers will not emerge from university well versed in psychology, philosophy, sociology, government, anthropology, political economy and so on – subjects that might deepen and broaden their understanding, but also possibly make them critical of the service they are about to enter?

I do not intend to argue for either of those possibilities. I wish only to indicate that the discovery of an internal contradiction through an immanent critique can allow those questions to be posed as *serious* ones, not merely as matters of idle speculation, or as derivations of a cynical mind. And when posed as serious questions arising from contradictions, they give us the opportunity and means to challenge the supportive rhetoric, which has, as one of its purposes, the task of covering up contradictions. Thus we see that, to look for contradictions, and to pose questions or reinterpret situations in terms of them, attacks the ideology we are confronted with.

As a second example let us take an issue that has been most extensively covered in recent literature – that of the relationship between school curricula, school certificates and jobs. Because of the extensive coverage I shall merely present a simple, possible caricature, of the issue. Schools issue certificates, and they prescribe curriculum content for those certificates partly on the basis that such content is necessary (directly and/or indirectly) for the jobs the certificate will buy. Employers hire school-leavers on the basis of their certificates, but it is now well documented that what employers tend to want is the certificate regardless of the content. The internal contradictions are obvious, and begin to generate a series of questions. What is there about the certificate that appeals to employers? Why are two, or three, or four, or five, or six years of secondary schooling prerequisites for respective jobs if the actual content learnt in those years is relatively unimportant? Why do schools really proceed with job-oriented curricula, or else justify certain content in terms of job orientation, when the content is not necessary for the job?[31] One possible answer to the first two questions is that employers are employing 'character types'. For job A they might want the sort of person produced by two years of secondary schooling; for job B they might want the sort of person who can stick at secondary schooling and conform to its patterns for six years, and so on.

On this issue, Bowles and Gintis have shown that school grades are strongly correlated with students' personalities as well as with their mental abilities; and that the school system rewards the same personality characteristics as does the job market. Schools, of course, reward different personality characteristics at different stages (e.g. kindergarten, lower secondary school, university), but the characteristics rewarded at any stage are the same ones required and rewarded in jobs plucking students from that particular stage. Thus the personality characteristics rewarded in lower secondary school are also rewarded in jobs that require only lower secondary schooling. It is in this way that schools really man the work-force. At the bottom of the occupational hierarchy workers have to be subordinate, docile, punctual and conforming to authority. Further up the hierarchy, traits like self-control, flexibility, initiative and ability to work alone and make decisions become important. Schools in their hierarchy similarly reproduce these abilities, and so reproduce different types of personality, attitudes as well as behaviour in different social groups. Bowles and Gintis conclude that schools thus act as agents that reproduce social stratification and inequality – curriculum content being relatively unimportant in the process.[32]

Our third example is the obvious contradiction between school content and school structure. Schools in liberal democracies teach the value of liberal democracy, yet tend to teach it in the most totalitarian and autocratic of ways. It is hardly beyond the scope of our imagination, or experience, to conjure up the image of a teacher who spends a term painstakingly teaching the development of the British judicial system from pre-Magna Carta days to the present, and who then, having ducked a paper plane aimed generally in his direction, arrests a boy, charges him, prosecutes, allows no legal defence, acts as judge without a jury, sentences, and then executes the sentence, all behind a closed door.

The contradiction in schools between content and structure is well known: schools do not practise what they preach. This raises several questions for us. Can they practise what they preach? The supportive rhetoric would try to overcome the contradiction and show that they can, given more money, better conditions, better planning or whatever. Or is it that the contradiction is inbuilt; either in that schools *can not* practise what they preach, or that schools *in no way ever intend* to practise what they preach? We will leave consideration of those issues to the next chapter.

For our final example take the matter of schooling, IQ and subsequent rewards. Part of the supportive rhetoric surrounding schooling is that schools distribute their rewards largely according to intellectual ability. The smartest stay on longest, master the most difficult content, and get the best rewards for this in terms of professional well-paying jobs. However, as we have recently noted, Bowles and Gintis (and others) have exposed a contradiction in this thesis. Getting the best jobs requires staying on at school longest; but longevity and success at school correlate strongly with personality, sex, race and social background, yet only minimally and tenuously, if at all, with IQ. Schools, it would thus appear, while operating as status-sifters, do not sift according to intelligence as they claim to do.

Having noted this contradiction between rationale and practise we might now seek to find the criteria that schools actually do reward, and we might also ask why there is such emphasis on cognitive success and intellectual attainments in schools. If grades correlate strongly with personality *and* intelligence, could the cognitive emphasis simply be disguise in the best ideological fashion? Schooling promises to reward the intelligent, and those who are rewarded are intelligent (although not all the intelligent are rewarded): thus what is said to be the case really does seem to be the case. Yet it could be that, while the intelligent

121

are rewarded, they are actually being rewarded for some other factor or factors, and the cognitive/intellectual aspect of schooling is merely a façade to give the impression that schools are cognitively oriented, and educate in the best liberal fashion.

Before closing this section we can quickly consider another means of exposing internal contradictions and thus mounting immanent critiques: the idea, simply, is not to look at what is included in the position under scrutiny, but to focus on things that are missing from it. For instance, it is a cherished ideal and practice that all adult Australians (give or take a few categories) have the right to vote. But strangely, the ideals that give them that right also deny them the right not to vote. There is a similarity between this situation and compulsory schooling; for schooling, like the franchise, was introduced as a *right*. We are now in the strange position of being legally compelled to exercise our rights, and on both issues we face penalties if we don't. This line of thinking opens up large possibilities for criticism. And the same thing can happen if we slice through standard debates to pick on what might seem at first to be esoteric or unrelated points. For instance, there is a fairly well charted list of arguments for and against school uniforms – but rather than entering into those, something can be achieved by stepping out of the framework, casting the problem into the context of 'serving of interests', and asking: 'who really benefits if school pupils wear uniforms?'

It is hardly being suggested that these particular enquiries might reveal anything of great substantive significance. It is the principle we are concerned with. Given the pervasive effect that ideology has on us, it can really be countered only in radical ways, by criticism that it neither expects nor encourages, and by methods and attitudes that the supportive rhetoric can easily brand as irrelevant and cynical. One further method of this type is to reinterpret the rhetoric in a logic not of its own, or even to cast one's investigation in terms of a whole different logical apparatus from which to study the world. We shall now examine such a method and apparatus; one that challenges the very pre-suppositions and worth of the logic and rationality that create the context in which we usually think, theorise and criticise. In doing so we shall also extend considerably what has already been said about immanent critiques and internal contradiction.

Dialectics

Dialectics, like formal classical logic, is a context, embracing a series of laws, in which the world can be known and spoken about in a meaningful way. Traditionally, the laws of classical logic have been taken to be a set of *a priori* truths about the world; but this view has been recently challenged in two important ways. On the one hand, a school of Polish logicians has put forward the claim that our grounds for belief in a system of logic have nothing of the *a priori* about them, and are of the same order as those required for belief in any theory.[33] On the other hand, Engels, among many others, has challenged formal logic on the grounds that violations of classical logic, or logical contradictions, *can exist in the real world*, and that therefore classical formal logic must at best be an *idealisation*, and not a set of *a priori* truths about the world. This position of Engels's is the one we are accepting, but necessarily, in this context, without displaying the full justification for such acceptance.[34] We are also accepting, in a similar fashion, that the three basic dialectical laws are not trivial or nonsense (as some would have them), that they are not simply confusions about formal logic (as others would have them), but rather that they represent non-trivial universal valid descriptions of the world.

It is hardly to our purpose here to give a detailed account of dialectics, or to chart major and minute differences between the theories of its proponents: we shall instead paint fairly broad brushstrokes, consider mainly one aspect of dialectics, and point out differences, and advantages, in the dialectical approach to 'contradictions' and 'negation' as compared with the formal logic approach.

Dialectics, whether taken straight from Hegel or passing through the materialist emphasis of Marx, is simply part of a conception of reality as process or development, wherein everything, without exception, undergoes internal change. The world is thus seen to be dynamic (this whole conception, it will be recalled, underlies our research programme), and the world is seen to be constantly in a state of change as a result of our investigations into and interactions with it. We interact with the world on the basis of our knowledge of it, but this interaction also changes the world for us, and leaves us having to know again.

The first law of dialectics is the law of the unity of opposites; as Lenin puts it, 'the recognition (discovery) of mutually exclusive, opposite tendencies in all phenomena and processes of nature (including mind and society)'.[35] By this it is meant that the interaction of such opposite tendencies is both the motor for the development of all processes and at the same time the stabilising factor of these processes. In Mao's words: 'The interdependence of the contradictory aspects present in all things and the struggle between these aspects determine the life of all things and push their development forward.'[36]

The important notion for us to pick up from that is 'contradiction'. Dialectical contradiction is by no means the same as logical contradiction; rather it is based on the recognition or premise that all things are impelled by contradictory forces, and exist at any particular time in the form that the struggle between those forces takes at that particular

123

time. More technically, dialectics speaks of contradictory situations, or unities of opposites, wherein at least two causal tendencies, which are opposite in the sense that each tends to produce a result nullifying the other or its effects, are operating.[37] This is taken to be a universal state of affairs; and when we apply the principle to specific instances, interesting things can emerge.

It should be obvious now that, when we examined internal contradictions and spoke of applying immanent critiques in our previous section, we were largely applying the principles of dialectics in exposing the contradictory forces at work in given situations. We can now place those findings in a new context or terminology. Given that the interdependence of contradictory elements, and the struggle between them, determines the life of all things, it is clear that schooling, or anything, from this viewpoint can be understood *for what it is* by recognising and highlighting the nature of its contradictory internal aspects. Job-oriented curriculum content that employers don't want, cognitive orientation yet reward of non-cognitive factors, and contradictions between content and practice can now be seen not just as pointing up a few little problems with schools: from the dialectical approach they are seen *as revealing the very nature of schooling itself*. And if the nature of schooling, or anything, is revealed in terms of its contradictory aspects, then it is clear that patchwork, in the form of supportive rhetoric and internal repairs, must be ineffective with regard to serious change if the contradictions that determine the nature of the institution, and impel its development, remain.

One further point can now be made. The dialectical approach, concentrating and focusing as it does on internal contradictions – contradictions within theory and within practice as well as contradictions between theoretical stances and practical outcomes – obviously works in the opposite way to ideology, which assimilates or glosses over contradictions. Dialectics, therefore, besides providing a clear revelation of the nature of the object under investigation, is also powerfully counter-ideological in yet another way. Thus on two counts it can be seen as a valuable weapon for fighting ideology.

There is yet a further aspect that can now be taken up, and that is the matter of negation. Negation is commonly recognised in the form of 'immediate negation', where 'yes' is simply replaced by 'no', and vice versa. The negation of exams is no exams; the negation of playing cricket is not playing cricket; and so on. Dialectic negation, however, does not work like this.

Consider again the contradictory elements existing in any situation as a unity of opposites. These elements are in struggle, each seeking causal predominance over the other. When one achieves this it negates the other; but it is crucial to recognise that, in doing so, it changes itself as well, and it changes the total situation. And thus we get a movement outside of the original framework, or an escape from the constrictive bounds of the prevailing theoretic and/or practical situation. Let us explain this by considering three examples, beginning with the classic case, capitalism.

Capitalism requires a class of capitalists and an industrial working class. In requiring this it does not invent a class of rulers, exploiters and oppressors on the one hand and a class of oppressed exploited workers on the other hand; for these clearly pre-date capitalism by thousands of years. What capitalism does require, and must create, is a class familiar with socialised and mechanised production and collective work, who, seeing the means of production necessarily passing into fewer and fewer capitalistic hands, will cry out for control of the means of production themselves. Capitalism, in other words, necessarily produces the one class that can make a socialist revolution; and if and when the unity of opposites cracks and the revolution comes, capitalism will be negated by what it itself produced. And not only does capitalism go, but with it go the oppression and exploitation that preceded it. We have, in Hegel's terms, a new synthesis, grown out of the negating contradictoriness of the old system.

It is of passing interest to note here that schools did not create teachers and children. But schools, in advanced industrial societies, do create, or require, a 'class' of children prepared to remain socially, intellectually and economically dependent for up to a quarter of a century; for many well into the time when they are socially and intellectually mature, and capable of being economically independent. As these 'children' gain the consciousness whereby they can begin to see themselves kept as children they could revolt against the aspects of the school system that determines them as such. Thus it could be that schools are necessarily producing the one 'class' that could overthrow the schools and bring about a learning and educational revolution.

For our second example, consider that in many parts of the Western world women are (or recently were) paid less than men for equal work. This led to the call from some people for an *immediate negation* – 'women should be paid the same as men for equal work!' – and largely this call has been successful. But as an immediate negation it simply works within the given framework or paradigm, and thus functions as fairly harmless internal criticism which can easily be accommodated and/or met. At the worst, employers might have to pay out a little more, and take a small drop in profits for a short time; at the best people will be satisfied that certain principles regarding human rights have been observed. And in all probability the new situation will be seen as more just, more fair and more humane. However, the call for immediate negation does not challenge the real basis or dynamics of the system as it

125

operates. Taking the issue on a broader front, the struggle between capitalists and workers over wages and working conditions, whether it takes economic, political or theoretical means (or all three together), may lead to success for workers when wages go up, conditions are improved and profits go down (for a while); but that very success, *if* it is gained, still leaves the situation, the now '*successful*' situation, within the very framework in which the struggle was generated. The key factors, the key issues, have not really been touched.[38] But focusing on the matter dialectically points up a different picture. The contradictory elements involved are employers and employees, and men and women. To negate the situation it is not just a matter of letting employers exploit women equally with men. What is required, eventually, is some sort of social reorganisation wherein there is no exploitation of workers by owners, and no differentiations in roles or expectations according to sex.

At this point our quick third example can turn us back towards education. As we noted earlier, one of the time-worn standard arguments within the supportive rhetoric on schools is whether they should be selective or comprehensive; and protagonists on either side try continually to immediately negate their opponents. The arguments usually take the form that schools should be either selective or comprehensive because in the particular way championed they can better fulfil a set of aims. Of course there is also much argument about the content of that set of aims. But while these arguments continue, the overarching framework is not threatened, and within the framework minor, or even large, concessions might be won. But if it could be shown, by highlighting internal contradictions, that schools, whether comprehensive or selective, simply cannot fulfil the aims that either side desires, then the constricting framework would appear as something of a paper tiger, and the negations really required would become obvious (which is not to say they would be put into practice).

We see here, and with the other examples, that another great beauty and value of dialectic argument, and the implementation of dialectic negation, is that it necessarily defines the successful outcome of criticism, struggle and the endeavour to know the world, *outside* the confines set by the very existence of that which it puts under scrutiny and criticises. It thus necessarily leads away from supportive rhetoric and prevailing ideology.

Conclusion

We have in this chapter indicated how we might recognise ideology when we are confronted by it; how choices of critical preference can be made among ideologies and ideological positions; and we have charted certain means whereby prevailing ideology can be attacked and criticised. Two points should now be recapitulated and stressed.

First, given that ideology is so thoroughly pervasive, (and that it is borne by individuals), it is unlikely to be perceived for what it is; nor is it likely that any clear need for criticism of it will become evident. Thus, recognising and attacking ideology requires a particular orientation to begin with - one must come into the arena suspicious and critical, assuming that things as presented might not be what they seem (that there may be faces lurking in the foliage of trees).

The second point is that, since ideology so easily accommodates the sort of criticism and thinking it encourages, it can be seriously attacked only by counter-ideological moves, such as defining aspects in terms of their contradictoriness; and applying criticism that necessarily leads outside of the particular ideological structure under question. Ideology can best be attacked by the application of theory, rhetoric and criticism which it does not encourage and which, by and large, it is not equipped to handle and cannot accommodate.

It would seem then, that if we all became suspicious, searched for the ideological, exposed false consciousness and applied counter-ideological methods of criticism, we could rise from our immersion in our prevailing ideology, free ourselves from distortions, especially interest-serving distortions, and come to embrace a better, clearer, non-distortive view of the world which really served our interests.

That, however, is neither the case in theory nor in practice. We have left out of our account three crucial points. First, as we have emphasised earlier, ideology is determined by social practices and is embodied in lived experience: this raises particularly difficult problems, which shall be attended to later. Second, what ideology does not encourage, and cannot handle or accommodate, it tends to de-legitimise, such that the threats and attacks are in some way branded pejoratively and are not taken seriously. This leads directly to the third point, which is that all counter-ideological moves, and even the possibility of making them, are negated almost thoroughly by the lived-ideology and theoretical ideology of education. Education, more than anything else, secures prevailing ideologies and makes them free from threat. That issue now requires detailed examination.

Chapter 5

Education

Introduction

'Education', it will be remembered, is being used in this work to refer, in a shorthand way, to formal institutionalised education; or to those learning experiences that are provided by or sanctioned by the state, that are transmitted in institutionalised settings, and are concerned to provide a broad understanding of the world. Thus what I shall be concerned with when speaking of 'education' is the sort of thing that almost all of us got, are still getting, or are actually giving, in approved schools, colleges, universities and other similar places.

Now education (as again indicated previously), whatever else it may entail, and whatever other ideals it may espouse, is essentially concerned with the transmission of knowledge. Its central concern is that the pupil, upon leaving, will know certain things that he did not know on arrival and that, in the interim, he did not pick up elsewhere. It would be a bad mistake, however, to view this knowledge only in terms of curriculum content, for as we shall see education transmits other knowledge as well; but it would seem fair to claim that education aims to overcome ignorance and to teach people about the world. It would also appear that education embraces the principle that it is better to have knowledge than to be ignorant, that it is better to be Socrates dissatisfied than a pig satisfied. There are a great deal more claims that education, especially education that claims to be liberal, would make with regard to knowledge, and to the benefits that particular knowledge bestows on the individual, but I shall not list these here for two reasons. First, they are already well enough known, and if not they can be found in any curriculum 'Preamble' or ministerial report. Second, I believe that they, like the ones I have listed, are pieces of rhetoric which blatantly distort the state of affairs. This shall become apparent when the real functions of education are displayed in this chapter.

128

Education *is* essentially concerned with the transmission of knowledge. What I shall argue, however, is that education, given the circumstances of a liberal democratic capitalist society, is concerned to transmit
knowledge that distorts people's views of the world; it is concerned to
create easily satisfied 'pigs'; and it is concerned to promote a pernicious
type of ignorance rather than to overcome ignorance. Helvetius said
that: 'Children are born ignorant, not stupid: it is education that makes
them stupid'; and he was essentially correct. Young uneducated children
are ignorant of the world; educated adults are usually similarly ignorant,
but because they have been given knowledge of a sort they fail to recognise their ignorance, and they mistake the theoretic relations they
bear for knowledge of the real world, and even for wisdom.

The preceding claims are clearly contentious and will have to be
argued for in some detail. I shall begin this argument in a rather strange
way, not by looking at the proposed virtues of education, but rather by
outlining and examining the case for the value of ignorance.

The value of ignorance

People didn't always believe in education, nor do all believe in it now,
and history presents us with an impressive list of arguments in favour of
ignorance. To begin with, there is the timeless notion that children are
happier than adults. Perhaps cavemen returning after an unsuccessful
day's hunting and worrying about where the next meal was coming
from saw their children playing happily with the bones of the last
meal, and rued the day they ever left such blissful ignorance behind.
Certainly today's adults worry about inflation, whom to vote for, what
a distant country's new foreign policy might mean to them, and whether
or not to buy shares that their broker has recommended; while their
children play on swings and in sandpits, and seem to have no other care
in the world. This familiar picture, however, does not usually extend to
a plea for total ignorance. Children, it is recognised, *will* grow up, and
since they cannot carry their childish ways within their adult bodies,
they do have to learn something about the world. But this need involve
only the most basic of skills required for survival, and it could be judged
good that the child be kept ignorant of everything else. If he can't read
his mind will not get filled with confusing or evil thoughts; if he does
not know of the great land across the sea he will not yearn to travel; if
he does not know economics the problems of foreign trade are not his
to share.

A second reason for valuing ignorance is closely related to the first,
the difference being that ignorance is equated with innocence, and this
brings with it a moral dimension. When innocence is closely associated

129

with moral and spiritual purity, knowledge can be seen as something that necessarily blackens the slate. Christ's statement that only as little children shall we enter the Kingdom of Heaven can be interpreted as a call to maintain not just moral purity, but the innocence, and the ignorance, that are supposed to go with it. That the statement has been so interpreted can be seen in the more extreme practices of the Anabaptist movement in the Reformation period. This sort of rationale is often used when ignorance is enforced through censorship; the deliberate suppression of information that may have a bad effect, and help to destroy the innocence of the would-be respondent. It is along the same sort of lines that certain matters are not spoken of 'in front of the children', and other matters are discussed only within specialised groups of initiates who presumably are beyond corruption. The central point, however, is that ignorance can be seen, and is often seen, as having a moral quality to it: the tiny infant, it has often been claimed, dies pure and untainted; kings once kept idiots at court, believing they were more blessed by God; and many people today glory in their ignorance of lewd literature, heretical writings and anti-establishment politics. This moral quality lies behind the speech of the carpenter in Chaucer's 'Miller's Tale':

> Ye, blessed be alwey a lewed man
> That noght but oonly his bileve kan!

Another argument in favour of ignorance is that simple folk don't get hurt. Three highly learned American astronauts are killed in a rocket firing; three similarly highly learned Russian cosmonauts die on re-entry into the earth's atmosphere; but (so it is argued) you don't get killed on Henry Ford's production line. Academics and schoolteachers have nervous breakdowns, but fishermen don't. West Point officers, not farmers, get killed and injured in wars. And it's scientists and would-be scientists who get their heads and limbs blown off, not simple folk who don't tangle with explosives, electricity and new-fangled contraptions. The less you know, and the less you try, the safer you are.

Closely associated with this argument is a variant of the common 'The bigger they are, the harder they fall' theory. One needs knowledge to become president of the United States; and the ignorant child who never left his subsistence farm in Tennessee lived longer than J. F. Kennedy, and never had to suffer public humiliation like Richard Nixon. In Tudor times it was Sir Thomas More's superior learning that brought the axe to his neck; the ignorant peasants of the time took Henry's oath of allegiance, which they probably didn't even understand, and lived happily ever after; which could not be said for the learned Wolsey, Cranmer or Cromwell. If Martin Luther King had remained an ignorant Harlem dweller he might still be alive. While ever history tends to record the triumphs of 'great men' it also spells out the message that the higher you rise (often through being knowledgeable), the harder you can fall. And thus we get a record of people killed, imprisoned, humiliated and in other ways destroyed because of their knowledge and position; people who would have presumably escaped such harm had they only remained ignorant. Knowledge brings positions of prestige and/or the ability to articulate arguments against positions of prestige: either way it puts you at risk. And when they're burning at the stake those who have read a heretic's pamphlet, or rounding up those suspected of underground subversive activities, it's most advantageous to be an illiterate or the village idiot.

> Where ignorance is bliss
> Tis folly to be wise

The next argument that we shall consider in favour of ignorance is the claim that all one needs to know is already known: this could apply either to the individual or to knowledge itself. As far as the individual is concerned, learning usually involves effort (and perhaps dissonance), and a simple means of avoiding such effort (and/or dissonance) is to claim that one already knows everything, or at least all one needs to know. This often takes the form, in adulthood, of rationalisation. Faced with the exponential growth of knowledge, or even the emergence of new authors or new schools of thought, it does seem reasonable for an adult, at some stage, to say: 'That's it!' and give up learning, which requires effort, in favour of the television set or golf. Academics often retreat from the new knowledge in their field by taking up positions that are almost exclusively adminstrative. But the argument, as noted, can also be applied to knowledge itself. The Bible tells us that: 'The thing that hath been, it is that which shall be; and that which is done is that which shall be done: and there is no new thing under the sun.'[1]

Our point here is not to undertake biblical exegesis, but simply to note a significant idea in a document that has greatly influenced man's thinking, and that has, in certain times and places, imprinted the belief that there is nothing new to be known. This interpretation has abounded in history, reflected as it is in hymns like 'Give Me That Old Time Religion', in admonitions not to stray from the ways of our fathers, in general suspicion of anything new, and in the very strength of tradition and superstition. The Augustan tradition in literature, continually looking back to the classics as it did to find truth and perfection, could also be taken as an instance of this belief.

Closely allied with 'there being nothing new under the sun' is the admonition of Jesus to 'Beware of false prophets' who shall be known by their fruits.[2] It is a very easy thing to apply the label 'false prophet' to anybody bearing new fruits, and to reject their knowledge in favour of one's own ignorance. Matthew Arnold noted that: 'We like to be suffered to lie comfortably in the old straw of our habits, especially of our intellectual habits, even though this straw may not be very clean or fine.'[3] One of the most notorious of our 'false' prophets was Charles Darwin, who bore the fruit of evolution, and who in many quarters, and for a long time, was soundly rejected. The famous Tennessee Monkey Case was the result of anxious adults wanting their children, and themselves, to remain ignorant of 'false' teachings. History fails to record all of the false prophets who were burned at the stake, imprisoned or forced to recant; whose books were burned or whose equipment was destroyed; or who carried a few fruits around in their heads but were simply afraid to articulate them. History does, of course, record those who have broken through, but it shows clearly that the Luthers, Freuds and Marxes had a hard time of it; and there are still a great many who do not want to taste of their fruits.[4] (Incidentally, there is something a little strange about Jesus's admonition, for, as we have shown earlier, the truth or falsity of prophets (theories, theorists) cannot be determined by fruits (evidence) alone. The admonition, when issued or referred to today, can be seen as having distortive ideological force.)

A variation on this particular theme is that *certain things* are simply not for us to know. God, we are told, moves in mysterious ways, and the ways of God are not for man to know: but the idea does have secular applications as well. Let us take Chaucer's carpenter again, and record more of his speech:

> Ye, blessed be alwey a lewed man
> That noght but oonly his bileve kan!
> So ferde another clerk with astromye;
> He walked in the fieldes for to prye
> Upon the sterres, what ther sholde bifalle,
> Til he was in a marle-pit yfalle;
> He saugh nat that.

To put that less eloquently, but in more modern idiom, 'keep your nose out of things that don't concern you, or else you'll end up in the shit'. Thus it is variously decreed not only that men ought not meddle in the ways of God, or seek to learn the mysteries of the stars, but also that workers ought to keep clear of the ways of management, that children should not know of the economic affairs of their families, and that wives ought to keep their noses out of what goes on in masonic lodges: simply because there are some things that certain groups should, for their own benefit, be kept (and keep themselves) ignorant of.

We have now outlined a number of reasons commonly given and perpetuated regarding the positive value of ignorance. In a sense they are all encompassed in a single line in the Bible: 'For in much wisdom is much grief: and he that increaseth knowledge increaseth sorrow.'[5] To put that negatively, and in modern idiom: *what you don't know won't hurt you*.

The problem that confronts us now is the none too simple one of countering these arguments; for they must be countered if one is to come out in support of education and argue for the value of *increasing* knowledge and *overcoming* ignorance.

Some of the arguments are easier to dismiss than others. For instance it can be shown (and needs to be shown) that, within the confines of any particular socio-historical context, the 'what you don't know won't hurt you' theory is very badly misleading, as is its close relation that 'simple folk don't get hurt'. It can very easily be established that in wars it is the 'ignorant' privates who get killed and maimed, not the enlightened generals; in modern industrial societies it is the workers who get crushed by machinery, not the inventors of machines; in electrified communities people ignorant of the working of electricity get shocked, not electrical engineers. This might provide some good arguments against wars, machines and electricity, but not necessarily against knowledge – but there are instances that can be applied to all socio-historical contexts. Diseases, for instance, are usually spread through ignorance; and history provides us with a parade of societies that have been wiped out through lack of knowledge about erosion, nutrition, defence and so on. What you don't know *can* hurt you; and simple folk *do* get hurt. (The history of simple folk, however, is rarely written.) But what can be done with notions like 'children are happier than adults'; that we must be protected (kept ignorant) of things that might harm us (physically, morally or intellectually); or that it is bad and dangerous, especially given the presence of false prophets, to seek new knowledge?

The standard approaches and answers to these questions have largely been formulated along metaphysical and/or ontological lines; and attempt to show that there is something about the nature of man, and/or existence, that requires that man should continually replace ignorance by knowledge if he is to fulfil his vocation on earth. Aristotle, in antiquity, and Freire, in modern times, are powerful proponents of such views. Another influential line, running from Kant through to Peters, argues that having knowledge (or certain types of knowledge) is intrinsically worthwhile; while the Platonic tradition simply equates knowledge with virtue. In all cases it is agreed that it is far better to be Socrates dissatisfied than a pig satisfied.

It seems to me, however, that none of these positions can really be justified, and that none of them counts heavily, against the arguments we have already noted *for* ignorance; against the notion that satisfied pigs should be left satisfied and happy; or especially against the idea that satisfied happy people in self-sufficient yet 'backward' socio-cultural milieux should be left as they are. I therefore want to leave aside notions of intrinsic worthwhileness, ontological vocations and calculuses of pleasure, and approach the issue in a completely different way; that is, by casting it in terms of the research programme in which this whole discussion is set.

If we envisage a social formation as made up and characterised by conflicts of interests and differentials of power, it is hardly likely, wherever ignorance is valued or prescribed, that it is the whole of a particular society that values and prescribes such ignorance (even though there may appear, on the surface, to be consensus in the matter). It is more likely to be the case that there will be a ruling group prescribing such ignorance and deeming it valuable, and that there will be a ruled group for whom ignorance is prescribed, and which (hopefully, from the point of view of the ruling group) comes to accept that such ignorance is in its interests, or that its ignorance is simply part of the way things are and should be. For instance, the church might decree, as it has throughout history, that there are certain things (complications?) the laity would be better off not knowing; professions keep their knowledge esoteric ostensibly on the grounds that 'a little learning is a dangerous thing'; ('the man who defends himself in court has a fool for a client'); men decree that women should not know of economics and financial management; various authorities apply censorship so that certain books will not be read and certain films and plays will not be seen; and schools do not teach certain topics or certain authors.

Now three possibilities emerge here. In the first place there could be cases where the ruling groups prescribe ignorance which appears really to operate equally in the interests of all. If there is a battle that, of necessity, must be fought, then it would appear that it is in everybody's interests (on the one side, that is) that as few people as possible know the precise time, place and strategy of its occurrence. Or, to be a little more extreme, if a deranged homicidal maniac, who is goaded by noise and confusion, is part of an audience of thousands listening to a violin recital at Festival Hall, and plain-clothes policemen enter, announce their purpose to the management and unobtrusively close in on him, it would be a crazy management that took the stage from the soloist to inform everybody of what was happening. Nearer to home, if the Treasury decided to devalue the society's currency, while that action would not favour all equally, keeping everybody ignorant of the precise time and rate of devaluation would at least go closer to favouring all interests equally.

At the other extreme, there could be cases where the ruling classes prescribe ignorance and suppress dissemination of knowledge in order to protect their own interests especially. As an example of this, consider this statement quoted by Freire, and attributed to a Mr Giddy:[6]

> However specious in theory the project might be of giving education to the labouring classes of the poor, it would be prejudicial to their morals and happiness; it would teach them to despise their lot in life instead of making them good servants in agriculture and other laborious employments; instead of teaching them subordination it would render them fractious and refractory as was evident in the manufacturing countries; it would enable them to read seditious pamphlets, vicious books and publications against Christianity; it would render them insolent to their superiors and in a few years the legislature would find it necessary to direct the strong arm of power against them.

This, at least on the face of it, is a little different from the celebrated Sir William Berkeley's: 'Thank God there are no free schools or printing . . . for learning has brought disobedience into the world, and printing has divulged them . . . God keep us from both.' For Mr Giddy openly wants servants, labourers, and inferiors *kept in their place*. After all, 'How *are* you going to keep them down on the farm, after they've seen Par-ree?'

On a slightly different level, consider this example of a government keeping its constituents ignorant of its actions, in a rather trivial matter. The tactic is the familiar one of 'No comment' and/or 'Nobody knows'; and was reported in the press as follows:[7]

> The Federal Government would not comment today on widely published speculation that radio and television owners will soon pay up to $90 a year in licence fees.
>
> The Victorian secretary of the Amalgamated Metal Workers' Union, Mr John Halfpenny, said this week that a reliable source working in the Government Printing Office had told him that licences were being printed.
>
> Mr Halfpenny said the fees were $25 for radios, $50 for a combined radio and black and white TV licence and $90 for a combined radio and colour TV licence.
>
> The former Minister for Posts and Telecommunications, Mr Garland, said he had no comment to make.
>
> A spokesman for the department said he knew of no discussion on licences during Cabinet meetings or high-level talks.
>
> The Treasurer, Mr Lynch, would not comment on the licences.
>
> The Government Printer, Mr F. Atkinson, said: 'I couldn't tell you if we were printing them.' He was confident that nobody in his office would leak the information.

135

We are not dealing here with top secret defence issues. The licences were either being printed or they weren't, and Mr Garland, *the spokesman*,[8] Mr Lynch and Mr Atkinson all *knew* - they had to know - what the case actually was. (Interestingly, Mr Atkinson and his employees seem somehow to be not allowed to tell the public what they are doing, even though, as government printers, they are ostensibly working for and on behalf of the public.) Now if the licences were *not* being printed, the government's interests were hardly under threat, and there was surely nothing to be lost by admitting this. But if they *were* being printed the Government's interests would have been under threat; for the electorate, learning of this, would have been quite hostile. It is reasonable to assume, then, that the Government was printing the licences, and like Mr Giddy wanted to keep the public ignorant to protect its (the Government's) interests.

The third possibility, and the one that must cause us most concern, is when the ruling classes claim to be keeping some groups ignorant for those groups' own good, or for the good of everybody, *and where such claims are questionable*. Censorship, for instance, is often enforced ostensibly for the 'moral welfare of the whole nation'; certain knowledge might be suppressed or be made available only to specialised groups, supposedly to protect the general run of people from misusing it, or to relieve them from the burden of carrying it; and so on. Such cases are usually bolstered by the sorts of arguments we have just looked at; that a little learning is a dangerous thing, that knowledge increases sorrow and the ignorant are happier, that certain knowledge destroys innocence, that false prophets abound *from whom people should be protected*, and that there is nothing new under the sun; arguments that are virtually impossible to refute (or verify), and that tend to lead to vague, unsatisfactory and (epistemologically) profitless debate. How, then, can we determine if and when the promotion of ignorance in such cases really is in the interests of the ruled groups and/or in the interests of everyone?

As it turns out, there is quite a simple solution to that problem, for when it is looked at in the context of our research programme the question can be seen to be a spurious and mystifying one. In terms of our research programme, where the absolute notions of 'altruism', 'benevolence' and 'impartiality' are necessarily denied,[9] no ruling group would prescribe or encourage ignorance in general, or take on knowledge itself yet deny it to others, unless such ploys served, or at least were thought to serve, the ruling groups most in the form of maintaining ruling interests and stabilising the *status quo*.[10] So the crucial point to note is that one does not have to tangle with a calculus of pleasures or interests, for it really does not matter whether keeping knowledge from a ruled group is actually in that group's interests or not: people might be happier not knowing the complications of the world; they might be better off unaware of the full range of possibilities open to them; and so on. What does matter, and what we can say unequivocally in terms of our research programme, is that promoted and/or enforced ignorance (always promoted and/or enforced by a ruling group) must necessarily favour, or be thought to favour, the enforcing ruling group most. Thus the tactic is always class interest-serving in a class society; and the arguments we have previously noted that favour ignorance can now be recognised and judged as interest-serving ideological rationalisations which serve a particular social function – namely protecting the *status quo* by deterring people from gaining the knowledge that might make them capable of threatening and challenging the existing order.

It will be noted that nothing so far has been said in favour of either being knowledgeable or being ignorant. However, the obvious can now be added; the more ignorant one is within a socio-historical context, the more easily one can be exploited and manipulated within that context; the less information one has, the less one can counter other views; the less one is encouraged to question, the less likely it is that one will question, and so on. Thus, *if* a ruling class wanted to exploit the ruled, give them false impressions, have them work and live against their own best interests, not question the *status quo* and so on, it would do well to keep them ignorant of certain things. This it could do directly, by repressing knowledge and information; but as we saw earlier, repression is generally a clumsy and ineffective technique. A better means would be to institutionalise, and disguise by supportive rhetoric, the promotion of ignorance; and this brings us to education in capitalist liberal democracies.[11]

Education as political manipulation (i)

Education, as was stated in the 'Introduction' to this work, whatever else it may entail or involve, is essentially concerned with the transmission of knowledge. It is necessary now to develop two aspects regarding this claim in order to lay the ground for what will shortly follow.

In the first place, the transmission of knowledge, within education as defined, has two factors to it: a content factor (the substantive knowledge transmitted) and a process factor (how the content is transmitted). And this has led some recent writers, such as Illich, to argue that there are thus two curricula – the overt one and a hidden one – operating at the same time.[12] The point we seek is much in accordance with this; namely that both factors must be recognised in looking at education, and that neither of them can be isolated, separated out or considered apart from the other. In being educated one does not just learn the content of, say, geography, history and mathematics: one also learns how to learn geography, history and mathematics; and this is not meant to refer only to the disciplinary methodologies. One learns who decides what aspects of geography are to be learned, how to behave in geography classes, where to give respect and obedience (and on what grounds), how to address and react to different members of one's class, whose favour is worth currying, whose opinion is worth attending to, and so on. Thus knowledge is also gained from the process, and this has to be added in with the knowledge about monoclines and synclines to complete the picture of what knowledge is transmitted. There might, of course, be serious disjunctions and contradictions between content and process, as when pupils learn the content of democratic principles in a totalitarian setting, or when university students are required to memorise a particular text as part of their critical free enquiry after knowledge. But regardless of these disjunctions, content and process are inextricably intertwined to make up the totality of the knowledge that is transmitted.

There have been those, of course, who have sought to cut this Gordian knot, or who at least claim that in principle it can be cut. We shall argue later that there is something to be said in favour of isolating 'process' for separate consideration, since process is largely consistent across varying bodies of content; but the more common ploy is to attempt to isolate content, and to look at education as being essentially concerned with the transmission of the content of curricula. There are many people who, as we shall see later, see the central concern of education as curriculum content, and who seek to establish or find the basis of education in epistemology and epistemological theories. Prominent among such theorists is P. H. Hirst, who sees liberal education as the development of mind, which in turn is initiation into 'forms of knowledge' that have become differentiated out over human history.[13] But there is a common fault shared by most of these theorists[14] which leads us to our second introductory point.

Epistemological theories, as Frankena has well argued,[15] are *neither necessary nor sufficient* to establish conclusions about education. They are neither necessary nor sufficient even to establish conclusions about the *content* of education, i.e. about what knowledge shall be transmitted. Conclusions of such kinds must derive from normative or value premises, but not necessarily from epistemological ones. Aristotle realised this long ago; and Frankena concludes: 'Hence, as Aristotle said, it is ethics and politics that determine what is to be studied, by whom, and to what extent – not epistemology.'[16] Epistemology may provide relevant considerations in determining answers to educational questions, but education is, at bottom, based on ethics and politics, and even the content of education is politically determined. Although education is essentially concerned with the transmission of knowledge, it does this not in a vacuum or in a mystical epistemological realm, but rather within the material conditions of existing social relations, which determine what shall be transmitted, and how; such that education serves as a major factor in the production of *certain kinds of knowledge*, which in turn serve the particular interests of particular societies. In this way education is, first and foremost, a political act.[17]

Identifying education as essentially a political act should be little cause for surprise. Education, as defined, is provided by the state. And those educational institutions that are not directly run by the state are monitored by the state, and are allowed to function only by fiat of the state which can close and terminate the operation of any institution it wants to. So education is state-controlled, being provided either directly by the state, or indirectly for the state by acceptable entrepreneurs.

Now if the state were a neutral body, serving all members impartially, it could come to pass that education too might be neutral, and many people do see the state and education in this way. As Benton indicates, 'the notion at work' here is that:[18]

> education like the rest of the institutions of the state . . . is neutral with respect to the struggles and conflicts going on elsewhere in society. The state as a whole is a neutral arbiter, an honest broker, which stands above the multiplicity of competing interests and pressures at work in civil society. If the state as a whole must remain neutral, then even more must this be so for the complex of educational institutions to whose care is entrusted the tender, impressionable mind of the new generation. Education must be kept out of politics and politics out of education.

But such a notion (as Benton also demonstrates) is built on an ideological distinction between what is considered to be educational and what is taken to be political; a distinction that is both misconceived and misrepresentative, as well as facile. It is also built on a false ideological construct of what the 'state' is, a construct we tend to easily reinforce every time we reify 'the state' in our ordinary language (as I have done many times in the last couple of pages). But if we put aside beliefs about neutral, reified 'states', and see education instead as being provided to serve the ruling interests in a society, we find that on two counts education is a non-neutral political act. It is an act that always encompasses and is built on a particular theory or view of man and the world, and on particular interpretations of what is good for man and the state; and it is an act that necessarily brings into play and involves economic and political power in fostering, producing and perpetuating these particular views. Gintis sums up this aspect of education well:[19]

> The function of education in any society is the socialisation of youth into the prevailing culture. On the one hand, schooling serves

to integrate individuals into society by institutionalizing dominant value, norm and belief systems. On the other hand, schooling provides the individual competencies necessary for the adequate performance of social roles. Thus educational systems are fundamental to the stability and functioning of any society.

But in a class society, a further factor could and would be expected to come into play. Education, provided as it is by the ruling class, would stabilise the functioning of the society and help to maintain and perpetuate a *status quo* which would essentially serve the interests of the ruling class. And if the society in question were a capitalist society, then education would serve the ruling class by helping to ensure the stabilisation and continuation of the capitalist mode of production, which requires, as we have seen, that the majority of the population live and work in a manner that is against their own best interests. But if the society were also a liberal democracy and/or espoused the ideals of liberal democracy, then this mass of people would have to be convinced, by 'positive' means, that what was occurring in society was in their best interests too. Thus education, in exercising its stabilising function, would have to do two specific things, regardless of whatever else it might do. It would have to disguise certain things, like the real basis of social relations; and it would have to deal in ignorance as well as the transmission of knowledge. In short, it must keep some things hidden away, and transmit other things in a disguised and distorted form. Freire makes a telling comment on this necessarily political function of education:[20]

In a class society, the power elite necessarily determine what education will be, and therefore its objectives. The objectives will certainly not be opposed to their interests. As we have already said, it would be supremely naive to imagine that the elite would in any way promote or accept an education which stimulated the oppressed to discover the *raison d'etre* of the social structure. The most that could be expected is that the elite might permit talk of such education, and occasional experiments which could be immediately suppressed should the status quo be threatened.

To put that in a more general way, education in a class society is a political act having as its basis the protection of the interests of the ruling class. It is a 'mechanism' (and that word hardly does it justice) for securing the continuation of the existing social relationships, and for reinforcing the attitudes and beliefs that will help ensure that those social relationships will continue to be accepted. Education is thus more than a 'mechanism' - it is an ideological force of tremendous import. On the one hand it is a *lived-ideology* which, in modern liberal capitalist democracies, everyone is compelled to live through for a long period of time. On the other hand it generates theoretical ideology, as all lived-ideologies do, but in the most influential and insidious of ways. To some extent one can question and reject the theoretical ideology generated by living in the family ideology; to a far greater extent (today) one can reject both living in the church ideology and the theory generated there. But education's very function is to instil in people a particular way of seeing the world; it takes those 'tender, impressionable minds of the new generation' and implants in them the master mental set – *see the world this way*. In this way it brings about the large-scale consensus spoken of previously; and in establishing a mental set it both opens up certain ways of seeing the world, and also closes off others: it both reveals and conceals as it promotes the production of certain knowledge while excluding the production of other kinds. Education is the manipulation of consciousness (a point that must be agreed with even by those who would see 'manipulation' in a non-pejorative way), and it functions largely without serious opposition of any sort. While education is universal and compulsory, and while only knowledge gained through education is legitimated in a society (rewards being offered for attainments in educational institutions, and status being conferred on the educated), the knowledge, values and views transmitted by education can only be seen as the right ones, the proper ones, and the most important ones to have and hold. Education legitimates itself *and* the way of seeing the world that it promotes and produces. Thus, when it is universal and compulsory it emerges as the major means for securing and promoting the consciousness that will perpetuate and secure the existing social relationships out of which the institution of education itself grows. Althusser, then, is correct in categorising education as the *number one* 'dominant ideological State apparatus' of the present day.[21]

One immediate conclusion to leap from that recognition is that education is not merely useless, it is positively counter-productive in fighting and overcoming ideology. Education forms and reinforces the dominant ideological views in a society and the consciousness that accompanies them: it can never 'raise consciousness', or create the conditions or promote the 'critical awareness' whereby the dominant ideology of an era can be recognised for what it is, let alone be attacked.

Education, although the most powerful, is only one of those lived-ideologies and institutions that form concepts, habits, attitudes and values in the individual that are appropriate to the place that individual has to occupy in society. But as we saw in our discussion of 'ideology', the existing system of social relations is laid before the consciousness of the individual, through ideological mechanisms, as given, and as right. So, while the reproduction of ideologies contributes to the reproduction of social relations, it also masks or disguises the reproductive aspects;

141

it presents the relations as natural, given or self-generative; and it presents the reproductive agents as if they have quite different functions and purposes. Education, then, like all ideological mechanisms, functions as a perception-altering drug, affecting the way one sees the world, but also (in this instance) affecting the way one sees oneself, and the way one sees education. It is largely for this reason that much of what has been said above concerning education will not be readily accepted by most people; for most, especially the well educated, are still under the influence of the education ideology or drug; and in seeing themselves as freely choosing individuals rather than drugged bearers of disguised relations instilled by ideological mechanisms, they have assimilated the tenets of education, and the rightness of education, without recognising or querying its essentially reproductive nature, in regard to both social relations and ideas relating to social relations. Most, for perfectly good reasons, would still hold that education is provided by a benevolent state to give all an equal opportunity to live and rise in society; that education aims for enlightenment and frees the mind from ignorance; that education mainly provides knowledge that adds to the quality of life; that education raises the standard of living of everyone; and so on. Most would probably concur with Scheffler, especially in sentiment, when he says: 'In teaching, we do not impose our wills on the student, but introduce him to the many mansions of the heritage in which we ourselves strive to live, and to the improvement of which we are ourselves dedicated'[22] and fail to notice the ominous undertones that Scheffler himself seems not to be aware of. Most would not attempt to give an account of education in terms of its contradictory aspects, or attempt to see it in ways other than those legitimated by education itself.[23]

Given that most people are in such a position, and have an 'education-developed consciousness' (or research programme) of what education is and does, it is necessary for us to show at some length what education really does. In the remainder of this section we shall stay mainly with the process aspect of education, recalling to begin with that, whereas process and content cannot be completely separated, process is largely consistent over all aspects of content (and is thus more pervasive than any single aspect of content), and can, to some extent, be spoken of in isolation. We shall look first at the effects of the process of education on individuals, all individuals; and then at the effects collective individual learnings have on social relations.

Education in a capitalist liberal democracy instils a series of beliefs in virtually all the educands who experience it, and it forces people to live an ideology wherein they must accept, and thus are likely to see the 'necessity' of, certain broad principles. Education instils the notion that control of the learning process must be in hands other than the educand's, and must be mediated through a hierarchy of controllers with clear stratified lines of authority. Thus the educand learns that he cannot learn for himself, and that if he does at least the real important learning should occur and does occur through education. Schools, etc., monopolise teaching/learning resources, and it is their certificates that have cash and status value. The educand also learns that the learning process is fragmented socially and technically; socially in that some people have particular functions and status because of their position (professors, teachers, pupils), and particular rights because of their age; and technically in that learning occurs in established classes (according to age, ability, etc.) and follows an institutionalised timetable regardless of teachers' and learners' interests or motivation. The seven-year-old who says, and many do, 'I can do running writing but I'm not allowed to till next year' has internalised all these things. The educand also learns that motivation and reward do not generally stem from intrinsic satisfaction in the learning process, but rather from extrinsic factors like marks, grades, certificates and approval. Recent studies of arts students in universities show that even there the notion of learning for personal satisfaction or the 'joy of learning' is largely a myth: students begrudgingly do whatever someone else requires of them if it counts towards a grade, and look forward to the day they 'get out', when they can follow their own interests.[24] Educands also learn that rewards are distributed unequally, and almost always to individuals, and that, as educands, they are in a situation based on competition rather than co-operation with others. For many, most, this is pointless competition. A child, through diligent study, might move from twentieth to fifteenth in class, but knows he can never be top. Many may succeed at one level but fail at, or do not attempt, the next level. Thus, while competition is the prevailing ethos, and while there are fewer and fewer places the higher one goes, most educands (and the majority leave on reaching the minimal legal leaving age, or on taking the lowest possible certificate) are consigned to failure, and thus see themselves as deserving only of the crumbs after others have taken the cake. Educands also learn the value of punctuality and continued attendance. Breaches of the former are punished, as are breaches of the latter, and learning outside of the institution is not an acceptable excuse for being absent from the institution.[25] Finally (although not exhaustively), the educand learns that non-learning factors are rewarded. Rule conformity is required, and certain 'good behaviour' or personality traits are rewarded; different ones, as we noted, at different stages of education.

Now, obviously, in keeping away from content we have not told the full story. But what implications arise from the part we have told, the 'socialising' aspect of education, into which virtually any content could be inserted? Well, obviously someone who lives through and internalises

143

this ideology at a time when consciousness is relatively unformed is very well set up to move into the workplace; that is, into the conditions of the capitalist relations of production, where, not coincidentally, the work process is in the hands of others in a stratified hierarchy; the work process is fragmented socially (bosses, foremen, labourers), and technically (division of labour, starting and finishing times); motivation is external to the process (wages rather than job satisfaction); rewards are distributed unequally to individuals; competition (often pointless) rather than co-operation is the norm (i.e. competing for better jobs); and punctuality, continued attendance, rule conformity and appropriate good behaviour are highly rewarded along with job skills.

Clearly, then, the conduct and process of education in a capitalist society corresponds neatly with the conduct and process of the workplace; and so what is learned via the process of education can be carried over directly by and in individuals as part of the ongoing perpetuation of the existing modes of production and social relations. The state makes such education compulsory, and provides massive economic support for it, creating a monopoly, and monitoring it carefully. Education then produces people who either positively accept or are passively resigned to their future given conditions of work and living; for ten years or more they have lived an ideology, and are ready to continue on in a similar one with the same principles. Or to put that a little more technically, education produces a consciousness that is in complete harmony with the consciousness determined and required by social existence (education, being a lived-ideology is, of course, part of that social existence). Thus education, in process, is essentially and decidedly political; and this would hold in all types of societies. In a capitalist society education simply produces a particular consciousness; one suited to the capitalist mode of production. Thus Toffler:[26]

> Mass education was the ingenious machine constructed by industrialism to produce the kind of adults it needed. The problem was inordinately complex. How to pre-adapt children for a new world – a world of repetitive indoor toil, smoke, noise, machines, crowded living conditions, collective discipline, a world in which time was to be regulated not by the cycle of sun and moon but by the factory whistle and the clock.
>
> The solution was an educational system that, in its very structure, simulated this new world . . . The most criticized features of education today – the regimentation, lack of individualization, the rigid systems of seating, grouping, grading and marking, the authoritarian role of the teacher – are precisely those that made mass public education so effective an instrument of adaptation for its place and time . . .

The school-child did not simply learn facts that he could use later on: he lived as well as learned, a way of life modelled after the one he would lead in the future.

The argument being developed here has not quite been completed, but before doing this let us turn to our second aspect: the effect that the process of education has, in a broad sense, on social relations.

It is hardly likely that anyone, even the staunchest liberal defender of education, would argue completely against what has been said above. It would be recognised that there is a *status quo*, and that children have to be, to some extent, socialised, i.e. made ready to take their place in the world as it exists. What might be argued with is the deliberate and one-sided way in which education has been set up as an arch villain. Defenders would probably draw attention to the content of education (which we shall deal with in the next section); but also, the very role of education would be viewed differently. Liberal apologists are quick to point out that universal education gives everyone a chance, an equal chance; that some people are not as smart as others; that some people are not cut out to be neurosurgeons; and that education, in offering equal opportunity, or near-to-equal opportunity, and a liberal curriculum, serves three functions *along with* the obvious and necessary function of maintaining an overall framework of stability. Education also acts as an agent of social *mobility*. Next, it serves as an agent of selection, putting people in their right places (in the best Platonic manner), the most able in the most demanding situations, the less able in situations they can handle. And finally, it raises the quality of life for all, *especially* the less able, to whom it gives literacy and culture. (They might also point to education's effect in combating less desirable forces and agencies in society.) Let us examine the first two of these claims, taken together.

Ever since the beginnings of universal compulsory education there has been the feeling around, at least in some quarters, that the first two claims might be subject to question; but only recently has substantial evidence been brought against them in sufficient quantity and with sufficient force to constitute a really serious challenge. It comes, once more, from the work of Bowles and Gintis: let us here consider just three of their most important findings in this area.[27]

To begin with, Bowles and Gintis demonstrate, via analysis of a huge amount of their own and other researchers' data, that education's role in increasing mental performance does not explain why people with higher education receive higher income. Now this is not to deny that education (years of schooling, etc.) is not closely associated statistically with cognitive attainments; nor is it to deny that the more education one has, the better one's chance of economic success. What Bowles and Gintis challenge, however, and find wanting, is the *causal* relationship between the higher cognitive attainments of the more educated people and their better economic chances. And what Bowles and Gintis demonstrate is that *only a very minor portion* of the substantial association between education and economic success can be accounted for by the school's role in producing or screening cognitive skills. They argue that the mental skills demanded of work are *limited*, and that the possibilities of acquiring these skills on the job are great. Such acquisition is also easy for the well educated who, through their education, have *broad and varied* skills. Thus the skill attainments and skill difference among the educated are of little import; and employers are thus able to choose employees from among the educated on grounds other than skill attainments: race, sex, personality traits, family background, credentials and references appear to be the most significant ones.

The second and third findings have been discussed earlier, and so we shall only note them here. Bowles and Gintis have shown, in brief, that, while increased income is closely related to years of education, it is related only tenuously, if at all, to ability as indicated by IQ; and education really rewards children according to race, sex, personality characteristics and especially social background, and not necessarily according to ability. Finally, Bowles and Gintis have demonstrated that school grades are stongly correlated with students' personalities as well as with their mental abilities; such that education can be seen as rewarding the very same personality characteristics that are sought and rewarded by the job market as it plucks students from different rungs on the educational ladder; in this way education in capitalist societies produces different types of personality and behaviour in different social groups, and so reproduces social stratification and inequality – thus contributing to the maintenance of social and economic stability.

Research findings of this type tend to indicate that education is hardly an agent of social mobility – it is, rather, an agent for social stability. This is a point that is well disguised by the liberal rhetoric, because education can and does bring about minor re-shufflings across social strata; and the rhetoric or ideology, characteristically fastening on to instances that are the case (as part of the general mystifying tactic of jumbling together illusory representations with real representations), constantly and disproportionately calls attention to those people who really do rise from the slums to positions of high prestige in society. And yet even these rare cases themselves can be seen as instances demonstrating education's *stabilising* function; for what really happens is that certain people who are particularly endowed in certain ways are removed from a class whose consciousness they might 'disturb', and are placed in a class in which they are led to believe they 'rightfully' belong. Thus the minor mobilisation can be seen as an integral part of large-scale stabilisation, wherein the submissive consciousness required of the working classes is further ensured by removing from their ranks those people who do not or will not adopt, or appear unlikely to adopt, the required consciousness.

The research findings under consideration also indicate quite strongly that, while education clearly is an agent of social selection, it does not select according to the criteria the liberal apologists highlight. Education selects not so much on ability and effort applied in the process, but more in terms of social and endowed factors brought *to* the process. One final point we can take from Bowles and Gintis's research is that, despite a long theoretic tradition in favour of liberal education reform, and despite continuous sincere propagation of the belief in equal opportunity in and through education, things have hardly changed at all since the beginning of this century with regard to education's role in bringing about mobility and offering equality of opportunity to all. So much then for the first two liberal defences.

We have argued in this section that education is essentially political manipulation, and that in all times and places it would operate as a lived and theoretical ideology whose function would be to stabilise and perpetuate social relations (and ideas pertaining to them) that ensured the continuation of the dominant mode of production in a society. The particularly insidious thing about this in a capitalist liberal democracy is that education must ensure the growth of capitalism, which is against the direct best interests of the non-capitalist classes, and it must give the overt impression of liberalism and democracy. To achieve both ends it must fool most of the people most of the time. Education has to instil the belief in all, workers and capitalists, that the *status quo* is 'given' and immutable; and it must instil the belief in the workers that the *status quo* is not working against their best interests but is serving them rightfully. Further, it has to indicate, again to all, that the *status quo*, and education itself, are democratic and do not favour any particular interests. Thus education in a capitalist liberal democracy is an ideological instrument which promotes false consciousness, promulgates distorted representations of reality, keeps people ignorant of those things that otherwise might enable them to recognise and challenge the actual social relations underlying the *status quo*; and which does all of this, and thus protects the *status quo*, not by repression, not by overt indoctrination, but by disguising what it does behind proclamations of liberalism, enlightenment and equality.

We have spoken so far only of the process of education. But surely (and we remember the third liberal defence not as yet considered) the content of education in a liberal democracy would count against such an interpretation, rather than help sustain and support it? Well, let us see.

Education as political manipulation (ii)

It might appear from the previous discussion that it would hardly matter what content was plugged in to education, provided that it suited society's technical needs, provided that it did not contravene society's moral codes too sharply, and provided that it did not contradict the process of education too much and too openly. This is essentially so, but strangely (and yet it is not really strange), it is the matter of content that probably promotes more educational debate and concern than any other aspect. Now curriculum content is part of what the educand comes to learn and know through education, and that content, along with the means whereby it is transmitted, assists in forming the consciousness of the individual. Thus curriculum content is also a form of intellectual and political manipulation. And curriculum content has two aspects to it: what goes into the curriculum, and what stays out. But before examining this let us consider the status of curriculum content.

Clearly, those who are concerned with formulating educational curricula are all guided by at least one common principle. While they might disagree strongly about the substantive nature of the content they seek to include, they all believe that the particular content they champion is the most important content that can be included in a finite and severely limited curriculum. Thus those who seek to include woodwork and metalwork in a vocationally oriented curriculum are quite like those who wish to see liberal education introducing people to each of the distinguished 'forms of knowledge', in that each sees something to be the most important thing that children, adolescents and even adults should learn. The content of education, then, varying though it might from time to time and place to place, emerges as a carefully selected corpus of what has been deemed, by certain power figures, to be the most important and worthwhile knowledge that educands should have, and should carry with them into adult life.

Identification of the most important and worthwhile knowledge is an issue not to be taken lightly at the practical level, which is largely the reason why there is so much debate and concern with curriculum issues. Educational institutions are severely limited; the whole educational process is temporally finite; and curricula have to pick the eyes out of an infinite body of knowledge. Thus all people concerned with curricula implicitly ask Herbert Spencer's question: 'What knowledge is of most worth?' and answer it on a series of different criterias, and in diff 'nt ways. Spencer wanted education based on and around science, Matthew Arnold plumped for the humanities, M.V.C. Jeffreys envisaged a religious centre for education, F.R. Leavis saw literary criticism as the central discipline, Herbert Read sought education based on art; the Harvard Report (*General Education in a Free Society (1945)*) saw education as developing the logical, relational and imaginative modes of thinking; A.D.C. Peterson goes for the logical, empirical, moral and aesthetic modes of experience; Hirst and Peters champion their particular forms of knowledge or modes of experience; Oakeshott wants education to tune into the voices of practical activity, science, poetry and history; Cassirer and Phenix have their own ideas; and so it goes on.

The variables involved in trying to answer the question, 'What knowledge is of most worth?' and the criteria by which it might be answered are numerous and complex. This explains, in large part, the continuance of, and the increasing importance placed on, curriculum debate and study. It also indicates, for the debators at least and those who encourage them, that the *particular content* of education is what is seen as crucially important.

But the increasing attention paid to curriculum matters, and the continual display of new and modified curricula as panaceas for education's ills, can be seen in another light. Curriculum debate is internal criticism and supportive rhetoric, the results of which can hardly affect the structure and effects of education. It is thus safe criticism, to be supported and encouraged (which explains why its occurrence is not strange). It shows that something is being done; it draws fire away from other areas; and it serves very neatly the function of mystification. It places content at the heart of education, or makes it seem that way, thus hiding the notion that education would serve its same social function, and affect the individuals *qua* individuals who pass through it in very much the same way, provided only that the particular content that was transmitted in the classrooms fell within extremely wide-ranging boundaries and made some concessions to prevailing technology and to prevailing moral codes.

But it is not the curriculum debators alone who see the content included, or to be included, in education as the most worthy, important and valuable of all content; and the key feature of education. Educands come to believe this too. This is not to say that they necessarily become interested in or enjoy or even value the content (in a long-term sense). But they all know, or quickly come to learn, one of two versions of the education game. Getting *that* job requires having a certain certificate, which requires passing certain exams, which requires knowing the particular content on which those exams are based. Or, survival in school with the fewest possible hassles requires concentrating on and attempting (even if in the most desultory manner) to master the curriculum content at hand, and ignoring other things. Thus, for the educand there are two categories of knowledge content: that tiny one that constitutes his curriculum, and that containing all else that is excluded. And if the educand is playing the education game, which he almost certainly is since he is living the education ideology, then the former becomes of

far greater importance than the latter. Thus, regardless of which particular variety of the education game is being played, the student comes
to learn and internalise one thing if nothing else; namely that curriculum
content is the most important and worthwhile knowledge, and the
knowledge that must be, first and above all, attended to, learned and
internalised. If the educand learns not even one iota of the content of
his curricula, he still learns that curricular content is important content,
represents important knowledge, and provides the key to success.
(He even learns these things if he openly thumbs his nose at, and refuses
to co-operate with, the education game.) Thus we find a series of general
attitudes among educands: schoolwork should be finished before hobbies
are attended to; interesting but non-curricular studies are to be taken
on *after* term ends; things that immediately motivate are to be put aside
because of forthcoming exams; and so on. And as mentioned earlier,
the content of education, packaged as it is especially with regard to
time units, leaves little space or time for following up other areas of
knowledge (or for examining and questioning education itself). Thus
education not only brands its own content as the most important, but
it also leaves little opportunity for educands to follow up external content, if they ever feel the need or desire to. One of the clearest manifes-
tations of this is seen in undergraduate university students who, although
supposedly carrying out research and undertaking a free enquiry into
truth, tend to stick religiously to set texts and read only from within
their prescribed reading lists.

Given that the educand learns at least one thing, namely that curriculum content is the most important content, let us examine what
follows from this, quite independently from considering any particular
content.

The first thing to note is something we have already drawn attention
to in a slightly different context. The educand has no control, or no real
control, over his course content. He might be able, in places, to choose
between courses, or to assist in formulating the curriculum, but by and
large the curriculum is decided *for* him. This is the second thing he
learns about content. And having accepted and assimilated this state of
affairs, as he must, the educand immediately finds himself placed in a
rather passive relationship to knowledge, trying to assimilate what
others think he should. Added to this he finds knowledge tied up in
little parcels for him, in two ways. First, the structure of the educational
institution demands set class times, yearly programmes and so on; and
so the educand pursues knowledge according to timetable demands
(regardless of interests and motivation), and according to courses (not
being able to do certain things till next year, and so on). Thus he learns
that others determine not only what he shall learn, but also when he
shall learn it, in what order, and in accordance with what groupings.

Second, the knowledge is almost always tied up in *subject* parcels with fairly strict parameters. Thus the educand learns that knowledge is fragmented; he learns what counts as mathematics or history or sociology; and he learns appropriate methodologies for approaching these individual subjects, and what is irrelevant in so doing. Yet in different institutions, especially universities, these parcels might be categorised quite differently. The educand is thus often led, on two counts, to confuse institutional demands with intellectual and epistemological ones.

This whole issue (the control of the 'what' and 'when' of learning) leads to a particular general intellectual attitude in the educand. He gains a passive approach to learning, and comes to expect to be provided with information to be learnt. He comes to develop a basic mistrust of his own judgment of what's worth knowing, learning (and doing), and when it is done well; and he comes to look upon the educator as the necessary mediator between himself, the world and standards. It follows from that that a heavy official-educator-orientation develops, whereby the educand looks to the educator for approval, and does not hold the opinions of others to be as worthwhile or important as the educator's – thus there is little horizontal learning or sharing of information in educational institutions (and when it does occur it is often called 'cheating' – even 'plagiarism' at higher levels). Students tend not to be concerned with peer opinion, knowing full well that it is the marker's opinion (the official educator) that really counts – even if he is not intellectually respected. And it also follows quite often that the educand forsakes his own ideas, opinions and knowledge (perhaps temporarily) in order to ensure approval from his educator by giving him what *he* wants, or what it is though that he wants. Following down this line we also come to see that the educand develops a consumerist view of learning and knowledge, and a wage-labour approach to gaining knowledge. Things not on the course are not worth knowing, things not on the exam are not worth learning, and eventually, learning might be undertaken only for the sake of extrinsic rewards, like grades, or not incurring the teacher's displeasure.

Much of what has been mentioned above has been covered by Freire in his identification of the 'banking concept' of education, where the passive student becomes a depository for storing bits of knowledge that he might then withdraw and make use of in later life.[28] But the general points also have a particular relevance to our overall thesis. Given what has been said, it is clear that the educand is likely to view knowledge as something that is to be gained or assimilated, in the sense that it exists essentially outside of himself and somehow has to become internalised.[29] He is thus not likely to see that knowledge can be viewed as a product of human labour power; nor, through being kept in a passive relationship to learning, is he likely to view himself as a producer of knowledge. The best he might hope for is to become the subject or 'possessor' of information that others have thought worth handing on (and the more he possesses the better, as far as his grades go); but he is unlikely to recognise his potential for acting on the world through theoretic labour and the production of knowledge, which itself can be a prelude to other forms of labour and action. Thus in his day-to-day schooling the educand both experiences a comparatively degenerative research programme concerned with knowledge, and comes to adopt a 'sponge' mentality wherein his capacity and propensity to labour and act, are nullified.[30]

The overall effect of the general issue we have been discussing is well summed up by George Molnar:[31]

> The worst influence school has is not on the excluded or the truants, but on those who stay on for at least the compulsory ten years. The bulk of these young persons emerge from their experience *dispirited*, grossly lacking in intellectual self-confidence which only some of them manage to re-acquire later in life at great effort, diminished in articulateness, stultified in imagination, gullible vis-a-vis authority figures, always undervaluing their own capabilities, and ready to express their accumulated intellectual frustrations in some compensatory and irrational way. The typical fifteen year-old school-leaver is turned off inquiry; he is a philistine, an enemy of the high culture of his society, and, saddest of all, a person robbed of any ability to see himself as the source of intellectual creativeness.

It is interesting to compare that with two other statements. The first is a century old, and comes from Matthew Arnold:[32]

> Knowledge and truth, in the full sense of the words, are not attainable by the great mass of the human race at all. The great mass of the human race have to be softened and humanised through their hearts and imagination, before any soil can be found in them where knowledge may strike living roots.

But Arnold at least had faith in culture and education, 'which saves the future, as one may hope, from being vulgarised, even if it cannot save the present'.[33] The second statement is contemporaneous with Molnar's, and looks at the situation after four decades of the universal compulsory education which Arnold pinned so much faith in. R.S. Peters says:[34]

> The majority of men are geared to consumption and see the value of anything in terms of immediate pleasure or as related instrumentally to the satisfaction of their wants as consumers. When they ask the question 'What is there in this for me?' or 'Where will this get me?' activities like science and art have no straightforward appeal. For they offer sweat and struggles rather than immediate delight and their instrumentality to the satisfaction of other wants is difficult to discern

It seems as though Peters (a staunch defender of modern liberal education) and Molnar (a severe critic of it) are describing very much the same scene. And it would appear, if their readings are correct, that four decades of compulsory universal education has not produced sweetness and light, softening, humanisation or fertile soil, but rather a generation of satisfied pigs. So much then for the third liberal apology of the previous section, namely that the content of liberal education raises the standard of living and culture for all, but especially for the less able.

Actually this matter can be approached in yet another way; for it can be shown that this particular liberal claim is built on a contradiction; one that is clearly evident in, and that mars the work of, one of today's foremost liberal apologists, the above-quoted R.S. Peters.[35] Peters characterises education, in part, as the disinterested pursuit of worthwhile curriculum activities. Schools, he then says, are essentially concerned with education, i.e. with the production of educated people. These people, in turn, would lead desirable forms of life as exhibited in their conduct, judgments, commitments and feelings; they would understand principles; their knowledge would be broad and not harnessed purely to utilitarian or vocational purposes; and they would have a concern for standards, and a cognitively transforming view of the world.

But if this were to come about it would cause tremendous problems; for, as we have already noted, Peters admits that in a modern industrial democratic society '*vast numbers*' of people have to be trained to undertake the menial and instrumental tasks performed by slaves and metics in ancient Athens. Now Peters seems to think, given good schools, that such people could be educated as well as trained. He also gives us examples where well-trained cooks, carpenters and glass-blowers can function as educated men while they appear to be doing what could also be done purely instrumentally. However, he fails to consider the wharf labourer, the forklift driver, the person on the production line at the biscuit factory or at General Motors, the barmaid, the cleaning lady, the shop assistant, the bus conductor, the night carter, the dustman, or the street sweeper. They have very difficult jobs to transform cognitively, to see intrinsic worth in, and to take much pleasure from doing well, with skill, delicacy and an understanding of principles. What's more, and what's more important, they are tasks that no educated person would undertake, or would undertake for very long. Peters, in talking about people being attracted to things of comparable quality, says:[36]

> A mathematician might find himself drawn more to music and philosophy. But *it would be odd if, in his right mind, he took up sweeping the streets*, unless there was some special explanation or background for sweeping, e.g. he was doing it as emotional release or to the glory of God.

It certainly *would* be odd if an educated man, in his right mind, took up sweeping the streets! And this notion underpins everything Peters says about the educated man: a person, being educated, goes for certain sorts of activities which can be pursued in certain sorts of ways.

It follows from this that if we want people to spend large proportions of their lifetimes going for other sorts of activities (mindless menial tasks like sweeping the streets) in other sorts of ways (instrumentally for financial gain), then we should be very careful *not* to educate them. If a society requires vast numbers to undertake instrumental and menial tasks, then it is in the interests of that society to ensure that vast numbers remain uneducated, at least in Peters's sense of the term. What then of initiation into worthwhile curriculum activities? Clearly, if education pursued the practice of initiating children into such activities, the real hope would be for a very low success rate. And the low success rate could, of course, be explained away on many grounds within the supportive rhetoric - poorly trained teachers, lack of funds, not enough research, etc. But it could also be explained by reference to the contradictory aspects that determine the character and nature of education. On the one hand, there are fine ideals continually expressed by people who would sincerely and seriously wish to see those ideals manifested in schools and other institutions. On the other hand, there is the capitalist society which requires vast numbers of people to undertake mindless menial instrumental tasks (and to remain unaware of, and powerless to criticise, their real relations in and to the world). Education, as an instrument of this society, is thus powerless to practise what it preaches, for it is characterised by the contradiction that it cannot produce the products it theoretically desires and ostensibly strives for within the society that it is charged with reproducing. This is not to deny or belittle the efforts and ideals of countless thousands of teachers who strive to produce liberally educated people; it is merely to note that their failures result not only from deficiencies within the system, but also from a contradiction within the larger system - no capitalist liberal democracy wants too many liberally educated people about.

What has been said so far in this section, in examining the issue of content but without touching on specific content, reinforces our earlier point that, in education, process and content are largely inextricable. Some of the things that have been said about content would apply to education in virtually any social system; whereas those that could be pointed out as being characteristic of education in capitalist liberal democracies would largely call out some of the same conclusions that were highlighted in our discussion of the process of education. There might be point, however, in indulging in near repetition, both for emphasis and in order to highlight the new aspects that will emerge when we turn shortly to consider the substance of curriculum content itself.

In brief, then, curriculum content is always justified by the planners in terms of its particular and specific worth to the individual and the state; and while this might always be sincerely believed in by those people, the rationale given actually mystifies the real function that curriculum content serves; for the rationale emphasises 'education' (however defined), while the function emphasises socialisation into the prevailing culture and ensuring the stability of the society. And the educand learns much from curriculum content before any matter is plugged in. He learns that others decide what's worth learning; that he cannot learn or initiate learning for himself; that what others decide *really is* most important; that knowledge is gained passively and not actively through things like *praxis*; that learning is a secondary feature subordinate to institutional demands; that knowledge cannot be gained or shared laterally but rather comes in a hierarchical form; that the person above in the hierarchy is the one to learn from, to follow and to impress; that there must be an *official* external mediator acting between one's knowledge and the world one knows; and that knowledge and learning are to be undertaken for extrinsic rewards.

An educand who learns all this is ready to take his place in the workforce as a passive, subordinate, unconfident, respectful, deferential character, bowing to institutional demands and dictates from above and persisting in doing what he is doing for the extrinsic rewards it brings. He is, in other words, ready to enter capitalist society.[37] That, as such a person, he stands in marked contrast to the ideal end product espoused by proponents of liberal education should not now surprise us. But it still has to be shown how the content within the process of education, or liberal education, assists in forming *this* character rather than in producing the liberal ideal.

Education as political manipulation (iii)

Education is essentially concerned with the transmission of knowledge; and through education it is hoped that one will come to see the world not just differently, but in a *better* way; for education is always a deliberate attempt to modify the individual for the better, or in terms of what is thought to be desirable.[38]

There is no such thing as value-free education; nor, as we have seen, can there be any such thing as neutral education, although many teachers think they are being neutral, or strive as hard as they can to be neutral leaving aside contentious issues, or always telling 'both sides' of the tory). But education always implies a concept of man, a concept of what is good for man, and a serious desire to do something definite to bring that good into being. The concepts may change from time to time and place to place, but the principle doesn't - if it did we would no longer have education: Illich's deschooled society would somehow have materialised from dream to reality. Education is a deliberate attempt to produce a certain type of person who sees the world in a particular way (although education in any society might want to produce more than one type).[39]

Now education is clearly a revelation, of a sort. It lays before people ideas, knowledge, values, viewpoints, attitudes, skills, beliefs, etc.; and thus, via its content, it provides knowledge of the world. But this is not the marvellous thing it was once taken to be; and to understand this we simply have to recall a few points discussed at length in our first two chapters.

Given the faults in empiricist epistemology, the impossibility of reading a given world and the place of the problematic (mental sets or paradigms will do) in knowledge production, education can hardly be seen as a neutral mediator which puts the given world before the student, so that the student might read it, or have it read for him, and then internalise facts about it. But education *is* a mediator; it is one of that set of things that, we argued, must necessarily mediate between the world and our knowledge of the world. Education, like experience, concepts, prejudice, theory, delusions, mental sets and so on, is one of the filtering mechanisms that operate between us and the world, determining what knowledge we shall gain of the world ('gain', not 'produce') and how we shall gain it. (It could also be likened to a problematic in that it fixes the theoretic raw materials and theoretic tools available for theoretic labour.) But education is a particularly powerful mechanism and mediator.

We argued earlier that in order to investigate something we must have a concept or theory of the object under investigation; that the concept influences our methodology of investigation, and thus that our methodology for gaining knowledge is always theory-laden. Theory becomes the key element in knowing and in ordering knowledge; and when we come to know the world we come to know it in a certain way - we come to know it from the perspective of a particular theoretic stance.

Now education, as defined, encompasses and influences many of the filtration mechanisms previously listed: it forms part of our experience, it gives us concepts, prejudices, theories, methodologies and mental sets - and it legitimates those that it gives us. Thus, overall, it attempts to get people to know the world from the perspective of a particular theoretic stance. And, as with all learning situations, it provides a mental set, saying: 'see the world *this* way'. The real difference between education and other means of revealing or presenting the world to others lies in the degree of formality, systematisation and legitimation. All attempts to influence the consciousness of man are

attempts to get man to see the world in a particular way, with parti
concepts, and from a particular theoretic stance. Education is sim
very effective means; because it has a captive audience serving long sentences; because it employs professional consciousness-manipulators; but
most important because it is legitimated, and thus the knowledge and
consciousness it produces are the ones that are considered to be of most
worth (whether or not one has succeeded in attaining and retaining much
of them).

Education, then (and we can now be seen as concentrating mainly on
the content), should be looked at not in terms of knowledge ideals that
are tied to truth or objectivity (i.e. as an attempted revelation of what
the real world is really like), but rather as a deliberate attempt to get
people to see the world in a particular way, through particular glasses,
or in terms of a particular set. This in itself should be no cause for
alarm; nor should it alone bring down any negative judgments on education. However, if education said 'see the world in this particular way',
and that particular way could be shown to be distortive, misrepresentative of real relations and against the best interests of the educand, then
negative judgments could be made against education.

It should go without saying by now that education in a capitalist
liberal democracy does present a way of seeing the world that is distortive, misrepresentative and against the best interests of the educands.
Education, as a state institution, is controlled by the ruling class, the
capitalists, to serve their interests, and thus it functions against the best
interests of the majority of educands. Education, again as a state institution, serves to disseminate and reinforce the received view or prevailing paradigm, which again is in the interests of the ruling class. But in a
liberal democracy these interests cannot be overtly declared, or enforced
by repression, for those tactics would make it more difficult to convince
people that we still have a liberal democracy. The view, and the interests,
therefore, are disguised; and educands are then given a way of perceiving
the world that disguises, distorts and misrepresents the actual relations
that are occurring. The educand comes to perceive the world from a
perspective that indicates that his interests are being served when they
are not. He is, then, being manipulated, and drugged into accepting a
distorted and misrepresentative perception of the world as if it were
reality.

Interestingly, as earlier discussion would have suggested, the particular content of education, given the process, is not as important a factor
in achieving this as might be first thought. Two particularly important
points should be noted here. First, education today need not play its
traditional role in disseminating content, for we are living in the first
historical age wherein an educand can get almost all of the content of
his 'school learning' outside of school, much of it more effectively and

157

efficiently elsewhere. It is also the first historical age (although a later stage of it) wherein education has been universal and compulsory. This points us towards an interesting internal contradiction. Why, at this particular point of time, is an educand required and compelled to get this content, or even to get it again, within educational institutions? (Even at traditional universities attendance on campus is allegedly compulsory.) The supportive rhetoric could, of course, account for this in terms of expert teachers, graded curricula, properly structured learning situations and so on; but there is another possible explanation. Could it be that what is *really* important is the educand's physical presence within the institution, rather than his learning of curriculum content there? Full-time obligatory attendance not only keeps the educand away from other experiences, but it also immerses him in the education experience wherein he comes to learn all those things previously listed that are related only contingently to curriculum content. It would seem feasible to suggest, given the contradiction we have noted, that education is concerned primarily with, and could be characterised by, submitting its charges to a *process*, and that *within* this process the learning of specific curriculum content (which could be learnt elsewhere) is at least of secondary concern.

The second important point to note is that the lack of blatantly obvious connections between the actual content of education and the effects of education is a mystifying factor built into education to disguise what education does. If a defender of the system asked us to point out which parts of the content were distortive and misrepresentative, we would have a hard time answering him; and yet his question seems a legitimate one, for it would surely appear that if education is going to distort and misrepresent it would do so through its substantive content. That, however, provides a beautiful instance of the way that education influences the manner by which education will tend to be investigated – the stress on content within education leads the educated to take content as the focus for investigating the effects of education. But even though our previous discussion has indicated that distortions and misrepresentations can lie and occur elsewhere (and mainly elsewhere, as with the individual seeing himself as an assimilator rather than producer of knowledge) answers can still be given in terms of content; and in providing them I shall consider four areas: inter-ideological support, content as ideology, benign content, and exclusion. I shall examine each of these in turn, but none in any great detail.

As indicated earlier, people live in a matrix or an ensemble of ideologies, the theory and practice of which support one another, and all of which support and reinforce the dominant received view of a particular society. Thus when education offers content that supports kindred ideology it is assisting the overall ideological representation (or misrepresentation) that arises out of the totality of the existing social conditions. For instance, lessons on the family (a topic on most social sciences curricula) support the family ideology; lessons on religion (and religious instruction) support the church and religion ideology; lessons on applying for jobs, and how to approach job interviews, support the work ideology; and so on. Such content becomes an integral part of seeing the world in a certain way; but if that way is distortive, and if the distortion is disguised, then the distortion in the particular content will hardly be obvious. It will not, and does not, present itself as what it is; or, to pick up an earlier analogy, it alters perception so that it is not (and cannot?) be seen for what it is.

Content that is clearly ideological is much easier to pick out, but it appears as though less and less of it is now being left in an immediately obvious form. Schoolchildren rarely assemble each morning to pledge loyalty to their God and country these days; and some of the worst of sexist, racist and imperialist overtones have been removed from curricula. But one still does not have to look far to see just how much remains, and at times how insidiously ideological notions are built into curricula. Numerous recent studies have pointed out sexism and racism in virtually every imaginable curriculum, even science (Madame Curie, in one version, is pictured helping her husband discover radium). A quick jaunt through any mathematics curriculum will pick up the emphasis on interest, profit, discounts and investment; schools still teach neoclassical economics, and even universities have a hard time getting political economy courses on their books; and history which teaches that Hadrian built the Roman wall in Britain, that Columbus discovered America, that Captain Cook is to be praised for taking possession of Australia in the name of George III, that *our* soldiers were heroes fighting for freedom and that generals win battles is reinforcing a series of distorted views of the world. So too is history and social science that views imperialism and exploitation as the spreading of Western culture and religion among the underdeveloped barbarians and heathens of the world. Even more obvious is the way curricula emphasise, and initiate children into, particular social, political and moral theories and viewpoints, and, where it is allowed, into specific religious outlooks and beliefs as well. And even the teaching of something as apparently neutral as mathematics, and possibly science, can be seen as serving particular and specific ideological purposes when mathematics is presented as a model of rationality, and when a particular 'scientific method' is stressed as being both 'scientific' and as the best (and correct) way of gathering data.[40] A child emerging from school believing that men are smarter and better than women and that whites are smarter and better than blacks (after all, how many female, or black, scientists, mathematicians, explorers, artists, generals, war heroes, state leaders, etc., did the child learn about in school?); that the

159

whites, having colonised the world, *rightly* colonised the world; that profit is an important goal; that the history of the world is forged by great men (name one of Wellington's troops!); that our side was right in the war; that a vote every three years indicates democracy; that politicians and pioneers are good men; that one must work hard at one's job; that empiricism is the heart of 'scientific method', and that one must follow the religious and moral code of one's society, and be rational, in a particular way, in all things has learned a very great deal indeed.

Much of the content that the educand is faced with, however, is ideologically benign, or near enough so to be taken as such. Its inclusion in curricula is justified on many positive grounds as being essential for a liberal education, and it is often pointed to as demonstrating the non-ideological and non-distortive nature of education – but it too can be looked at in another way. If we accept that certain content is not serving any direct distortive ideological purpose (as content) there are three possibilities open to us: the content may be serving noble liberal aims like establishing critical powers, introducing the educand to one of the many mansions of his heritage and so on; it might be thoroughly unimportant, and simply be acting as coal for the process fire; or it might harmlessly be taking up space in order to exclude other things. It is, of course, impossible to arbitrate on this issue without taking substantive example after substantive example and putting each to thorough scrutiny; and there is, of course, neither time nor space to do this here. It should be noted, though, that those who see schools as essentially existing to teach children to tolerate boredom would go for the second alternative; and anyone looking at the utterly benign nature of certain curricula might be inclined to agree with them. Also, when it is recognised that the vast majority of people in liberal democracies complete their education early in the piece, either as soon as they can legally quit or on the taking of their first certificate, we see that most don't get much of a liberal education at all. The ideals of liberal education sound fine when followed through to higher levels; but for the child who leaves school at fifteen to work in a factory, which is the fate of most children, what really was the point of sitting through those hundreds of hours of index laws and trigonometrical ratios, learning the periodic table of the elements, studying the grasslands of Africa and the tundras of the north, and memorising the main imports and exports of Argentina and Portugal? Perhaps these things could contribute to a liberal education *but also* be utterly benign (simply allowing the process to go on), and thus serve both aspects of the contradiction within liberal education; namely that, regardless of outspoken ideals, or even ideals as practised by educators, schools must produce vast numbers of compliant and uneducated people if capitalist society is to be perpetuated and survive in the form desired by the ruling class.

The final issue to be considered under the heading of content is that of exclusion. Educational institutions, we recall, are always running up against the demands of time, and from the infinite body of content available they can choose and include only a small part. Thus if there must be a choice between X and Y, and X is included, then educands will be kept ignorant of Y.

Now clearly, while education is an organ of the state and the ruling groups in a society, and while it serves to perpetuate and protect the interests of those groups, it will not include as content anything that would seriously work against the vested interests of those providing education. Thus the content of education is partly, but necessarily, established by the process of censorship. Deliberate exclusions, or bodies of censored material, are of course hard to find; for any education system that boasted liberal democratic aims like free enquiry, open discussion and the pursuit of truth wherever it may lead would not want also to display a box of censored material which must not be enquired into or pursued. And again, the absence of such a box bolsters the liberal apologist's case, and makes ours even harder to clinch. Once more, it would take an enormous amount of empirical work to pin a case for deliberate exclusion,[41] and again it is work we will not undertake here. But it could be noted that all areas of learning have their orthodoxies or prevailing paradigms which accommodate certain types of studies and exclude others. If one is in a neoclassical school of economics political economy will not be studied; in a stimulus–response behaviour-modification school of psychology there will be no place for the psychoanalysts and humanistic psychologists; in a school of 'ordinary language' philosophy metaphysics will be out; and so on. This much is known. What is also known is that it is those in power, represented as they are through professors, school boards, principals and curriculum departments, who decide what goes in and what stays out. And in deciding what stays out they thus determine certain things that people shall be kept ignorant of. It would not be surprising, then, to find little or nothing in curricula that would allow or assist people to discover the real nature of relations in society or the underlying aspects of the social structure (which even the curriculum planners are probably unaware of). Education, then, promotes a pernicious type of ignorance rather than overcomes ignorance. And it can continue to do this in the neatest of covert ways: material can always be left out, either on 'neutral' epistemological grounds (although they are neither necessary nor sufficient for the task), or because of expediency, provided one can continually keep coming up with material that *must go in*, and with good reasons why that material must go in. Thus, in these times of knowledge explosions it is an excellent tactic to set up curriculum boards consisting of liberals, with a few vocationally oriented ones among them, and let them fight it out for their particular preferences. They will, for all their differences, engage in supportive rhetoric, remain strictly within the prevailing paradigm, and provide an excellent example of theoretical ideology supporting practice. And there will be no possibility of any radical reformulation of educational content emerging.

One final thing needs to be said about exclusion of content. Content that is excluded from curricula is excluded from much else as well. When we recall that education establishes the importance of its own offerings, and by being compulsory forces people to live in its own ideology and so keeps them away from other experiences, two things emerge clearly. First, non-curricular content becomes branded as inferior, less important and not worth knowing. And second, non-curricular content is hard to get at, even if anyone seriously engaged in and with education wanted to get at it: there is little, if any, time available; and since education monopolises resources, the content itself might not be available either. Publishers tend not to publish books that are not on courses; libraries and bookshops order according to courses and demand (which is determined by those *running* courses); and so on. Thus education, through its curricula, provides a much more pervasive notion of 'what knowledge is of most worth' than appears on the surface; and so again emerges as a powerful agent of political manipulation.

And yet there is still a strange paradox surrounding the content of education. Education appears to be primarily concerned with the transmission of content. Educational achievements are measured, or are said to be measured, in terms of content mastery – certificates are awarded on the grounds of various assessments, almost all of which assess the degree to which one has learned and mastered curriculum content. But, as has been shown earlier, content, especially at the school level, is hardly relevant to the jobs that certificates buy, and employers don't necessarily choose employees on the grounds of their mastery of school content. And, as has also been shown, the content of education, and education itself, has hardly produced, at least to this point in time, a race of people meeting and living up to the ideals of the liberally educated person (and if education is to perpetuate the existing social relations under capitalism it is essential that it doesn't produce too many of these people).

Finally, we might add that people forget the content they gained via education, or at least large parts of it. I wonder how many people reading this page still know who discovered the Castlereagh River, how to differentiate an equation, what the halogens are, what a savanna is, where the Boro live, and so on; despite the tremendous efforts that they, and their teachers, put in *at the time* to get that knowledge imprinted. More to the point, how many of those who dropped out at fifteen, and are not likely to be reading this work, still remember these things? It would appear that, while the major role of education is *said* to be concerned with transmission of content, and while most effort goes into teaching and learning specific content, the content, in the long run, is unimportant and expendable. If this is so, then we have hit on a large internal contradiction, partially hinted at earlier, which could assist in revealing, understanding and defining the real role of education in a capitalist liberal democracy. Education does not exist to produce liberally educated people (even though its spokesmen and apologists claim it is doing this); it does not provide direct and relevant occupational skills (except in very specific cases); and it appears to put its stress on those aspects of its content that most people either forget or fail to learn in the first place. The stress on content reinforces the ideology of 'education', but also mystifies education's real purpose and nature: that is, to induct people into a set of ongoing social relations; to legitimate these relations and present them as necessary and given; to get people to perceive the world in a certain distorted way whereby the real existing relations are disguised; and to keep people ignorant of what is really going on and how it works against their best interests.

Conclusion

Education, as an institution, works in the way all institutions do. It atrophies the capacity of people to think of alternatives. Thus, paradoxically, while education is supported by a rhetoric that talks of developing critical thought, and while education does transmit critical methodologies of a sort, it also stops people thinking of, devising and legitimating alternative learning possibilities. Just as the family produces people suited to family life and unable to think of alternatives, so too does education produce schooled people good for school, and unable to envisage alternatives. Education, like other lived-ideologies, perpetuates itself, and continually establishes the claim and 'right' to its own sole legitimacy over knowledge and learning. As an institution it does what Illich suggests all institutions do: it becomes an instrument of social control by manipulating the content of man's imagination. For Illich:[42]

> The school system today performs the threefold function common to powerful churches throughout history. It is simultaneously the repository of society's myth, the institutionalization of that myth's contradictions, and the locus of the ritual which reproduces and veils the disparities between myth and reality.

But education is a particularly influential manipulator of imagination and consciousness, for this is its specific, deliberate, outspoken purpose and function. Like all lived and theoretical ideologies, but in a far more effective and persuasive way than any other, education 'dissolves the normative dimension of human experience into the existential order of things. "What ought to be" is reduced to the acceptance of "what is".'[43]

Education, by serving the ruling interests in a class society, and by doing this in a disguised way, actually gives people a distorted view of the world, and offers a misrepresentation of reality. Through its process, its content and its political power in bestowing social rewards, it presents a conceptual scheme and methodologies – ways of perceiving the world – that largely ensure that people will take their place in the existing world as well-fitting members of the *status quo*, without questioning the *status quo* or perceiving the real relations on which it is built. Education achieves this particularly well by forcing all people to live through its ideology for a long period of time, by matching this lived ideology so well with the lived ideology of the workplace, by promoting theoretic ideology designed to legitimate and stabilise the *status quo*, by establishing its own offerings as the only legitimate ones, and by atrophying one's capacity to imagine and establish alternatives.

Education is not a revelation of truth, an activity touched with visions of greatness, an initiation of barbarians into the citadel of knowledge or a means of getting to know oneself and the world and the best that has been thought and said in the world; it is not the gaining of virtue, the liberation of the mind from ignorance or the creation of free men.[44] Education is a perception-altering drug: it is a deliberate, systematic process *that aims to get people to perceive the world in a certain way*, by providing certain offerings and by keeping people ignorant of other possibilities. In a class society, the 'certain way' in question will favour the ruling class. In a liberal democracy this must be kept hidden and disguised. Education, then, in a capitalist liberal democracy is a deliberate systematic process that aims to get people to perceive the world in a certain way that favours the ruling class, while at the same time having them believe that they are seeing the world 'objectively', seeing it as it really is, in the best, and perhaps the only, way that it can be seen. Education promotes a distorted and illusory view of reality in the name of enquiring into truth. And since it does this in a deliberate and systematic way, its offerings and products can properly be characterised as a structured misrepresentation of reality; a misrepresentation that educands subsequently become bearers of.

Chapter 6

Possibilities

Introduction

In our previous chapter we argued only one thing: that education in a capitalist liberal democracy instils in people a distorted misrepresentation of the world. We did not mean to suggest that this process was unique to capitalist liberal democracies (although some particular features *are*), or that education in capitalist liberal democracies lay towards the negative pole on some continuum of distortiveness and misrepresentation. Education provided by some totalitarian states, such as that initiated by Hitler, and education in certain primitive tribes, based as it is on myth and superstition, would be distortive and misrepresentative too, although in somewhat different ways (the latter would be unlikely to be deliberately exploitative in a class-serving manner). There would be little to be gained, however, in congratulating ourselves in that our education is 'better' than theirs; but comparative studies are not to our point - our only point is that *we* give our children a distorted and misrepresentative way of perceiving and knowing the world; a structured misrepresentation of reality, which favours one section of society and works against the interests of other sections, and yet does not seem to be that way.

Two questions arise from this. First, ought we do anything about it; and second, can we do anything about it?

The obligation to change

Most people in today's capitalist liberal democracies are reasonably well off materially, and by and large they are happy. So why not simply leave them happy? Why trade their satisfaction for dissatisfaction; their contentment for discontent; and their blissful ignorance for disturbing

165

knowledge? This is an argument commonly heard, and it is a difficult one to counter. As suggested in the previous chapter, I don't think the argument can be countered successfully on metaphysical or ontological lines, or even on utilitarian lines concerned with calculi of pleasures. There is really only one thing that can count against it: the more ignorant one is, and the more satisfied one is in one's ignorance, the more easily one can be exploited by those less ignorant. This in itself is sufficient argument for raising the consciousness of those 'satisfied pigs' in situations where exploitation may arise, no matter how happy they are; unless, of course, exploitation of people by other people could itself be justified, which I hardly think possible. Now at this point two crucial matters must be faced. First, as we have already noted, exploitation and deception are *necessary* features of the social relations that exist under capitalism; and so under such a system the 'satisfied pig' *is* being exploited and deceived, regardless of his material comforts and happiness. In Jean-Paul Marat's words in the play by Peter Weiss:

> Even if there's no poverty to be seen
> because the poverty's been hidden
> even if you ever got more wages and could afford to buy
> more of those new and useless goods
> which these new industries foist on you
> and even if it seems to you that you never had so much
> that is only the slogan of those
> who still have much more than you.[1]

The second thing to recognise is that the biblical admonition that 'he who increaseth knowledge increaseth sorrow' is not necessarily correct: the choice is not always between blissful ignorance and sorrow; and it does not necessarily follow that those who gain more knowledge, or undistorted knowledge, or who learn how to produce knowledge, must suffer for it. We can conclude then, that in an exploitative and deceptive situation (given that exploitation is bad) there is a *moral* obligation to do away with those aspects that aid exploitation: one such means would be to increase the knowledge, consciousness or awareness of the exploited; and this itself need not necessarily doom them to unhappiness.

Increasing knowledge, consciousness and awareness, however (as we recall from our first two chapters), is not merely a matter of reading more of the world, or adding to our bag of truths or facts about the world. The key lies rather in replacing, or adding to, research programmes, so that the world comes to be perceived, interpreted and known from the perspective of progressive, and more progressive, research programmes. Now, is there any obligation to do this, other than what is involved in decreasing and overcoming deception and exploitation?

Again I think metaphysics, ontology and even epistemology let us down here in that they cannot provide sound reasons or justifications as to why we ought to seek more, and more progressive, knowledge of the world. Replacing static or degenerative programmes with progressive programmes is, of course, a pre-condition of a certain sort of advancement or progress, but seeking that sort of advancement and progress in itself cannot, I think, be cogently argued for or justified. It seems to be more a matter of faith - a faith certainly not shared by all peoples and all cultures in the world. But if this faith is grounded in some programme concerned with general human wellbeing, like raising the quality of life for all, then it too takes on *moral* overtones; and even though what it advocates in substance might be badly misplaced,[2] its motives can be supported by argument and be shown to be ethically viable. Some people base their life's work around such motives and become teachers and/or educators; seeing it as their (moral) obligation to advance learning for the general wellbeing of others.

So the answer to the first question - Ought we do anything about the state of affairs brought about by education in a capitalist liberal democracy? - has been answered as well as it might be: if we recognise the obligation to decrease and eliminate exploitation among people, and/or if we recognise the obligation to expose deception and lead others to perceive the world from the perspective of more progressive and less distortive research programmes, and/or if we believe it is in everybody's interests to promote the advancement of learning in a particular way, then we ought to do something, and the obligation in each case is a moral one. And there is, of course, much that needs to be done. There is even more that needs to be done in those situations where the exploited and deceived are neither happy nor in a state of material satisfaction; a situation that applies not just to capitalist-dominated areas of the underdeveloped Third World, but also to significant sectors of advanced Western capitalist societies.

The question remains now as to whether we can do anything, and if so, how? This question is more complex than may appear at first glance, and will be tackled on a number of fronts.

Must one's programme provide the answers?

We have indicated previously that discourse and interpretations called out by a theory can be judged negatively only from the perspective of another theory or research programme that is (or appears to be) more progressive than the original theory. We have also suggested that argument within a particular programme or paradigm (internal criticism) is more suited to refining that paradigm than it is to bringing about critical judgments with regard to that programme or paradigm itself. It is necessary now to indicate two things; first, that criticism internal to a paradigm need not be, and is not always, entirely worthless; and second, that judgments from outside a paradigm can be critically preferable without necessarily coming up with 'the answers'. Let us illustrate these points by means of a practical example.

Imagine that a person P confronts the Minister for Public Works with large-scale systematic evidence suggesting that the Sydney Harbour Bridge will fall down in a very short space of time. The Minister, and his experts, study the report and find it *compelling*. Now it would be the height of stupidity for the Minister to tell our person to go away and design a better bridge, before anyone does anything about it. It would be just as absurd for P to withhold his evidence because he himself cannot design bridges. Clearly, then, criticism can be valid and worthwhile, even though the critic *himself* can come up with nothing better to put in the place of what he is criticising. The scientists who discredited the theory that the extinction of the dinosaurs was brought about by sudden vegetation changes on earth have not come up with a better theory as yet, and this does not detract from their criticism.

Criticism from within a paradigm, if it is compelling, will almost always suggest possible alternatives, replacements, solutions or improvements of a sort. In our example, if P's evidence is compelling it will indicate *why* the bridge is about to fall down, and this in turn will suggest what repairs might be put into action to keep the bridge standing. However, the solutions implied and the repairs undertaken need not necessarily work. P might find the roadway to be cracking: the obvious solution is to prop the roadway up with another pylon; but this in turn might alter the whole moment of forces, cause cracking in other areas, and might still bring the bridge down. But regardless of whether the solution works or not, the point to note is that P's criticism, being within the prevailing paradigm, can only lead to patchwork within the paradigm, thus refining the paradigm; and the criticism will be worthwhile only if that patchwork holds, and if what it holds is worth holding up (but P, of course, does not have to indicate the type of patchwork necessary to do the job). Criticism of this sort can thus be valuable when it leads to repairs; it is limited and counter-productive, however, when it leads to repairs of things that would be better pulled down; and coming from within a paradigm it necessarily tends towards and thinks in terms of repair. At this point let us now introduce M, who is outside the paradigm: he sees that P is right, but he also sees that, regardless of whatever patchwork is undertaken, there will still be holes left when all the putty is used up, and that a bridge in this particular position simply cannot last for more than fifty years. His advice is to pull the bridge down before somebody gets hurt.

Now M, even more than P, is open to the foolish charge of negative or destructive criticism: knocking things down without putting anything in their place. And M will probably find it far more difficult to have his criticism recognised, both because he is working from outside the paradigm and because he is working against all those who have a vested interest in the bridge being, and remaining, where it is. But given the circumstances of our example, and given that both P and M are right, M's judgment is clearly critically preferable, although M does not have a 'constructive' answer.

At this point N might come along with a plan that either indicates how traffic can be moved across the harbour more effectively and efficiently *without* the bridge, or removes the need for traffic to cross the harbour at all. N, in true dialectical fashion, has defined the successful outcome of the situation outside the boundaries of the situation that gave rise to the problem. But N, we might expect, would hardly be listened to until P and M were found to be right: we tend not to burn our bridges while-ever we can still convince ourselves that they are working satisfactorily.

Our education system, by its very nature, produces a lot of reformist P's, and very few M's and N's (who are usually consigned to whistling in the dark) - but the points we are really concerned with, and have shown, are that criticism from within paradigms need not necessarily be worthless (even though it is limited), and that critically preferable judgments can knock down without replacing, and still be critically preferable. Seeing what is wrong does not require knowing what is right.

Consciousness-raising

In this section we shall temporarily put aside talk of knowledge and awareness and instead embrace the term 'consciousness-raising', which has recently been popularised by Freire. The basic notion here is that some people's consciousness has been arrested and fixed at some point, and that others, with raised consciousness of a situation, can step in and help the former to understand the situation properly. Or, to put this just a little differently in the Marxian terms we employed earlier, some people have false consciousness, which can possibly be put right by those whose consciousness is not false. Now, as we also noted earlier, arbitrating as to whether consciousness is true or false is a very tricky matter; and this has led to much criticism of the notion of consciousness-raising. One objection to this notion is put most clearly by Peter L. Berger; and since what he says neatly encapsulates most of the prevailing arguments and issues against 'consciousness-raising' we shall quote him at some length:[3]

Whose consciousness is supposed to be raised, and *who* is supposed to do the raising? The answer is clear wherever the term is used in political rhetoric: It is the consciousness of 'the masses' that must be raised, and it is the 'vanguard' that will do the job. But who are these people? 'The masses' are, of course, whatever sociological category has been assigned the role of the revolutionary proletariat by the ideologists of the putative revolution – industrial workers (in countries where this particular assignment seems plausible), peasants, landless rural laborers, even white-collar 'wage slaves' or students. The 'vanguard' consists of the ideologists – typically intellectuals, who may be defined for our purposes as individuals whose major preoccupation is the production and distribution of theories. Such people have usually gone through a long period of formal education and usually come from the upper midde or upper classes of their societies. It may therefore be said: 'Consciousness raising' is a project of higher-class individuals directed at a lower-class population. Moreover, the consciousness at issue is the consciousness that the lower-class population has of its own situation. Thus a crucial assumption is that lower-class people do not understand their own situation, that they are in need of enlightenment on the matter, and that this service can be provided by selected higher-class individuals.

Concretizing the concept in this way reveals that it is not necessarily linked to the political Left. In the United States, for example, a left-wing ideologist may be convinced that he understands the real interests of the working class much better than most workers do. But a right-wing politician or a middle-of-the-road liberal social worker may be animated by precisely the same conviction in dealing with other clienteles. 'They don't understand what is good for them' is the clue formula for all 'consciousness raising', of whatever ideological or political coloration – and 'we do understand' is the inevitable corollary. Put differently, the concept allocates different cognitive levels to 'them' and to 'us' – and it assigns to 'us' the task of raising 'them' to the higher level.

That is a strange piece, wherein fundamental errors and shrewdly correct judgments are intricately interwoven. It *is*, of course, the consciousness of the masses that is to be raised, and if this job is to be done it will be done by the vanguard. Also: 'They don't understand their situation' or 'They don't understand what is good for them' *is* the clue formula for consciousness-raising. But to reduce the matter to dichotomies like lower class/upper class; little educated/well educated; worker/ theoretician, and to speak of 'cognitive levels', is simplistic to the point of caricature – it is also an excellent example of distortive ideology or supportive rhetoric at work.

Our previous discussion has shown clearly how, in certain political situations, ideology, and education, bring about the conditions whereby people *do not* understand the situation in which they live, nor do they understand what is in their best interests. To so mystify, we argued, was part of the very point of the functioning of ideology, and education, in capitalist societies. Our earlier discussion has also indicated that there can be, and are, good grounds whereby one ideology or set of beliefs can be judged as being a better or worse representation of the world than other ideologies or sets of beliefs. Thus it is possible, both in theory and practice, to make judgments of critical preference among ideologies, and to make those judgments on acceptable and valid criteria. This being the case, it is quite possible to have a vanguard whose consciousness is developed to the extent that it can make such judgments of critical preference; and, given that ideology, and education, serve their purpose only if they influence the vast majority of a society, it would be expected that this vanguard would be small. But it need not come exclusively from the intellectuals, or from the 'higher' classes. One necessary prerequisite for having a 'higher consciousness' or a critically preferable view of the world is not to be immersed in the prevailing paradigm, received view, or dominant ideological matrix of capitalist societies. A second prerequisite is to have a more progressive ideological perspective, research programme or view of the world. Now, just which people are so placed, and how they become so placed, would in all probability be a difficult thing to determine, but a few feelers can still be put out. First, the intellectuals, having been educated more than most, are not good contenders for stepping outside prevailing research programmes (which it is largely their job to make prevail) in order to cast judgments on the ideology they themselves embody, bear and sustain. Second, the 'higher' classes (ruling classes?) are those that have most to gain by perpetuating the *status quo*, and again would be poor candidates for the vanguard. The vanguard, if and when it is to come forward, might contain a few disenchanted 'radical' intellectuals who are either young and/or not wedded to the prevailing paradigmatic way of seeing things;[4] and it might contain a few well-meaning Robert Owens from the ruling class; but it would in all likelihood emerge from the exploited and deceived who somehow, by anti-educational means,[5] were able to discover the real relations and conditions of their existence. It should be hardly necessary to point out that one does not have to be well educated, or be an 'intellectual' in that sense, to be perceptive or intelligent or to have a raised consciousness: actually, not being well educated in the formal sense could be a distinct advantage here.

The anti-educational means spoken of do not, as we shall see, deny the intervention of 'intellectuals' or others as teachers or consciousness-raisers in the first instance, or even on a continuing basis. But then again, the whole notion of 'consciousness-raising' is hardly a matter of intellectual imperialism. Carl Bereiter identifies the problem we are up against here when, in another context, he makes this perceptive appreciation of the modern teacher's role (an appreciation, it might be added, that not too many teachers articulate):[6]

> Teachers have been assigned the task of saving the human race by educating a superior new generation who will rectify the evils created by past generations or at least not succumb to them. But the same humanistic ethos that tells them what qualities the next generation should have also tells them that they have no right to manipulate other people or impose their goals upon them.

This, in its own way, reinforces Berger's notion regarding who has the right (and on what grounds) to tell other people how to live, and what is good for them. But let us take Berger a little further, as he talks about 'defining the situation' very much, to begin with, in the terms we outlined in our first two chapters:[7]

> A crucial question, therefore, is: 'Who does the defining?' Every 'definition of the situation' implies specific theoretical presuppositions, a frame of reference and in the last resort a view of reality. Once a situation has been defined in certain terms a number of practical options are foreclosed. It is a very limited notion of participation to let an elite define a situation in complete disregard of the ways in which this situation is *already defined* by those who live in it - and then to allow the latter a voice in the decisions made on the basis of the preordained definition.

Now Berger would be correct here if it were the case that situations were defined *by those who live in them.* But it was the burden of much of our previous discussion to indicate that, in certain political circumstances, situations are defined *for* those who live in them (largely through the effect that social interests have on theoretic production), and that such definitions disguise the real nature of the situations, to the extent that people simply (to pick up Berger's earlier statement) 'do not understand their own situations'. Part of the disguise and mystification lies, of course, in the implanting of the consciousness that one actually does, freely and actively, define one's own situation, and that one is perfectly well aware of what the realities of the situation are. Berger simply defends and perpetuates such mystification.

Now if it is the case that situations are defined *for* people, and are defined for them against their best interests, then consciousness-raising, that is stepping in and helping people to see the realities of their situation and how it works against their best interests, can not only be defended positively in terms of an obligation to overcome exploitation; it can also be defended against charges of academic or intellectual imperialism, and against charges of merely replacing one form of exploitation and manipulation by another.

The defence, and the justification, cannot of course rest in terms of 'if they do it, so can we': it must start from the recognition of the way in which consciousness is actually formed; for only when this is recognised, and its effects are identified, can we have the possibility of true consciousness-raising, and hope to avoid the dangers of imperialism and/or alternative forms of exploitation. But even then, the operation of consciousness-raising must be guided by very tight criteria. To begin with, the consciousness-raiser (and we shall use 'teacher' now simply for convenience) must be fairly well assured that his research programme or way of seeing the world is more progressive than the one embodied and employed by those whose consciousness is to be raised. If his programme is more progressive it will, by definition, be able to explain the success of the prevailing programme in interpreting the world (and thus why it has been adopted), and it will be able to account for at least some of the anomalies and contradictions that the prevailing programme assimilates, glosses over or cannot account for. The teacher, then, armed with his more progressive programme, should be able to understand the beliefs people have, why they have them, and why those beliefs appear to present a satisfactory picture of the world. This makes available to him his first step, which is simply to get people to see how their consciousness has been formed, and why they believe what they believe. There is nothing, at this stage, that in any way resembles intellectual manipulation in the sense of exchanging one set of beliefs for another.

The next step, however, is far trickier. There would be little point in getting people to see how their consciousness was formed, and if necessary making them aware that their consciousness was false and distorted, unless the intention was to do something about it. And this is where the problems arise for the teacher; for here he faces the danger of simply saying: 'See the world *my* way' - which is precisely what the dictators, the ideologues and the educators say. Where then do the differences between education and consciousness-raising lie? Basically they lie in the two crucial areas of content and method. As far as content goes, consciousness-raising must begin with the actual situation of the people as it is lived and experienced, with its problems, its troubles, its rationalisations and so on. The teacher must aim to make people aware of why the old programme that they have assimilated does not account for the real lived situation well enough, mainly by concentrating on anomalies and contradictions; and given success there he can then present his programme as a better weapon for accounting for all the situation's facets. If it accounts for everything the old programme accounted for, and more, and if it accounts for anomalies between the lived situation and the old programme, it should emerge as a better programme. So what the teacher is handing on is a new critical methodology which can be applied to the content of lived experience. Rather than saying 'See the world my way', he is saying 'Look at *your* world in a different way' – methodology is being stressed, and the *content* is being drawn from lived experience. It is not, like educational curriculum content, being imposed on lived experience by others; nor is it being imposed in spite of lived experience. The teacher is not defining the situation *for* people; having helped expose the weaknesses of the old, imposed definition, he is supplying a methodology whereby people might define their own situation *for themselves* in a better way.

The second difference concerns the actual method of consciousness-raising. We remember from our discussion of education that content and process cannot be isolated from each other, and that process has a great deal to do with the forming of consciousness: if this is so then conciousness could hardly be raised by using the same processes that were employed to instil and form the existing consciousness. Thus the teacher, in saying 'Look at your world in a different way', has to employ a new pedagogical form, one that does not embrace any of the features that necessarily resulted in other pedagogical processes leading to distorted views of knowledge and the world. At least two such forms have so far been suggested to us.

One is very new, and is given to us by Freire. Freire recognises that consciousness-raising, or removing distortions, can hardly be carried out by any power élite, or by any official teachers working for, or on behalf of, the power élite. Consciousness-raising has at its heart the interests of the recipients, and it is carried out on their behalf, to serve their interests, in the situation in which they are living. It requires not an authority-type teacher setting or teaching an obligatory curriculum made up of areas of his own expertise; but rather a teacher entering into dialogical relationships with people in terms of their own situation and their understanding of it. The aim, eventually, is for people to come to understand what was false about their consciousness, and then to take on a different theoretic perspective which provides a better picture of the world. But Freire also claims that, for all the intervention of 'consciousness-raisers', a liberating pedagogy for the oppressed must be spawned and carried through by the oppressed themselves, once they come to realise their real situation.

The second form is hardly the product of the new revolutionaries or Marxist apologists. It goes back as far as Plato and *The Meno*, where Socrates gives us two principles for overcoming false consciousness and replacing it with raised consciousness: (1) disabuse the holder of false knowledge or consciousness (whether it be the belief that doubling the side of a square doubles its area, or the belief that the world is flat, or the belief that the state is an impersonal 'body' which treats all people equally), by leading the person to see for himself that what he believes is not correct; (2) fill the void, or relieve the numbness, by entering into dialogical encounters, wherein teachers and learners together come to discover the real relationships that exist in the world they are exploring, and together come to learn which tools are necessary to discover and reveal particular relationships.

It turns out, then, that consciousness-raising, on this model, is not intellectual imperialism, for people are led to discover only what they themselves thought they knew, but now realise they need to know. And the teacher is merely helping to expose errors from the perspective of a more progressive research programme, and joining in a quest for real understanding (rather than providing answers that he may not, and need not, have). Consciousness-raising refers, methodologically, to the removal of error or distortion; and substantively to what each particular situation presents as content. Freire says:[8]

> The starting point for organising the programme content of education or political action must be the present, existential, concrete situation, reflecting the aspirations of the people. Utilising certain basic contradictions, we must pose this existential, concrete, present situation to the people as a problem which challenges them and requires response . . . .

Socrates put it this way (I omit Meno's replies):[9]

> At the beginning he did not know the side of the square of eight feet. Nor indeed does he know it now, but then he thought he knew it . . . he felt no perplexity. Now however he does feel perplexed . . . Isn't he in a better position now in relation to what he didn't know? So in perplexing him . . . we have helped him to some extent towards finding out the right answer, for now not only is he ignorant of it but he will be quite glad to look for it . . . Do you suppose then that he would have attempted to look for, or learn, what he thought he knew (though he did not), before he was thrown into perplexity, became aware of his ignorance, and felt a desire to know? . . . Now notice what, starting from this state of perplexity, he will discover by seeking the truth in company with me, though I simply ask him questions without teaching him.

The content of 'consciousness-raising', then, begins with posing problems, and can be seen as emerging from the actual situations people are in, their aspirations, and the things they need to know as presented to them by those situations. The 'consciousness-raiser' goes hand in hand with the people to discover answers. Thus process and content are in harmony; just as they are also in harmony when authoritarian state teachers impose obligatory curricula on children who are compelled to study them regardless of their needs or interests. But consciousness-raising can now be seen to emerge as a viable alternative to education, allowing as it does for people to gain undistorted knowledge by interacting with the world in terms of their *own* interests (rather than in terms of other social interests), and in terms of the needs that are actually inherent in and arising from their own lived situation. The distortions normally brought about by the social dimension of knowledge production should be eliminated, such that people can come to perceive their world as it really is.

Needs, power, authority and learning

For all of the emphasis in the preceding section, our acceptance of Plato does not go very far at all. Plato advocated dialogics mainly because of his belief that knowledge was innate/inherent in individuals; and teachers, like midwives, could deliver but not implant knowledge. But knowledge, as we have argued, is neither inherent in individuals, nor can it be implanted in them by others; rather it is gained through personal interaction in and with the world, and is produced essentially as a response to particular needs in particular historical–social contexts. And since people's needs vary from time to time and place to place, their knowledge of the world would also be expected to vary in much the same way. It would be reasonable to suggest, therefore, that if external imposed sectional social interests were eliminated from knowledge production, we could gain, or aspire to gain or produce, that particular knowledge that we really needed in order to continue to interact with the world. But the knowledge we gain, or are given, via education as *we* experience it does not arise that way at all. The significant feature of education is that someone decides for the learner what he needs to know, and this is in direct contrast to consciousness-raising, which begins with the actual situation and needs of the people whose consciousness is to be raised. No consciousness-raiser would ever move in on an unexploited, self-sufficient, healthy, isolated, peaceful primitive tribe, and give them literacy, 'scientific method', Western culture and Christianity (that is, impose an alien social dimension as a determinant of what they need to know); this is the job of imperialists, missionaries and educators. The key feature of education is imposition – deciding what someone needs to know, and then attempting to ensure that he comes to know it.

Now at this point we have to be very careful in determining just where the problem with this lies. It is not being suggested that the acts of deciding what someone needs to know, or ensuring that he comes to know it, are necessarily bad in themselves: in countless individual cases this might be a good thing, even though it would be hard to justify in principle that anyone ever has the right to impose learning on another. And we are not suggesting that content becomes distorted as content simply because it has been imposed: (x^2-y^2) would be equal to $(x+y)$ $(x-y)$ regardless of the way that it was presented. But what imposition changes is the nature of the learning experience and the social dimension of knowledge production, and herein lies the key to the problem. Imposition necessarily implies power: it establishes the primacy of power over needs, and it generates learning situations where power, content and knowledge become inextricably intertwined. Knowledge is sought and arises essentially as a response to needs, and is gained and produced by interaction in and with the world; but if power (imposition) usurps 'needs' and takes its place *as part of that interactive process*, then a distortive element is mixed in with the knowledge produced; the knowledge is produced, at least in part, in terms of a social dimension which includes a need to submit to power. Let us consider an example.

A person can learn X (that less dense liquids float on more dense liquids). He can also learn X in a power situation, where someone determines that he shall learn it and someone makes him learn it – even if in the most pleasant of ways. In both situations he comes to know X; but in the second situation he also comes to know Y (that someone determined that he shall learn X, and that someone made him learn X). Now X and Y, in this situation or any similar situation, cannot be totally disentangled, and so gaining knowledge of X is to some extent distorted, since *part of the experiential situation of coming to know X is knowing Y as well*: Y is integral to the production of X (whether it is seen consciously that way or not). And since part of the experiential situation of coming to know X was *not* 'needing to know X' – that part being replaced by 'needing to submit to power' – the way that X is really produced is thus distorted. This is a fine but most important point, for in the gaining of knowledge, process and content are inextricable to the extent that process actually becomes an inherent part of the content. Limiting cases in such a situation would be where Y was the predominantly causal factor in the person's learning of X, so that the person comes to know X only because he was forced to; and where a person knows X in the sense that he can simply repeat it, and considers it to be correct and worth repeating only because a teacher says that it is the case. But the question that now arises is whether it is possible and/or desirable to have learning situations wherein a person may learn content in the absence of power.

It is, of course, eminently possible; and most of us engage in such situations just about every day of our lives, as we experience and learn things by ourselves. It is obvious, however, that if we gained our knowledge of the world *only* through self-experience, this would severely limit the amount of knowledge we could gain, and it would prove to be a very inefficient means of gaining knowledge even in the areas that we could get access to. To overcome both of these problems there is obviously a need and a place for authorities; but the point to note particularly about this is that, in introducing authorities (or authority) into learning situations, one does not necessarily re-introduce power.

There are, as has often been documented, two notions of authority.[10] One can be *in* authority, and one can be *an* authority. If one is in authority one necessarily has power,[11] but this is not necessarily so if one is simply an authority. Now being an authority never in itself provides the right or sufficient justification for teaching others; and so in education systems as we know them the two senses are merged and conflated. He who is an authority is legally put in authority by the state in order to teach. But since educational institutions, especially schools, do more than just teach children content, this second function, of being in authority, fits very well. Up to a stage attendance is compulsory; up to and after that stage educands must follow an obligatory curriculum; they must be in set places at set times, attend to the imposed business of the time, and obey all the rules of the institution. And there are no policemen in the institution. The teacher is simply placed in *loco parentis*: he has to see that the rules are kept, that pupils are in the right places at the right times, and that they are diligently following the curriculum imposed on them. This is education as we know it, and as such it requires and needs teachers who are *in* authority, and are thus power figures. In such a situation teachers are necessarily power élites, who are also representatives and servants of the greater power élites in society (even though few see themselves in this way); and so in many related ways they transmit distortions and misrepresentations as knowledge.

But learning situations do not always have to be like this, regardless of the insistent way ideology, and the educational ideology, present the *status quo* as given, right and immutable. Whether educational institutions can ever dispense with power–authority figures will be a matter for later consideration; but what we can recognise now is that the education model is hardly the ideal that all learning situations might measure up to. It is both theoretically and practically possible for us to gain knowledge of the world through intermediation and dialogue with authorities who have no power, and/or who bring no power to the learning situations. This happens all the time – in peer interaction, in discussion groups, and whenever we consult experts or those more knowledgeable than ourselves, even in simple matters like seeking directions in a strange town. On the other hand, we very often act as authorities who teach without the use of power, and while few of us might ever emulate Socrates, we all tend to do our little bit, if not among close friends then possibly with our own children. When knowledge is freely shared with those who seek it, when they seek it, we have learning situations without power - and situations that might provide a more appropriate model to look up to.

Such an argument will not satisfy everyone, of course, because there is still a strong prevailing belief that children, or even adults, will not learn if power is not being exercised over them. That this belief still prevails is not surprising, given that the people who hold it have usually experienced only the power-based education ideology; and in this way their claim is akin to a suggestion that people will not work unless they are watched over by armed guards, if it is made only from observations and experience in prisons. (This, incidentally, is an excellent example of the working of theoretical ideology - fitting instances, even hypothetical rationalisations, into the ambit of a perpetuating and unquestioned theory.) The claim, of course, can be backed by some substantial evidence; by pointing to the many attempts that have been made to remove power from classrooms, and even schools, and the resultant failure wherein, in most cases, something approaching chaos has ensued. And yet this is only to be expected when the attempts are isolated, sporadic and piecemeal. What would happen if power were totally removed, and with it obligatory curricula, fixed time periods, etc., nobody knows or could have much idea of knowing. But if we freed ourselves from the theoretic education ideology that people learn only when forced to, and from the gloomy theoretic ideology going back at least as far as Hobbes that man without controls is a pretty miserable creature, and from the religion ideology that man is tainted by original sin, and possibly from others, there seems to be no *prima facie* case that people would not learn unless forced to. Further, if learning and gaining knowledge were geared to people's actual existential needs and interests, it is difficult to see why power would be necessary at all.

We turn now to our second consideration - is it desirable to remove power from the learning situation? The answer to this is clearly 'yes' on two counts. In the first place, as has already been shown, the association of power with content has a distortive effect on that content, and the removal of power would remove that particular distortion. But the second count is far more important. Gaining knowledge of the world serves either the interests of the individual gaining that knowledge, or interests external to him. (It may serve both interests, but it must serve one more than the other). When power is brought to the learning situation it can be taken that that situation is designed and contrived to serve the interests of the power figure most,[12] (just as education is provided by the power élite to serve their own particular interests and to get people to see the world in a way that serves those particular interests). In a power situation, then, the learner comes to learn things that are imposed on him, things that serve the interests of others, and thus things that may not accord with his needs, and that may distort his perception to suit the needs of others. The removal of power, however, would necessarily lead to people knowing the world, or coming to know the world, in terms of their real needs and never in terms that are imposed to distort knowledge and consciousness in order to favour particular sectional interests. The absence of power in a learning situation might not guarantee that the resultant learning will be free of illusions, errors, distortions or misrepresentations; but it must surely guarantee (unless incredible chance factors are operating) that the knowledge gained in such situations will not embody misrepresentations and distortions that are particularly favourable to a ruling interest group.

But surely the defenders of education will once more gather forces here, and argue that it is a *good* thing that power establishes primacy over needs in learning situations. Most people, it will be argued, do not know their real needs, or what is in their best interests, and this is why we have educators making curricula. Also it is often suggested that if children were to follow their interests or needs in schools they would indulge in frivolous and trivial activities and would never come to see what was worthwhile; 'essential' disciplines would not be studied,[13] and, not having been enlightened and 'protected' by appropriate education, the children would be *more open* to exploitation by others in positions of power. These are, of course, ideological defences and rationalisations, given our previous argument that education does not overcome ignorance but rather creates a pernicious form of ignorance and submissive consciousness whereby exploitation can take place. But once more we have very little idea of what would really happen if pupils and authorities got together to work out curricula collectively in terms of what needed to be known. The authority, of course, could take a leading part in this without exercising power by doing as we suggested he should do - begin from the needs arising out of the concrete existential situation as it is lived and experienced. It is possible that some studies might go by the board, but one can only wonder about the status of such studies if no one felt the need to pursue them. And we could have few serious grounds for predicting that technology would suffer (it might change, however), or for envisaging the emergence of a new race of illiterate uncultured morons who devote their lives to bingo and billiards, simply because learning was based on their needs and interests and not on the needs and interests of the power élite. Interestingly, that race has already been identified *as the product of modern education*, by both its defenders and its detractors.[14] And we might add, in conclusion, that we would not be merely swapping one power élite for another; for the authorities we envisage to lead and guide learning, and to help people to discover knowledge of the world, would be acting without power, and on behalf of no other power. They would simply be what every one of our idealistic manuals claims that teachers today are or ought to be (but cannot be); people helping others in the *common pursuit* of knowledge.

We can now consider one final issue with regard to authorities; namely what a child, or anyone else, does when faced with the very common situation where authorities conflict and disagree with each other. As a naive educand there is very little one can do except recognise what everybody should recognise: namely that authorities, while they are knowledgeable, do not possess proven knowledge, nor do they function as bearers of objective truth. Authorities, like everyone else, necessarily see the world from a particular point of view. Thus, when taking notice of an authority, it is also essential to take notice of how he views things, what his interests are, whose interests he is serving, and what research programme he operates under. Two of the greatest failings (or successes?) of our education system are the instillation of the belief that the teacher or lecturer is always right, and the deification of print – such that, if the book says so, it must be right! School pupils are continually told to look up reference books for material, but rarely are they told that those books contain only one person's perspective on the issue, let alone how to identify and be critical of that perspective. And university students are notorious for filling their essays and theses with quotations from reference books, rather than arguing their own case, as if quotations from famous authors were, *ipso facto*, good, right and better than anything the student could come up with himself.

Let us consider here a quick, and slight, example of authorities disagreeing. Shakespeare's biographers commonly note three things: (1) of the first eighteen years of his life hardly anything is known; (2) on 27 November 1582 an entry appears in the Bishop's Register at Worcester announcing his coming marriage to Annam Whateley; (3) the next day two farmers bind themselves for the legality of Shakespeare's marriage to Anne Hathwey. How shall the discrepancy be explained? One biographer, after noting the lack of data surrounding the period, says: 'That Whateley is a scribal error for Hathaway is *certain*.'[15] Others see no such scribal error. They see two farmers learning of the proposed marriage to Whateley and, knowing Hathaway to be three months pregnant to the bard, holding William literally to a shotgun wedding. Now it is most unlikely that we will ever find out what really happened at Stratford in November 1582; but interestingly we can learn more about the authorities who interpret the event than the event itself. An examination of their social–historical–intellectual backgrounds could indicate why specific authorities interpret the same data in different ways, and why some make Shakespeare out to be a bit of a lad with the girls, while others cover up this possibility.

The point can now be generalised. Just as our own knowledge of the world is the result of our interaction in and with the world, filtered in all the ways we have seen, so too is any authority's knowledge. Thus in all things it is essential to take note of what an authority says, and to determine as far as possible why he comes to say it as he does. Products of our education system tend to do the former (possibly because they learn in power situations) and neglect the latter: thus they gather and assimilate facts, that is internalise other people's knowledge statements, and misunderstand what knowledge of the world (theirs, the authority's and knowledge in general) really is.

In conclusion, it is hardly being suggested that a naive educand, or possibly even a reasonably sophisticated one, could probe the depths of each authority's interests and perspectives; what is important, however, is that a learning situation should embrace and illuminate a proper understanding of authorities, so that what they say can and will be taken as what it always is – a view of the world from a particular perspective. This explains, in part, why authorities disagree; and understanding of that would begin to equip the educand to arbitrate with regard to their differing opinions.

There are many things that have not been sorted out in this section, such as which of the infinite number of 'needs' that people have should be given priority in learning situations, and on what basis;[16] and how are our authorities to be selected and designated. These, and others, are important questions, but would take books of their own to be answered properly. Here we shall merely stick with our point and our theme: while the lived-ideology of education is based, even in part, on power, and serves the interests of the power élites or ruling classes in a society, it must necessarily transmit both substantive knowledge and a particular idea of what knowledge is, which gives the educand a distorted and misrepresentative view of the world. Removing all power from educational situations, and basing those situations on the needs of the educand rather than on the needs of the power élite, would represent a shift from the social to the theoretical dimension of knowledge production, and would constitute a necessary beginning to removing those distortions and preventing their recurrence.

Can education be changed?

Eventually one has to face a realistic and, unfortunately, pessimistic conclusion: education, as provided by capitalist liberal democracies, will not change from providing structured systematic distortions of reality to bringing people non-misrepresentative knowledge of the world. There are a number of basic reasons why this is so. I shall simply list two.

To begin with, education is an instrument of the state, and serves the ruling interests and power élites of the state. Its job is to maintain and stabilise the social order, and it does this in interaction with other institutions and ideologies; and there is no way that education could possibly extract itself, become autonomous, and then dictate to the social order. Many well-meaning people have looked to education to bring about a better world by raising literacy, culture, etc., but it is the height of naivity to think that education can take on a promotional role and drastically change the social order itself. This naive tradition is epitomised in G.S. Counts's famous pamphlet, *Dare the School Build a New Social Order?*[17] which, while it might have raised the blood pressure of many, should also have strained their credulity. While education is set up by the power élites to serve their own interests, it is hardly likely that they would voluntarily relinquish their hold – or allow the conditions to develop that would threaten their hold over education, and thus over people's consciousness.

Second, change in education requires initial recognition that something is wrong, followed by a long process of de-mystification; and it is difficult to imagine how either of these could occur. We noted earlier that one's concept of the object under investigation leads to theory-laden methodology of investigation, and also that in certain cases the object can interfere with the investigation at the most basic level by acting back on the investigator. Education, we argued, was one such case. Education gives us a point of view for seeing things, *including education*, and thus largely influences the way we shall criticise education, and the sorts of things we shall take as being up for criticism. The education ideology thus presents and legitimates a picture of what is *acceptable criticism* of education; and this picture is set solidly within the parameters of a prevailing paradigm. Education, in providing us with legitimate content and methods for criticism, simply cannot legitimate any critical content or method that is capable of criticising what it itself has legitimated. Thus, as noted earlier, education cannot be counter-ideological.

But the education ideology also gives us a picture of who the *acceptable critics* are. They are the people who have been most educated, those with degrees, and those with are high up on the academic ladder. These people, again as indicated earlier, are likely to be the least equipped to criticise education in terms of rising out of their immersion to make radical reappraisals, or of undertaking the long and complex task of de-mystification – dispersing the verbal and ideological mists and fogs that have been built up around education to conceal that it does something other than what it purports to do. And it is these acceptable critics, indulging in their internal criticism, who will be attended to, and who are most likely to be published and read. Thus education, in legitimating

183

its own expert critics, again cannot be counter-ideological.

Clearly, the ruling forces in a capitalist liberal democratic society will not bring about the sorts of changes in education that are required if education is to reveal the real relationships in such a society; and education, structured as it is, tends not to produce people who can see that distortions are prevailing *and* who will be attended to when they speak out. There are, however, some grounds for hope, slight though they may be.

Possibilities

Anyone who has read this far will have noted a contradiction. The very existence of this work tends to indicate that I have done that which I have claimed people could not do – I have written a radical reappraisal of education. But writing such a reappraisal is not the important thing; what really matters is having that reappraisal made public and having it legitimated. And of these two possibilities the former is far easier to achieve than the latter because of a contradiction within capitalism. Even though this work attacks capitalism and education, capitalist publishers are still likely to publish it if they believe they can make a profit out of it. But educators are of a slightly different breed. If this work were presented as a PhD thesis it would almost certainly be failed; that is, it would not be legitimated as a serious, scholarly dissertation on education, mainly because it calls into question and threatens the very academic ideology into which it would be placed for marking. (The actual reasons given for failure would, however, be quite different from that.[18]) And along the same lines, now that this work has been published, it is more than likely that expert educationalists will at first ignore it, and then, if it doesn't go away, will turn to print themselves to discredit and de-legitimate it (bad reviews in respectable journals, etc), since it cannot be accommodated within the prevailing education ideology that they maintain and sustain.

The important piece to take out of that paragraph, however, is the notion of 'contradiction'. In our fourth chapter we outlined certain moves whereby ideology could be recognised and fought, not that we placed all that much faith in people being able to apply them to the extent of overcoming distorting ideology. They offer us some hope however; and there is one that might be particularly useful in this particular context – namely recognising and working on contradictions. We would find, if we examined the whole canvas of ideology in capitalist society, that there are contradictions within each ideology, and contradictions between particular ideologies. We have already examined contradictions within education, but similar ones in other areas would be contradictions between thrift (and saving for the future) and conspicuous consumption, in the economic ideology; between the woman's right to consent, but there being no such charge as 'rape' against one's wife, in the legal ideology; and between the belief in family planning yet the outlawing of contraceptives, in some religious ideologies. But at least as important to note are the contradictions between ideologies, and here it should be recognised that as societies become more complex the boundaries between ideologies become less clear – thus our latter two examples could also be seen as inter-ideological contradictions, between the legal and the family ideologies, and between the family and the religion ideologies, respectively.

The important point to note is that education, like all other ideologies, does not carry out its functions smoothly, or achieve a 100 per cent success rate (even though it is more successful than other ideologies), because of these contradictions; and it is the inter-ideological contradictions that are increasing in number. As sex education and religious instruction appear in schools, contradictions occur between education, the family and the church; as education becomes less vocational, contradictions arise with industry. In times of unemployment, when certificates don't buy jobs, other contradictions occur; yet others are found when employers tell employees to forget what they learnt at school or university, or when the forces of repression act against the school-encouraged expression of political comment, or when people are discouraged from using the 'creative thought' that education insisted it was encouraging. These contradictions are very real for those who actually *experience* them. Now there is evidence to suggest that the contradictions will increase; and so there is hope that more and more people will experience them, and in the process question the legitimacy and the 'rightness' of the education ideology and recognise and challenge the illusions it produces. From this there could arise a call to abandon illusions about conditions, which, to paraphrase Marx, is equivalent to a call to abandon conditions that require illusions. That is one possibility; but not a very large one, for, as Randall Albury points out so well:[19]

> In spite of these contradictions, however, the overall result of the ideological process is to produce individuals who objectively function as effective bearers of the relations appropriate to specific places in a specific society, but who nevertheless experience themselves not as bearers of relations but rather as irreducibly unique personalities freely choosing the actions they perform.

and the overall effect of education, as we have seen, is to produce individuals who function as effective bearers of the relationships and knowledge appropriate to specific places in a specific society, but who experience themselves not as bearers of a specific imposed distorted perspective and viewpoint, but as unique intellectual personalities who see the world as it really is.

Are there any other possibilities? Like characters in a Beckett play we could just wait. After all, there is much in Max Planck's notion that significant changes occur not through convincing the opposition, but when the older opposition dies off, and the younger, less-entrenched 'radicals' are able to move up, gain access to publishing and to power, and establish *their* orthodoxy as the new prevailing paradigm.[20] Then again it does appear possible that problems with pollution, decreasing resources and energy crises might force us, for our very survival, to do away with the capitalist mode of production and replace it with one that does not require distortions, illusions and the disguise of social relations for its efficient and continued operation. This would result in new conditions of social existence, bringing about new consciousness, and with it new education. Finally, we could pin our faith in Marx, and trust that he was correct in predicting the eventual self-destruction of capitalism and the emergence of the socialist/communist world from the ruins: that too would give us the new social relations required to make unnecessary the distortions and misrepresentations we have identified.

But sitting around waiting can hardly be sufficient, and it was certainly not what Marx proposed. The new consciousness will not rise magically out of the ruins, if there are to be ruins, just as consciousness now is not a magical thing that appears mysteriously from the ether. We stressed in our discussion of 'ideology', and we cannot stress too much that ideology and consciousness have their basis in concrete lived relations and situations; they are rooted in them and arise from them. And unless the lived-ideologies give way to new ways of behaving and living, the theoretical ideologies, and consciousness in general, will not change. Also, without change in practice, or attempted change in practice, all the theoretical suggestions in this work regarding countering ideology and changing education must remain limp and unsupported.

The only real possibility is to prepare now, and to act now; but it might appear as though this declaration has placed us in the midst of a 'chicken and egg' riddle, for if social relations determine consciousness, from where shall we get the consciousness to live new social relations? The answer to that question can actually be found embedded within historical materialism, which is not the totally deterministic programme it is often taken to be. At its very simplest level the answer is that people create social circumstances just as much as circumstances 'make' people, and it is out of this very dialectic process that new consciousness and new forms of living can come about. The consciousness itself, or theoretic practice, is made possible because of the contradictions that exist within capitalist society; the necessary action i made possible when theoretic practice ceases to remain within the head, and when theoretic products become used as raw materials and tools for guiding action. Thus two things are basically required; first, a means of recognising existing social formations in terms of their contradictory elements, along with an adequate analysis of the formation and functioning of those elements; and second, a simple recognition that men and women, *ordinary* men and women, can and do change the world. In spite of education, and ideology, the contradictions exist and must continue to exist; the harder part, as suggested earlier, is to recognise them for what they are, and to take oneself seriously as an active participant in producing history. But both theoretically and practically, it is possible to gain the raised consciousness that can bring about new social relations, and also to create the new social relations that shall determine a raised consciousness.

And so with education, as with all aspects of social relations, the only real possibility *is* to prepare now, and to act now; that is, to engage in revolutionary practice.[21] 'Engaging in revolutionary practice' is, understandably, a concept that daunts many people who associate it with 'the forcible overthrow of all existing social relations'; but that is only one form of revolutionary practice. Revolutionary practice does require the overthrow of existing social relations, but force is not necessary on the part of the revolutionaries (at least not in the first place). What *is* required, however, is that new social relations be created and lived, or, in the terms used in this work, that we create *new lived-ideologies*. With education, then, we must create new lived-ideologies, where the *lived process* of education especially is changed, and changed in such a way as to remove all those factors that bring about and produce a distorted misrepresentation of reality.

The new lived-ideologies, however, would not be ideologies of *education*; for two reasons. First, as we have seen, there is no way that any significant change in education could occur independently, or in advance of a significant change in social existence and social relationships; and yet what we require is something that will drive, lead and actively bring about such significant changes. Second, the consciousness for the new lived-ideologies must be created partially by living in them, but everyone today is forced to live in the education ideology. So it is not a matter of overthrowing the prevailing education ideology, for there is no way that can be done (at least now). The only possibility is to begin in a far wider sense with general social *praxis*, and from that standpoint begin to create, and attempt to have legitimated, new lived-ideologies of anti-education which can compete with the prevailing education ideology. And just as education is interlinked with all other aspects of society, anti-education must also be so interlinked, so that it too might have possible correspondence with the workplace, the family, etc. Actually, anti-education, which could not be confined to its own institutions, would be well suited for that.

Anti-education is not deschooling (and while schools serve the role they do the power élite is not going to disband them). And anti-education is not alternative schooling, or 'progressive education'. Anti-education would have nothing to do with schools, at least not yet, while the predominant school ideology remains.

Anti-education can hardly be defined precisely at this point of time; but it would be a matter of people talking, acting and working informally among themselves; discussing their lives, their freedoms, their constraints, their situations, their visions and their knowledge of the world; discovering the world for themselves through experience and with authorities, and linking up with movements in other areas of society, in a gradual process of changing themselves, education and society. It would seek out new forms, new goals, new directions, new processes and new social relations for the transmission and assimilation of knowledge; and in doing so it would have to continually recreate its research programme as it sought, adopted and promoted new and (hopefully) undistorted ways of seeing the world. Anti-education would consist of people disinterestedly, and in community, trying to learn what they need to know, in contrast to people having to accept as knowledge a distorted and misrepresentative picture of the world.[22]

One should not realistically expect a rush on anti-education. Most people don't put a high value on informal talk and discussion of their very own problems, on self-discovery, or on activities that don't have an immediate pay-off. Most can't envisage real learning without an official teacher; many people don't think they have anything to offer or say in discussion, or they think their views are unimportant or illinformed. These are not natural qualities related to the 'condition of man', however—they are the direct results of education. Many people, especially those well endowed with material comfort, see no need to change the world, which is hardly surprising, considering the overall effect of education and ideological immersion. Many people have no time to undertake such a task, or make no time because of what they have been taught to believe is more pressing and important. If they are students they know the immediate relevance of their course material and shall leave such discussion till later. And later, as workers, they still have no time, for at the end of the day they are worked out and either want to relax or else, now rising and succeeding in the status race, they lose their objections to the world. Many people would not want a change, even if they saw the need for one, because of the chains with which they have attached themselves to the *status quo*, living and locked in as they are to the sorts of situations mentioned earlier, wherein time that has been served in a particular life-style 'justifies' serving more time in that same life-style; as occurs with mortgages and other loans, promotion, life assurance and endowment policies, superannuation, long service leave and so on. Those who are about to take a year's long service leave, or retire on full superannuation which they have worked and contributed towards for forty years, or have almost paid off their house; or have just gained, or suspect they are about to gain, promotion; or have finally 'settled into' their way of life, or even those who now have another mouth to feed are not likely to want any revolution just now, thank you very much. Many people distrust anything that is anti-establishment, for quite understandable reasons. And, as indicated before, institutions so control people's imaginations that they are unable to think of alternatives to the way things are anyway. Add to all of this the fragmentation of life under capitalism, not just in the workplace but in living in the individual isolated family ideology, and we find a whole life-style quite opposed to joining together in collective active discovery.

This all heads towards a most pessimistic conclusion. Distortion and illusion have so become the norm that they no longer appear as distortion and illusion. The means for challenging and abandoning them are de-legitimised, and few wish to challenge and abandon them anyway. Those that do face an enormous task of finding a methodology and research programme that can cut through or unwind centuries of careful tangling in the hope that reality can be revealed. Of those who continue, few expect success in their own lifetimes (which is always a daunting factor, for even those who are content to wait for delayed gratification usually want to experience some tangible sign of success). And all can expect internal struggles in their endeavour, with even their closest supporters turning against them; for anti-establishment projects are usually internally divided since they rarely share a common established research programme to begin with.[23] The odds are badly stacked; but even if some are overcome there are still the state's forces of repression to contend with when the threat begins to become serious.

The endeavour seems to be unenviable; and yet what finer task could there be for those who take themselves seriously, or who want to take themselves seriously, as teachers, as transmitters of knowledge, than to *remove* the illusions, disguises, distortions and misrepresentations that now characterise man's knowledge of the world, and to reveal the world as it might be seen from the perspective of research programmes that expose rather than build in such elements? The problem that remains, of course, is how to do that: how to expose a constantly and carefully legitimated view of the world as an illusion, and so help people to correct the distortions that now make up their consciousness.[24]

The answer is anything but clear; but two things at least can be suggested. First, what is sought will never be achieved in the classrooms and lecture halls of educational institutions as we know and experience them. Second, an essential part of the endeavour must lie in some people, or hopefully even in all of us, engaging in revolutionary practice; in *living*, or trying to live, new ideologies; and in attempting to view the world from the perspective of research programmes generated in and by those lived-ideologies. Until that happens, and until those people speak out, the rest must be mere speculation; for we can neither stand back and hope to predict or prescribe the consciousness that will arise from new lived experiences, nor hope vicariously to absorb it. We must either make those experiences for ourselves, or at the least listen to those who are undergoing them as a necessary prelude for our own action.

The task should not be viewed lightly, but then again it is not one of utter hopelessness. If we lived in a fairy-tale world we might hope simply to remove illusions from prevailing consciousness by openly declaring that the Emperor has no clothes on, and then live happily ever after; but things do not work that way in the real world. What is required in the real world is for revolutionary practice to be undertaken, yet to be undertaken within an arena depressingly littered by the premature corpses of the large majority of the previous combatants. At that level the thought is not appealing. What is more appealing, however, is that engaging in revolutionary practice is nothing more than attempting to live more fully. And yet, as Hegel has noted, to live fully is, at the same time, to risk oneself. That condition can not be avoided. There is no question that it is a matter of risk. The real question is how fully do we want to live, and how much are we willing to risk?

Notes

Chapter 1 Knowing and interpreting the world

1 P. Freire, *Pedagogy of the Oppressed*, Ringwood, Penguin, 1972, p.27.
2 Among Popper's works see especially *The Logic of Scientific Discovery*, London, Hutchinson, 1974, ch. VIII.
3 He could, of course, confine himself to collecting data about only one small aspect of the world, like the effect of heat on metals. But if he begins with the *a priori* hypothesis that metals will expand when heated (and that the phase of the moon is irrelevant in this process), he is not being strictly inductive.
4 I regularly pose this problem to my classes, and although I have kept no 'scientific' data a continual pattern is always seen to emerge. Almost all students count the pregnant woman as *one* person on the oval. Generally there is a division over the matter of abortion; but of the anti-abortionists there are always some who are anti because 'the foetus is a person', yet who refused to include the foetus in the oval count as a person.
5 A classic case of this in the area of supposedly academic and/or scientific 'objectivity' appears to be that of Sir Cyril Burt. See below, pp.103–4.
6 J.S. Bruner and L. Postman, 'On the Perception of Incongruity: A Paradigm', *Journal of Personality*, 18, 1949, pp. 206–23.
7 N. Hansen, *Patterns of Discovery*, Cambridge: University Press, 1958, p.7.
8 *The Tempest*, Act 1 Scene ii.
9 Our sentence oversimplifies the issue. As part of the growing literature on this subject see S. Cohen, *Drugs of Hallucination*, London: Paladin, 1971; and J.A. Vernon, *Inside the Black Room*, Harmondsworth: Penguin, 1966.
10 The theme permeates Laing's work. See especially *The Divided Self*, London, Tavistock, 1960; *The Politics of Experience and the Bird of Paradise*, Harmondsworth, Penguin, 1968; and *The Politics of the Family*, London, Tavistock, 1971.

11 The best account of the grounds that have variously been employed over the last 400 years in judging people to be insane is given by Michel Foucault in *Madness and Civilisation*, London, Tavistock, 1967.

12 There is considerable literature on this subject; but see especially the work of B. L. Whorf, in J.B. Carroll (ed.), *Thought and Reality - Selected Writings of Benjamin Lee Whorf*, New York: John Wiley & Sons, 1956. Note also this statement from R.F.W. Smith: 'Since the concepts people live by are derived only from perceptions and from language and since the perceptions are received and interpreted only in light of earlier concepts, man comes pretty close to living in a house that language built.' 'Linguistics in Theory and in Practice', ETC, (A Review of General Semantics), International Society for General Semantics, Chicago, Autumn 1952.

13 See below, pp. 39-40.

14 The literature on this subject is immense. A good starting point is G. W. Allport's classic, *The Nature of Prejudice*, Reading, Mass:, Addison-Wesley, 1954.

15 R. Rosenthal and L. Jacobson, *Pygmalion in the Classroom*, New York: Holt, Rinehart & Winston, 1968.

16 See R.D. Tuddenham and P.D. Macbride, 'The Yielding Experiment from the Subject's Point of View', *J. Pers.*, 27, 1959, pp. 259-71.

17 For consideration of this issue in a wider context, see R.D. Laing, *Self and Others*, Harmondsworth, Penguin, 1971.

18 See, among many others, E.E. Maccoby, T.M. Newcomb and E.L. Hartley (eds), *Readings in Social Psychology* (especially the article by Asch: 'Effects of Group Pressure on the Modification and Distortion of Judgments'), New York, Holt, Rinehart & Winston, 1958; M. Deutsch and H.B. Gerard, 'A Study of Normative and Informational Social Influences Upon Individual Judgment,' *J. Abnorm. Soc. Psychol.*, 51, 1955, pp. 629-36; R.S. Crutchfield, 'Conformity and Character', *Amer. J. Psychol.*, 10, 1955, pp. 191-8; D. Krech, R. S. Crutchfield, and E. L. Ballachey, *Individual in Society*, New York, McGraw Hill, 1962.

19 Pre-testing tended to indicate that they *could* make the necessary visual discriminations.

20 See M. D. Bogdonoff *et al.*, 'The Modifying Effect of Conforming Behaviour upon Lipid Responses Accompanying C.N.S. Arousal', *Clinical Research*, 9, 1961, p. 135.

21 A. S. Luchins, 'Mechanisation in Problem Solving', *Psychol. Monographs*, vol. 54, no. 248, 1942.

22 P. Feyerabend, 'How to be a Good Empiricist . . . ', in P.H. Nidditch (ed.), *The Philosophy of Science*, London, Oxford University Press, 1968, p. 27.

23 For a clear account of the positivist position see A.J. Ayer, *Language, Truth, and Logic*, Harmondsworth, Penguin, 1971.

24 All the ones we have noted can be found embedded in this single passage:

> The phenomena of learning and activation, like other topics in psychology, can be approached in a variety of ways. The following treatment is based on the assumption that psychology is the study of behaviour, taken in turn as the activity of the intact living organism. In the belief that psychology can imitate more advanced sciences like physics in its method, by analysing its subject matter as much as possible, behaviour is described in terms of stimuli and responses. A stimulus is defined as anything that can excite one of the organism's receptors, and a response as any part of behaviour with which it is convenient to work. With this approach, stimuli and responses are the raw data of psychology. Merely observing data is not enough, however, for the scientist also has to set down a record of his observations in a form which is not limited to the particular case and which he hopes will have some generality. This is where theorising comes into the picture.

The passage is the opening paragraph of *Learning and Activation* (John Wiley & Sons, Australasia, 1969), a widely set text in psychology, written by R.A. Champion, McCaughey Professor of Psychology at the University of Sydney since 1966 and head of that school in 1966–8 and 1972–5. One might, therefore, be tempted to guess at what counted as psychology in that school, and what students in that school took psychology to be, or knew as psychology. For discussion of this general issue, see below, pp. 73– 4 and pp. 137–63.

25 'History: the Poverty of Empiricism'; in R. Blackburn (ed.), *Ideology in Social Science*, London, Fontana, 1973, p. 113.

26 E.H. Carr, *What is History?* Harmondsworth, Penguin, 1974, p. 11.

27 Ibid., p. 22.

28 The last theory mentioned is the most commonly supported today by psychologists; perhaps the third theory is still popular in some areas.

29 This, of course, is in contrast to the way we usually do investigate the world. Francis Bacon's shrewd observation of 400 years ago, that we begin with hypotheses and then deliberately seek out the evidence that confirms them while neglecting the evidence that refutes them, still holds true today. A fuller account of this phenomenon will be given in our discussions of ideology.

30 Should the reader be concerned with the way that I have paraded evidence and facts (many even derived from empirical studies), I can only note that their conditional status has always been implicitly recognised, and the shorthand form of recording and reporting them has been employed mainly in order to make this work readable.

Chapter 2 Theory and critical preference

1 See, for instance, P. Feyerabend, 'How to Defend Society Against Science', *Radical Philosophy*, 11, Summer 1975, pp.3–8. Feyerabend argues this way in other places as well.

2 A large part of the point of this condition is to disallow, in principle and practice, that *ad hoc* hypotheses be used to account for anomalies, and thus to 'save' the original theory.

3 Such reification can often be interest-serving. On the general issue, see below, pp.76–7 and 99.

4 As an example of bringing this approach to the field of education, see the influential work of R.S. Peters and P.H. Hirst. See also below, pp.79–81.

5 See I. Lakatos, 'Falsification and the Methodology of Scientific Research Programmes', in I. Lakatos and A. Musgrave (eds), *Criticism and the Growth of Knowledge*, Cambridge University Press, 1970.

6 The notion permeates Karl Popper, *The Logic of Scientific Discovery*, London, Hutchinson, 1974; see especially his *Conjectures and Refutations*, London, Routledge & Kegan Paul, 1974.

7 See T. Kuhn, *The Structure of Scientific Revolutions*, Chicago University Press, 1973.

8 Lakatos, op. cit., p.104.

9 See Karl Popper, *The Logic of Scientific Discovery*, London, Hutchinson, 1974, sections 30–7.

10 See Lakatos, op. cit., p.107.

11 Ibid., p.116.

12 Feyerabend, op. cit., p.5.

13 'Possibly' – because the degree of difficulty in choosing is not constant. It is easier (using only Lakatos's criteria) to make judgments of critical preference at this point of time between astrology and quantum mechanics than it is to make judgments between behaviourism and psychoanalysis, or between the economic theories of Friedman and Keynes.

14 See K. Mannheim, *Ideology and Utopia*, London, Routledge & Kegan Paul, 1966, pp.97–165; and K. Popper, *Objective Knowledge* Oxford University Press, London: 1972, pp. 44ff. But note especially B. Barber, 'Resistance By Scientists to Scientific Discovery', *Science*, 134, 1961, pp. 596–602; where it is convincingly demonstrated that issues like paradigmatic allegiance, methodological conformity, religion, professional standing, seniority and political issues affect (or at least have in the past affected) what shall be acceptable and accepted discovery in science.

15 This conflates Mannheim's notions of 'ideology' and 'utopia'. See Mannheim, op. cit.

16 Knut Erik Tranöy, 'The Ideology of Scientific and Scholarly Conduct', in Raymond E. Olson and Anthony M. Paul (eds), *Contemporary Philosophy in Scandinavia*, Baltimore and London, John Hopkins Press, 1972, pp.307–30.

17 Feyerabend, op. cit., p.6. The original is in italics.
18 Another, and vitally important sense will be introduced below. See pp.86–93.
19 However, scientists, could not, of course, even at the risk of not making important breakthroughs, attend to every anomaly or unusual piece of datum that confronts them; for if they did their work could hardly go on.
20 To find the theory spelt out fully see R.S. Peters, *Ethics and Education*, London, George Allen & Unwin, 1970.
21 On the matter of anomalies as puzzles or counter-instances, see Kuhn, op. cit., p.79.
22 See, for example, 'The Poor Scholar's Soliloquy', *Childhood Education*, 20, 1944, pp. 219–20. The criticisms made of education here could have been made, perhaps less articulately, by any fourteen-year-old dropout. But no fourteen-year-old dropout could get published in a reputable journal; so their case is taken up here by a respectable academic (in disguise). The result, however, is humorous: it should be serious.
23 That, of course, is putting it far too simply. But for some of Marx's dealings with the problem of illusory representations, or the difference between appearance and reality, see *Capital*, vol.1, pp.307, 316 and 537; and vol.3, pp.797–809. References are to the Lawrence & Wishart edition, London, 1961–2.
24 L. Althusser, *For Marx*, Harmondsworth, Allen Lane, 1969, p.188.
25 Cf. Althusser: 'This practice is *theoretical;* it is distinguished from the other, non-theoretical practices, by the *type* of object (raw material) which it transforms; by the type of means of production it sets to work, by the type of object it produces (knowledges).' L. Althusser, *Reading Capital*, London, New Left Books, 1977, p.59.
26 Ibid., p.42.
27 Ibid.
28 See below, pp.97–8.
29 See below, pp.64–5.
30 It is possible that, in order to preserve and sustain certain social interests and practices, theoretical products or knowledge statements might be promulgated that actually do coincide with the real world. But if the production functioned to serve interests rather than to produce the real object, the coincidence is largely immaterial. As indicated below, it is the *function* of theoretical production that is of central concern.
31 If, as I have maintained (and will maintain again), theoretic practice can never be totally free from social practice, at least where there is underlying conflict within that social practice, it must follow that virtually all theoretic products (again barring chance coincidence) must be distortions of the real world. This is necessarily so (it would also follow from what we have said about selection, filtration and theory-ladenness). But the considerations listed above can be particularly useful in helping to determine the seriousness and the effects of particular distortions.

32 Perhaps I should point out the 'obvious' that very few seem to see. To show that certain social relations and practices necessarily give rise to a distorted view of the world in no way implies that I know what the real world looks like, or that I have to know what the real world looks like before I can begin.

Chapter 3 Ideology

1 L.S. Feuer (ed.), *Marx and Engels : Basic Writings on Politics and Philosophy*, London, Fontana, 1972, p.85.
2 Throughout this work 'interests' is used in its normative rather than psychological sense, to refer to what is concerned with the welfare of people rather than what they are psychologically attracted to or 'interested in'.
3 Many examples of this common phenomenon are found in the text below.
4 On this issue the reader is referred especially to the works of Reich and Marcuse; more specifically to Reich's *The Mass Psychology of Fascism*, and Marcuse's *Eros and Civilisation*.
5 It would be of interest to consider what functions these theories have served in particular societies, instead of wondering which, if either, is true.
6 Here is an instance where the 'treachery of language' leads us into unintentional reification. By 'society' is meant not a thing, but a 'complex, dynamic network of social relations'. That phrase, however, would produce much strain if it was used throughout this work. See above, pp.39–40.
7 We would have to be very much on guard, of course, against being caught up in illusions ourselves, or having our results influenced by the object under investigation.
8 No thorough definition of a 'liberal democracy' is intended here; but we take it that such a social system embodies at least the basic freedoms of speech and worship, bestows at least the rights to assemble and to withdraw labour, elects its government by means of a wide franchise in the society, and allows opposition representation within the governing houses. More generally, people are supposedly free to express their opinions, choose their government and be actively involved in decisions that are taken.
9 For example, the thirteen judges of the European Court of Human Rights, after five years of deliberating over the possible obscenity of *The Little Red School Book*, finally delivered a judgment (7 December 1976) which, in part, declared: 'Freedom of expression is one of the essential foundations of a democratic society and applies also to the expression of ideas that offend, shock, or disturb. Restrictions on that freedom must be proportionate to the aim pursued.'
10 This is by no means to suggest, however, that the received view

(ideas, beliefs, etc.) would be the causally predominant factor in such an occurrence.

11 Here the reification is most misleading.

12 When, for instance, the Communist Party appeared to present a threat, there came the infamous 'McCarthy witchhunts' in America, and a referendum to outlaw the party in Australia. One wonders to what size the Klan would have to grow before it was officially outlawed. (Note the reference to *Tribune* above, p.38.)

13 The concept of 'class' is being used very loosely at this stage.

14 British Common Law is often held up as having been formulated in this way; but any serious examination of its development reveals this to be a myth.

15 R. Owen, *A New View of Society*, London: Dent; (Everyman edition), 1966, p.14.

16 Ibid., p.3; my italics. This is the wording on the 1813 title sheet.

17 From *The German Ideology* quoted in D. McLellan, *The Thoughts of Karl Marx*; London, Macmillan, 1972, p.158.

18 See the reference to Barber's research above; p.194, n.14.

19 See below, pp.103–5.

20 Just as university students take as (say) psychology what ruling interests (professors) define as psychology. See above, p.193, n.24.

21 This counts heavily against the influential work of P.H. Hirst, whose notion of 'forms of knowledge' rests on the idea that 'our experience becomes structured round the use of accepted public symbols. The symbols thus having public meaning, their use is in some way testable against experience . . . .' Hirst's view of knowledge is dependent on a view of 'public' that would be difficult to sustain. (The quotation is taken from 'Liberal Education and the Nature of Knowledge', in R.F. Dearden *et al.* (eds), *Education and the Development of Reason*, London, Routledge & Kegan Paul, 1972, p.405; but the notion can be found as the basis for all of Hirst's epistemological writings.)

22 See below, pp.118–26 and 184–8.

23 See below, pp.106–8.

24 Once again, language problems occur. In order to keep this work readable, both 'shorthand' and anthropomorphisms are being employed. I am not accepting or suggesting any form of 'conspiracy theory' here or at any point; nor do I seriously propose that institutions (and later schools) are the real active subjects of the processes I attribute to them.

25 R.S. Peters, *Ethics and Education*, London, George Allen & Unwin, 1966, p.8; my italics.

26 Ibid., my italics.

27 P.H. Hirst and R.S. Peters, *The Logic of Education*, London, Routledge & Kegan Paul, 1970, p.3.

28 Ibid., p.9.

29 The conference in question is the International Seminar, Philosophy and Education, 23–5 March 1966, Ontario Institute for Studies in Education.

30 See T. Kuhn, *The Structure of Scientific Revolutions*, Chicago University Press, 1973, p. 122. Kuhn fails to adequately account for how the 'existence' of a paradigm is determined by social relations. It is of interest to consider what social practices and social relations might give rise to a study of education that necessarily 'left everything as it is'.

31 Note, of course, who it is that sets up the *official* commissions. Common Room talk, although it might be of a higher level, will not bring about changes unless it passes through such channels.

32 R.B. Prowse, 'The Educational Process From a Layman's Point of View', in *The Educational Process*, Melbourne, Australian Council for Educational Research, 1973, p.45.

33 E.B. Castle, *Ancient Education and Today*, Harmondsworth; Penguin, 1961, p.200.

34 J. Holt, *Freedom and Beyond*, Harmondsworth, Penguin, 1972, p.163.

35 A most important contribution to analysis of ideology has been made by Peter Stevens in 'Ideology and Schooling', *Educational Philosophy and Theory*, 8, 2 October 1976, pp. 29-41. Stevens distinguishes between 'ideology' and 'neology'; and that which we are about to discuss falls under his category of neology. Such a distinction, while too advanced for our present purposes, could hardly be ignored if a more detailed examination were being undertaken.

36 R. Albury, 'Ideology', *Tharunka*, 13 October 1976, p. 4. Note the connection here with empiricist methodology, which also 'reproduces the "given"'.

37 See L. Althusser, *Lenin and Philosophy*, London, New Left Books, 1971, p.165.

Chapter 4 Attacking ideology

1 R.S. Peters, *Ethics and Education*, London, George Allen & Unwin, 1966, P.170.

2 Even those statements I have just taken as scientific could be regarded as ideological. But on a more positive note, analytic statements could not be so regarded; e.g., 'A poor man has little money' is analytical and non-ideological, and it differs in many ways from 'The poor are happier than the rich'.

3 *Sydney Morning Herald*, 16 September 1975.

4 On the social dimension of knowledge production, consider just when it was that Hobbes 'came up' with his eagerly accepted theory. Why did the year 1651 not produce and *legitimate* a Marcuse?

5 We have considered only one specific issue, but similar yet generalised investigation could reveal that the actual law itself especially favours and protects the established ruling interests in any (class) society.

6   See A.A. Jensen, 'How Much Can We Boost I.Q. and Scholastic Achievement?' *Harvard Educational Review*, 39, 1, 1969; and *Educability and Group Differences*, New York, Harper & Row, 1975. See also R. Herrnstein, 'I.Q.', *Atlantic Monthly*, 228, 3 September 1971; and *I.Q. in the Meritocracy*, Boston, Little, Brown & Co., 1973; as well as H.J. Eysenck, *Race, Intelligence and Education*, Melbourne, Sun Books, 1971.

7   *Sydney Morning Herald*, 13 November 1976; all italics mine. See also the *Sunday Times*, 24 October 1976 and onwards till the end of November 1976, for the full *exposé*.

8   See S. Bowles and H. Gintis, *Schooling in Capitalist America*, New York: Basic Books, 1976, especially pp. 102-25. Extensive use of the research findings of Bowles and Gintis is made as this work proceeds. It is recognised, of course, that their work was carried out only in the USA, and that I am generalising far beyond the population from which the findings were drawn. The generalisations, however, are made in the contexts of, and are related to, similar economic settings rather than specific schools or schooling systems, and in this sense they seem reasonable ones to make.

9   For trenchant criticism of Jensen, and particularly Herrnstein, see the articles by Bowles, Purvin and especially Chomsky; in A. Gartner *et al.* (eds), *The New Assault on Equality : I.Q. And Social Stratification*, New York: Harper & Row, 1974. An extensive bibliography of material critical of Eysenck and Jensen is provided in *Radical Education Dossier*, 4 October 1977, pp. 17-18.

10 Peters, op. cit., pp. 310-11.

11 R.S. Peters, 'In Defence of Bingo : a Rejoinder', *British Journal of Educational Studies*, 15, 1967, pp. 188-94.

12 Francis Bacon, *The Advancement of Learning*, London, J.M. Dent, (Everyman edition), 1930, p. 103.

13 As an amusing illustration of this, some colleagues of mine and I once donned full-length white coats and proceeded to carry every chair out of a major domestic air terminal – not one person objected to our story that 'we had to move the chairs', and everybody just stood until the police brought the game to an end. Most students of psychology can probably tell a similar story arising out of their practical work.

14 *Sydney Morning Herald*, 13 December 1975.

15 *Sydney Morning Herald*, 15 November 1975.

16 I owe this example largely to Peter Stevens.

17 For instance, ideologies often have little scientific support and little commonsense support: they tend to gloss over anomalies, to concentrate on 'confirming instances' and to be stated in ways and to generate methodology that inevitably supports their contentions.

18 It is important to recognise that we are examining the mode of production, not the rhetoric that surrounds it. The rhetoric accepts that capitalism requires owners of the means of production and workers, but tends not to accept that these necessarily become

respectively rich and poor. If an owner becomes rich and a worker stays poor this is seen to be a contingent issue; for according to the rhetoric all can become equally well off, and certain owners can end up in poverty while some workers become rich.

19 As quoted in the *Sydney Morning Herald*, 16 September 1975.
20 *Sydney Morning Herald*, 9 October 1976.
21 It is unlikely that insurance companies really believe that God causes earthquakes, etc. What is of interest is that the rhetoric still prevails.
22 See above, p.43.
23 That these instances do occur, no matter how rarely, is yet another indication of the way ideology mixes together what really is the case with illusory representations of what is the case, thus making those illusions harder to identify as illusions.
24 See Bowles and Gintis, op. cit.
25 Peters, *Ethics and Education*, op. cit., p.252; my italics.
26 D.H. Lawrence, *Phoenix II*, London, Heinemann, 1968, p.586; my italics except for 'impossible'.
27 We dismiss as improbable that there is a statistically 'normal distribution' of abilities among humans that somehow neatly fits the ability requirements of a modern industrial society, such that each person has a 'level' that fits a particular niche, and that there are the right number of appropriate people to fit each particular niche.
28 For instance, if a particular job can be done by a person with a low level of education, yet now requires people to have a high level of education in order to gain it and hold it, job dissatisfaction usually occurs, and consequent negative feelings can pervade all areas of the person's life. Clerks, bank tellers, and even analytic chemists often find themselves doing what any normal fifteen-year-old could do, and are hardly fulfilled by their work; even less so because of their higher education, which ostensibly pointed to and prepared them for higher things.
29 They have been encouraged in other societies as well, e.g. feudal societies.
30 And in doing so destroy our research programme.
31 The justification is often quite implicit. Any teacher who mouths any variation of the extremely common utterance, 'If you don't do well in your exam you won't get a good job', is justifying learning certain content as a means or prerequisite for getting a job. The exam in question might be in French: the child might be seeking employment as a plumber.
32 See again Bowles and Gintis, op. cit.
33 See especially the work of Jan Lukasiewicz, in Storrs McCall (ed.), *Polish Logic*, Oxford, Clarendon Press, 1967.
34 Engels's clearest statement comes in *Anti-Dühring*. To develop this point would require another book, and so we shall merely note a couple of instances. The history of classical formal logic has been a parade of invention of *ad hoc* hypotheses to cover contradictions that exist in the world. One can write on one side of a piece of real

paper in the real world: 'The statement on the other side of this paper is false', and on the other side: 'The statement on the other side of this paper is true', the contradictoriness of which no *ad hoc* hypothesis of 'self-reference', even Tarski's, can alter. Hempel's famous paradox of the ravens, that the existence of a non-black non-raven (say, my blue pen) confirms that all ravens are black, shows the absurdity in the world of something that is logically sound. Further, it is logically possible that two independent confirming instances of the same hypothesis, when taken together, disconfirm the hypothesis. And it is logically possible for an instance that refutes a conjunction of two hypotheses to confirm each of them individually. Such logical possibilities reduce discovery of knowledge in the real world to chaotic shambles. For full discussion of these latter two examples see W.C. Salmon, 'Confirmation', *Scientific American*, 228, 5 May 1973, pp.75–83. Further, quantum mechanics is now posing problems whose solutions require the use of a non-classical logic.

35 V.I. Lenin, 'On the Question of Dialectics', *Collected Works* (ed.) Russ, Moscow: 1958, 38, pp.357–8.

36 Mao Tse-Tung, *Four Essays on Philosophy*, Peking; Foreign Languages Press, 1968, p.31.

37 Take for example the earth's orbit. The earth struggles to break away from the sun's gravitational force; the sun struggles against the earth's centrifugal force; and unity is maintained. Should any one factor gain control, however, the situation would change.

38 This may not be immediately obvious to those who have gained the benefits, and so are understandably thankful because they have never had it so good. See above, p.99.

Chapter 5 Education

1 Ecclesiastes 1:9.

2 Matthew 7 : 15–16.

3 Matthew Arnold, 'The Literary Influence of Academies', in R. Super (ed.), *The Complete Prose Works of Matthew Arnold*, vol. 3, Ann Arbor, University of Michigan Press, p.235.

4 Darwin (among others) provides us with an interesting instance of rejection followed by assimilation. When his theory was at last accepted it was neatly assimilated into the supportive rhetoric surrounding the Bible, especially Genesis 1 : 2–7 and 20–6, and Ecclesiastes 1 : 9. The theory that the earth was 4004 years old was discredited; the seven *days* of Genesis were interpreted as seven eras; and Darwin was seen as spelling out in detail the truth compressed in Genesis 1 : 20–6. There is nothing new under the sun.

5 Ecclesiastes 1 : 18.

6 In P. Freire, *Pedagogy of the Oppressed*, Ringwood: Penguin, 1972, p.102.

7 *Sydney Morning Herald*, 7 February 1976.

8 See above, pp.76–7.

9 Thus our earlier examples, where it was claimed that the interests of all were apparently equally satisfied, are open to question. Further probing would show that winning a battle, and keeping news of devaluation secret, do not favour all equally.

10 Doctors and lawyers are often quoted as expressing concern that the average person would only do himself harm if he attempted to apply law or medicine to himself or others. There is something in this as far as medicine goes, but far less with regard to law, where 'do it yourself' conveyancing, prosecutions and divorce proceedings are quickly gaining favour. If professionals were not, *first and foremost*, concerned about their own interests, they might undertake public education programmes to enable the general public to learn how to care for themselves.

11 C.f. John Stuart Mill: 'Men do not want solely the obedience of women, they want their sentiments. All men . . . desire to have . . . not a forced slave but a willing one . . . . They have therefore put everything into practice to enslave their minds. The masters of all other slaves rely, for maintaining obedience, on fear . . . the masters of women wanted more than simple obedience, and they turned the whole force of education to effect their purpose.' 'The Subjection of Women' in *On Liberty, etc.*, London, Oxford University Press, 1971, (World Classics edition), pp. 443–4. Mill might have generalised his case further.

12 See I. Illich, *Deschooling Society*, Harmondsworth, Penguin, 1973.

13 P.H. Hirst, 'Liberal Education and the Nature of Knowledge', in R.F. Dearden *et al.* (eds), *Education and the Development of Reason*, London, Routledge & Kegan Paul, 1972. See above, chapter 3, n.21.

14 Hirst himself is *not* one of the theorists at fault, for he recognises the limits of epistemological enquiry in the formulation of curricula – see his 'The Logic of the Curriculum', *Journal of Curriculum Studies*, 1, 2, 1969.

15 W.K. Frankena, 'A Model for Analysing a Philosophy of Education', in Jane R. Martin (ed.), *Readings in the Philosophy of Education : a Study of Curriculum*, Boston, Allyn & Bacon, 1970, pp.15–22.

16 Ibid., p.20.

17 The ethical aspect of education is not under question here; but ethical considerations could be shown to merge and mingle with, and thus be part of the political considerations.

18 T. Benton, 'Education and Politics', in D. Holly (ed.), *Education or Domination*, London, Arrow Books, 1974, p.10.

19 In R.C. Edwards *et al.* (eds), *The Capitalist System*, Englewood Cliffs, NJ, Prentice-Hall, 1972, pp.123–4.

20 P. Freire, 'Education, Liberation, and the Church', *Study Encounte SE/38, 9, I, 1973 (World Council of Churches), p.8.

21 L. Althusser, *Lenin and Philosophy*, London, New Left Books, 1971 p.153.

22 I. Scheffler, 'Philosophical Models of Teaching', in R.S. Peters (ed.), *The Concept of Education*, London, Routledge & Kegan Paul, 1969, p.134.
23 For instance, K.R. McKinnon, Chairman of the Australian Schools Commission, in noting how reform had failed to permeate Australian schools despite the influx of millions of dollars (a smaller-scale version of the American experience throughout this century), blamed the forces of rigidity and bureaucracy, including teachers being afraid to change their ways, for this failure. Like the American apologists, he failed to consider that the system, being as it is, cannot become what he wants, regardless of how much money is poured into it. See the report in the *Sydney Morning Herald*, 18 October 1976.
24 See, for instance, the study conducted by Masha Eisenberg at the University of Sydney, 1970–3: 'Student, Staff and University : a Study of Teaching and Learning in the Faculty of Arts'. The frequent use of the phrase 'when I get out' by students is highly significant.
25 A student of mine was once failed a course on 'Indonesian Culture' (he was refused permission even to sit for the exam) on the grounds that he was absent from all nine classes. He was in Indonesia at the time.
26 A. Toffler, *Future Shock*, London, Pan Books, 1976, pp.361–2.
27 See again S. Bowles and H. Gintis, *Schooling in Capitalist America*, New York, Basic Books, 1976.
28 Freire, *Pedagogy of the Oppressed*, op. cit., pp.46–7.
29 For discussion of 'models' whereby this might be explained, see Scheffler, op. cit. Scheffler also deals with 'insight', but not with production.
30 University students often complain about having to do 'the set essays' : the majority of them, however, experience extreme dissonance when told to make up their own topic and seek out their own reading.
31 G. Molnar, 'Voltaire of the Schools', *Nation* (Australia), 24 June, 1972, pp.19–21.
32 R. Super (ed.), *The Complete Prose Works of Matthew Arnold* (6 vols), Ann Arbor, University of Michigan Press, 1962, vol.6, p.72.
33 M. Arnold, *Culture and Anarchy*, Cambridge University Press, 1963, p.52.
34 R.S. Peters, *Ethics and Education*, London, George Allen & Unwin, 1966, p.145.
35 I argue this more fully in my 'Peters on Schooling', *Educational Philosophy and Theory*; 9, 1, April 1977, pp.33–48.
36 Peters, op. cit., p.147; my emphases.
37 Thus the process of 'education' is, for most, subtle socialisation for a working class role. Both the socialisation and the role, however, are given different titles: witness the clerks or secretaries who believe that *education* has brought them *middle-class* status, or the apologists who mouth this rhetoric.

38 Thus, as noted earlier, there is always an ethical dimension to education. So modifying the individual might also include attempts to counteract other moulding and modifying forces in society.
39 See M. Carnoy, *Education as Cultural Imperialism*, New York, David McKay, 1974.
40 See, for example, M.J. Macklin, 'On Hiding One's Curriculum Under an Ideological Bushel', *Australian Science Teachers Journal*, 19, 3 September 1973, pp.53–65, especially, 55–7.
41 One could begin by determining what books, and which authors, are not found in libraries, on course outlines or on reading lists.
42 Illich, op. cit., p.43.
43 S. D'Urso, 'Student Alienation: The Gathering Crisis in Secondary Schooling'; quotation taken from an unpublished version of the paper.
44 Metaphors abound through the history of educational thought : the last six are taken respectively from R.M. Livingstone, R.S. Peters, Matthew Arnold, Plato, Aristotle and A.S. Neill.

Chapter 6 Possibilities

1 P. Weiss, *Marat/Sade*, London, Calder & Boyars, 1965, p.63.
2 It might be that, had we arrested our knowledge 5000 years ago, we would today be living in peace on an unthreatened planet. One thing is sure: if man does destroy himself and the earth, it will not be the eastern mystics who do it.
3 P.L. Berger, *Pyramids of Sacrifice: Political Ethics and Social Change*, New York, Basic Books, 1974. This quotation is taken from an abbreviated form of the fourth chapter, which appeared as 'The False Consciousness of "Consciousness Raising"', in *Worldview*, January 1975.
4 See T.S. Kuhn, *The Structure of Scientific Revolutions*, Chicago University Press, 1973, p.90. 'Almost always the men who achieve these fundamental inventions of a new paradigm have been either very young or very new to the field whose paradigm they change.'
5 See below, pp.187–9.
6 C. Bereiter, 'Moral Alternatives to Education', *Interchange*, 3, 1, 1972, p.26.
7 Berger, op. cit.
8 P. Freire, *Pedagogy of the Oppressed*, Ringwood: Penguin, 1972, p.68. See also his *Cultural Action For Freedom*, Harmondsworth, Penguin, 1972.
9 *The Meno* 84 A–D; W.K.C. Guthrie (trans.), Harmondsworth, Penguin, 1964, p.135. It is hardly being suggested that the coincidence between Freire's ideas here and Plato's would carry over into all of Plato's epistemology, pedagogy or politics.
10 See R.S. Peters, *Ethics and Education*, London, George Allen & Unwin, 1970, pp.238–65.

11 The reverse does not hold: one can have power without being in authority.

12 This follows from our research programme. See the similar arguments concerning 'interests' and ignorance above; pp. 65–6 and 133–7 respectively.

13 Foremost among the proponents of this theory is R.S. Peters. For criticism of this view see C. Clark and P.S. Wilson, 'On Children's Interests', *Educational Philosophy and Theory*, 7, 1, 1975, pp.41–54.

14 See above, pp. 152–3.

15 B.H. Newdigate, 'Shakespeare's Life', in C.J. Sisson, (ed.), *William Shakespeare: The Complete Works*, London, Shakespeare Head Press, 1947; p.v., my emphasis.

16 For interesting discussion on this point see J. Gribble, *Introduction to Philosophy of Education*, Boston: Allyn & Bacon, 1969, pp. 80–6. See also R.F. Dearden, '"Needs" in Education', in R.F. Dearden *et al.* (eds), *Education and the Development of Reason*, London, Routledge & Kegan Paul, 1972, pp. 50–64.

17 G.S. Counts, *Dare the School Build a New Social Order?* New York, John Day, 1932.

18 For instance: not enough (unnecessary, pretentious) footnotes: failure to give sufficient attention to other respectable (yet possibly facile and erroneous) views; use of an assertive rather than tentative approach; insufficient 'academic distance'; employing colloquial language and metaphors, etc.

19 R. Albury, 'Ideology', *Tharunka*, 13 October 1976, p.4.

20 See M. Planck, *Scientific Autobiography and Other Papers*, (trans. F. Gaynor), New York, Williams & Norgate, 1949, pp.33–4.

21 'Revolutionary '*praxis*' is the more appropriate term, embodying as it does both theory and practice. While '*praxis*' is intended, the more familiar term 'practice' will continue to be used in the text.

22 There is very little anti-education around at the moment. Some heartening signs are the growth of communes that are running their own 'schools', the growth of 'counter-courses' in tertiary institutions, which are taken for interest and which offer no grades or credits, and the recent proliferation of informal study groups and reading groups. The nearest I have seen to large-scale 'institutionalised' anti-education is the complex at Tvind in Denmark (although I suspect the people there would not like what they are doing referred to as 'anti-education'): for a detailed account of this interesting place see my 'Tvind: Education on the Move', *Radical Education Dossier*, 3, 1977, 14–17.

23 It is possible, and likely, that this work will be attacked more strongly by various groups among the 'Left' than it will be by those defending the prevailing 'Establishment' paradigm.

24 The problem is hardly new. It lies behind the 'cave analogy' in Plato's *Republic*. Plato recognised that the 'prisoners' would ridicule, and even try to kill, anyone who tried to raise and correct their consciousness: the example of Socrates was fresh in his mind.

Index